THOMAS MANN'S
WORLD

THOMAS MANN'S
WORLD

By JOSEPH GERARD BRENNAN

NEW YORK
RUSSELL & RUSSELL · INC
1962

Copyright 1942

COLUMBIA UNIVERSITY PRESS, NEW YORK

PUBLISHED, 1962, BY RUSSELL & RUSSELL, INC.

BY ARRANGEMENT WITH COLUMBIA UNIVERSITY PRESS

L. C. CATALOG CARD NO: 61–13770

PRINTED IN THE UNITED STATES OF AMERICA

To ELFORD CAUGHEY
whose reading of *The Magic Mountain*
was the beginning of this book

ACKNOWLEDGMENTS

MANY PEOPLE have helped in the making of this little volume. I am deeply in debt to Horace L. Friess, without whose searching yet kindly criticism this study would have lacked even the imperfect organization it now possesses. James Gutmann and Hugh W. Puckett gave me the benefit of their scholarship. I derived stimulus from Houston Peterson and encouragement from Wm. Pepperell Montague (Dionysus and Prometheus!). Jeffrey Smith contributed some thoughtful suggestions. Hermann Weigand's study *Thomas Mann's Novel 'Der Zauberberg'* first suggested to me what a wealth of material for analysis lay in Mann's work. Merrill Moore, M.D., read and criticized the chapter on Disease. Thomas Mann himself graciously read the manuscript and supplemented his kind words with a welcome to his home. Alfred A. Knopf granted permission for extensive quotation from the English translations of Mann's works. Matilda Berg of the Columbia University Press gave me invaluable editorial guidance. My dear wife Mary helped to make the writing of this book a pleasant task, one which was doubly a labor of love.

J.G.B.

New Rochelle, N. Y.
July, 1942

INTRODUCTION

THOMAS MANN is more than an eminent novelist. He is one of those representatives of German culture whose writings reveal a speculative imagination of far-reaching dimensions that has the quality of synthesis. His genius reaches out into the realms of music, of morals, of politics; it raises fundamental questions as to the function of art, the nature of humanity. Mann stands at the close of the German cultural tradition which stems from Goethe on the one hand, from Schopenhauer through Nietzsche, Wagner, and Freud on the other. In its quality of synthesis, Mann's artistic direction is kin to the creative drive of his predecessors. Transmuting the influences of these *Kulturmenschen* within an intensely personal art and critique, Mann's achievement not only stands at the end of this cultural tradition, but is also a commentary upon it, a recapitulation, a summing up.

But Thomas Mann's work does not merely point backward into the past. He himself counts it most significant that all his predecessors, from Goethe to Freud, had an eye toward the future. In Mann's stern critical evaluation of the tradition to which he belongs, in his effort to bridge the gap between the problems of the nineteenth and twentieth centuries, in his own passionate hope for the future, there is revealed that forward nisus so often found in a creative genius of the first rank.

It is not the purpose of this study to abstract from Mann's writings a systematic aesthetic, although judgments concerning the nature and function of art are to be found in his works, nor a systematic metaphysic, although his books contain philosophic implications. In *Death in Venice*, Mann asks, "Who shall unriddle the problem of the artist nature?" The present study takes as its point of departure an examination of that problem. But Thomas Mann's attitude toward art and the artist cannot be considered as an element separate and distinct from other themes in his work. He himself has said that art is the quintessence of humanity and the artist the most human of men. The impossibility of detaching Mann's own view of art and the artist from his vision of life and humanity bears out that statement. As Mann's genius matured, his interest in art and the artist shaded over into concern with the broadest human problems. But it is impossible to point out just where the former leaves off and the latter begins. One implies the other and neither can be conceived apart from the other. Thus, in attempting to fix on Mann's doctrine of the artist nature, we find ourselves compelled to follow to their farthest limits various strands of thought which enclose his world view.

Our survey is not simply a compendium of what Thomas Mann *says* about the artist and his relation to life; it is also an analysis of Mann's own artistic personality as it stands revealed in his work. The problem is scanned against the background of nineteenth century German culture; Goethe, Schopenhauer, Nietzsche, Wagner, and Freud stand out as dominant influences. Specifically, our investigation of Mann's work examines the problem of the artist nature in reference to certain definite factors: its social environment, its deviation from the normal in personality and health, its reaction to questions of morals and politics, its relation to the kingdoms of music and metaphysics.

Since Plato, who observed that the poet's creative activity is akin to madness, it has become a commonplace to say that genius is never "normal." The divergence of the artist nature from the usual pattern of human life has fascinated Thomas Mann, and this theme is prominent in his work from "Little Herr Friedemann" to *The Beloved Returns*. The solitude to which the artist is condemned because of his fatal gift of insight, his consciousness of the gulf which separates him from his fellow men, his longing for that familiar ordinary world from which he feels himself cut off—these are notes in the motif of "isolation" which runs through the introspective early stories. Mann's treatment of the artist's isolation is strongly colored by elements drawn from personal experience which sharply reflect the character of the environment in which he grew up—that is, nineteenth century German bourgeois. Mann's consciousness of the bourgeois residue in his own personality has led him to reflect at length upon the effect produced by such a heritage on the character of an artist and the quality of his art. Mann has incorporated into his creative work the polarity between bourgeois discipline and creative élan—and he has used it as the basis of dramatic conflict.

Probably the most personal and characteristic of Thomas Mann's reflections on art and life is his concept of the relation between disease and genius. Upon an intuition that illness can be more human than health, Mann bases his conviction that genius often finds the direct and open approach to life barred, that its path must skirt perilously close to the dark realms of disease and death. We come upon numerous instances of this in his works. In a German town on the Baltic coast, Hanno Buddenbrook, a musical son of a proud merchant father, dies when his tender genius can no longer cope with the pattern of life into which he is being forced. By the sultry lagoons of Venice, the lonely writer Gustave von Aschenbach is driven to death by the conflict within his soul. In a tuberculosis sanatorium high in the Alps, young Hans Castorp finds his way to self-fulfillment amid the poisonous exhalations of sickness and corruption. Through parable and through open declaration our analysis follows the development of Mann's conviction that the artist, that humanity itself, has a spiritual as well as a physical bond with disease and death.

It is the *romantic* artist, Mann tells us, who seems most sensitive to the exhausting effects of artistic production. Romantic art has an equivocal character, an inclination to decadence. The music of Richard Wagner affected Mann profoundly; he calls the composer the "Arch-romantic." Reflections on Wagner lead to the question of the link between music and the romantic. Against the background of German romanticism, we arrange Mann's own romantic tendencies— his love for the nocturnal and his emphasis on feeling, his passion for music and his absorption of its technique into his own art. For all his romantic sympathies, we discern in Thomas Mann a vein of antiromantic criticism; we follow the development of his Nietzschean conviction that too much emphasis on feeling and "music"—particularly in the case of the German people—generates a certain danger which may carry over from art into life, and stand as a threat to humane values.

Just as it diverges from social and organic norms, so too the direction of the artist nature does not move wholly within the bounds of ordinary morality. Genius, Mann says, finds its morality not in cold self-control, but rather in abandonment, in yielding to the hurtful and the forbidden. The artist and the criminal have something in common. It is suggestive to place this dark view in conjunction with Mann's late insistence on the connection between art and morality in the common ground of truth.

The question of morals leads us to the question of politics, which is—or should be—civic morality. An extraordinary example of the development of an artist's political consciousness is Thomas Mann's orientation in the sphere of world politics. After the early hostility to politics and democracy, set forth in the *Reflections of a Non-Political Man,* we find a growing political attention in the Thomas Mann of the years following the first World War. This awareness, drawing strength from the innate bourgeois love of order and decency, is quickly actualized by the violent stimulus of German fascism. Uprooted from his native soil, the sometime *Unpolitische* carries on a crusade against a political evil which to him is at the same time a moral evil. Never a partisan of art of "social significance," Mann comes to the conclusion that when political degeneration menaces human values, the artist cannot remain indifferent to politics.

Without claiming that Thomas Mann builds about his own art products a self-conscious framework of philosophy, our analysis finds in his dualism of nature and spirit an extension in the direction of the metaphysical sphere of certain tendencies present in his work in concrete form. With reference to the generic headings of "nature" and "spirit," the perspective of Mann's work broadens. The polar "pedagogic" forces which influence the characters in his novels are viewed in the light of this fundamental antithesis. The stylistic device of irony is discovered to reflect a cosmic force, an *eros* which plays between the opposite poles of nature and spirit. Mann believes that the antithesis cuts deep into the world of art. The task of the artist is revealed as a hermetic mission between nature and spirit, the metaphysical function of art as its joining of the two realms.

The theme of isolation fades from Thomas Mann's mature work. Preoccupation with disease and death lessens perceptibly after *The Magic Mountain*. Suspicion of intellectualism is softened. Political aloofness gives way to political interest. As his literary career developed, growing consciousness of his own romantic tendencies brought about changes of emphasis in Mann's work. His history is one of a spirit born to a romantic heritage and powerfully stimulated by it—a spirit which gradually becomes aware of its own romantic inclinations and, subjecting them to critical analysis, allows some to die away after working them out in creative products, and guides others into new directions. Foremost of these new channels into which Mann has guided the creative drive of his late maturity is the *Joseph* story. Mann has said that one of the most romantic qualities of nineteenth century German culture is its interest in prehistory, its searching of "the romantical, prehistorical mother womb." The *Joseph* story is romantic in just this sense. In its retreat into the dusk of primeval time, in its delving into the subintellectual matrix of the unconscious, the *Joseph* saga reveals itself as the creation of a fundamentally romantic mind and art.

The present study, however, does not take us deeply into the problems of the *Joseph* story. While our analysis draws on all Mann's writings, it focuses more sharply on the long period of development which begins with the early short stories and culminates in *The Magic Mountain*. In the books of those years we find the problem of the relation of the artist nature to life most clearly presented. Of course it would be foolish to claim that there is no continuity between the *Joseph* novels and Mann's earlier work. Joseph has something of the artist about him. Even from the simple Bible story one receives the impression of a sensitive youth of delicate perceptions. In his tetralogy, Mann colors in this aspect of Joseph's character. The Joseph of the Mann stories has "that native tendency to idleness and dreams" to which his creator confesses in an autobiographical sketch. But the continuity must not be exaggerated. The *Joseph* story represents a certain major shift in the centre of gravity of Mann's work taken as a whole, a shift apparent in the withdrawal of emphasis from the problems of art and the fixing of attention on myth-psychology. In its double sounding of the well of historical time and of the depths of the unconscious, the *Joseph* saga represents a new and different phase of Mann's output and as such deserves separate examination or inclusion in a complete and final study of Thomas Mann's work.

Two independent creative works come between *Joseph in Egypt* and the final volumes of the Biblical series. They are *The Beloved Returns* and *The Transposed Heads*. Like the *Joseph* books, these late stories turn from the contemporary scene to bygone days—the former to early nineteenth century Germany, the latter to ancient India. *The Beloved Returns*, originally titled *Lotte in Weimar*, is a study of genius in the person of Goethe. This work gathers up into quasi-novel form a great many things about genius that Mann had already said in previous contexts; it represents no change in his earlier judgments concerning the relation of the artist to life. *The Transposed Heads*, titled in German *Die vertauschten Köpfe*, is a fantasy on an old Indian legend. Mann calls this piece "a metaphysical joke" and says that he wrote it for relaxation before beginning the final volumes of the *Joseph* story. We shall see later what bearing it has on our inquiry.

CONTENTS

INTRODUCTION   ix

ABBREVIATIONS   2

1. THE ARTIST'S ISOLATION IN A
   BOURGEOIS WORLD   3

2. DISEASE, ART, AND LIFE   37

3. MUSIC AND THE ROMANTIC   76

4. MORALITY AND THE ARTIST   109

5. ART AND POLITICS   134

6. ART AS MEDIATOR BETWEEN
   NATURE AND SPIRIT   161

BIBLIOGRAPHY   189

INDEX   195

THOMAS MANN'S
WORLD

ABBREVIATIONS

AS THIS STUDY is primarily for English-speaking readers, most of the references are to English translations of the works cited. The following abbreviations are used for works to which frequent reference is made. The original title and the place and date of publication of Mann's works are given in parentheses. Citations of the writings of Nietzsche refer to The Complete Works of Frederick Nietzsche, ed. Oscar Levy, London, 1909-13.

Bud   Buddenbrooks (Buddenbrooks, Berlin, 1901). New York, 1924.

DV   Death in Venice (Der Tod in Venedig. Berlin, 1911). Reprinted in Stories of Three Decades.

Eck   Eckermann, Johann Peter, Conversations of Goethe with Eckermann. Everyman's Library, London, 1930.

FGW   Freud, Goethe, Wagner. New York, 1937.

G-T   Goethe and Tolstoy (from Bemühungen. Berlin, 1925). Reprinted in Three Essays. New York, 1929.

MM   The Magic Mountain (Der Zauberberg. Berlin, 1924). New York, 1927.

PM   Past Masters. New York, 1931.

RH   Royal Highness (Königliche Hoheit. Berlin, 1909). New York, 1926; reissue, 1939.

Sk   A Sketch of My Life ("Lebensabriss," Die Neue Rundschau, 1930). Paris, 1935.

STD   Stories of Three Decades. New York, 1936.

TK   Tonio Kröger (Tonio Kröger. Berlin, 1903). Reprinted in Stories of Three Decades. New York, 1936.

WWI   Schopenhauer, Arthur, The World as Will and Idea, trans. Haldane and Kemp. Boston, 1883-85.

1

THE ARTIST'S ISOLATION IN A
BOURGEOIS WORLD

THOMAS MANN was born in 1875 in Lübeck, Germany, the second son of Johann Heinrich Mann, a well-to-do grain merchant of the city. His mother was Julia da Silva-Bruhns, a Brazilian lady of mixed German and Portuguese blood. Thomas grew up with his two brothers and two sisters in a spacious and stately dwelling. Summers were spent at the nearby seaside resort of Travemünde. The atmosphere in which the children were raised was one of dignity and comfort. Conservative, careful of his appearance, loving order and gracious living, Johann Heinrich was respected by all and held the office of Senator in the old Hanseatic town. He died, however, when Thomas was only fifteen. The family grain business was disposed of, and Thomas's mother, who had always loved the South, moved to Munich with the younger children. Thomas finished school in Lübeck, and then joined his mother in Munich. There he entered an insurance office as a clerk, and in the intervals between copying accounts he wrote his first stories. After a year, he left business to attend some university classes. Then he went to Italy to live for a while with his older brother Heinrich, who was also writing. It was during this Italian sojourn that Thomas began writing the novel *Buddenbrooks*, which was to bring the twenty-five-year-old author to the attention of the world.[1]

Although his path in life was not the one his father in-

[1] Sk, pp. 2-15.

tended for him, Thomas Mann retained a deeply fixed memory of the respected Senator and his love of order, comfort, and dignity. Something of the father had taken permanent root in the child. "I am the son of the German bourgeoisie," Thomas Mann declared years later, "and never have I disowned the spiritual traditions which belong to my origin." [2] This allegiance has plainly affected every turn of the novelist's life and art. Again and again in his writings, from the earliest stories to the most mature critical essays, we come across this term "bourgeois." [3] The concept is so deeply embedded in Mann's creative work that an understanding of its implications is necessary in any study of his art.

In its general sense, the word "bourgeois" stands for that social stratum commonly called "the middle class," which had its origins in the Renaissance, when the powerful forces of individualism were loosed against the old ecclesiastical-monarchical aristocracy. The rise of this class was coincident with the growth of capitalism, the summit of its influence was reached in the nineteenth century. In France, where the term "bourgeois" originally signified a freeman of a medieval *bourg* or borough and later came to be used as a label for the middle class as set off against the nobility, the bourgeoisie came into its own after the Revolution. Its laicism and middle-class ideals of equality were the source of its anticlericalism, as of its republican and antiroyalist convictions. Even though France returned briefly to the monarchy in the nineteenth century, one remembers Louis Philippe,

---

[2] "An Appeal to Reason," *Criterion,* X (London, 1931), 396.

[3] For the German *"Bürger"* (*Bürgertum, Bürgerlichkeit*). The English word "bourgeois," taken directly from the French, is not an exact equivalent of "Bürger" in meaning. Although both derive from the old German *"Burg,"* the French *"bourgeois"* and the German *"Bürger"* have a history of semantic change. To our ears today "bourgeois" has a derogatory flavor, because it has so often been used as an epithet. The German word, however, carries a suggestion of "patrician" as well as "middle class." But to avoid continual recurrence of the italicized foreign word, the English variant is used in this chapter.

who tried desperately to look like a businessman, and carried an umbrella. European businessmen liked the bourgeois regime, admired the "citizen king," whose doffing of the trappings of royalty was symbolic of his acquiescence in an age of practical business ideals.[4]

The rate of the German bourgeois ascendancy was slower than in other European countries, for the German states were hampered by political disunion and the caprices of the numerous petty princes and their courts. Moreover the German burgher retained an aristocratic bias, a high pride in station. Carl Brinkman points out that the German bourgeois class, in contrast with that of England and France, included some feudal elements—tendencies at once less individualistic and more solidly aristocratic than was typical of the same group in other European nations.[5]

European bourgeois society reached its halcyon days in the nineteenth century. In that expansive era, the cause of capitalistic liberalism was paramount and the bourgeois class was the repository of power and stability. But in the twentieth century the class was dealt a well-nigh mortal blow, as the Great War of 1914-18 shattered the spiritual order of the continent and left social ferment as well as dead bodies in its wake. From this wreckage, there rose Russian Communism, then Italian and German Fascism, ideologies whose common denominator was the repudiation of bourgeois values. After a lull of barely twenty years, another war struck the continent of Europe, apparently to lay waste what was left of the old order.

The European bourgeois class had its faults—philistinism, suspicion of the working class, preoccupation with material gain; but the fact remains that for some hundreds of years

---

[4] Johann Buddenbrook is an admirer of Louis Philippe. Bud I, 24.
[5] See the article "Bourgeois" in the *Encyclopedia of the Social Sciences*.

both order and progress depended largely upon it. And some day, when a final appraisal is made of the bourgeois contribution to world culture, its service as a matrix for a legion of artists will be acknowledged. Painters, composers, literary men, by far the preponderant number of these have arisen from the middle classes of Europe. This has been especially true of Germany.

Thomas Mann stands out prominently in the ranks of those German artists whose heredity and environment have been unmistakably bourgeois. Both in parable and in direct autobiographical reference, he leaves no doubt as to his own awareness of the significance of his origin. But this emphasis on the bourgeois element in his background is always coupled with corresponding emphasis on the nonbourgeois character which he claims to have inherited from his mother, a lady whom he says was "distinctly Romantic in type, in her youth a much admired beauty, and extraordinarily musical." [6]

Buddenbrooks, the first work on a large scale which Mann produced, is a bourgeois epic, full of autobiographical overtones. The long story actually appeared at the end of 1900, when Mann was in his twenty-fifth year, although it came out under a Fischer imprint of 1901. *Buddenbrooks* is largely an objective-naturalistic treatment in novel form of a merchant family of Lübeck. The book traces the Buddenbrook history through four generations in a manner which has suggested some resemblance to the Galsworthy technique in the *Forsyte Saga.*[7] The narrative is one of the decline and death of a family. The Buddenbrooks are grain merchants of the little Baltic city; their position is comfortable, solid, and respectable. Father and son may differ in outward tempera-

[6] Sk, 7.
[7] See "Buddenbrooks und The Forsyte Saga," a dissertation by Charlotte Rohmer (Nördlingen, C. H. Beck, 1933).

ment—Great-grandfather Johann is a French-speaking, fash-
ionably sceptical man of the world, and Grandfather Johann
is a Bible-quoting churchgoer—but they are one in their
deep loyalty to the family tradition, in which zealous attention to business and love of good living are inseparable. This
same combination of industrious devotion to work and cultivation of comfortable living is present in Thomas Buddenbrook of the novel's third generation. But with Thomas
comes the shadow of future decline. For there is a fatal
tension in his nature—he is conscious of elements in his
nature which are actually hostile to the bourgeois code.
There is his early inclination to Roman Catholicism, and his
youthful tendency to idleness and irregular living, to which
his good-for-nothing brother Christian has completely surrendered.[8] But Thomas has sternly repressed these wayward
impulses, and has endeavored to forget them in his redoubled
industry in building up the fortunes of the family business.
His antibourgeois instincts, however, have unconsciously
directed his marriage to the lovely and musical Gerda Ar-
noldsen, whom all the townspeople consider a little "queer,"
despite the large dowry she brings to the coffers of the Buddenbrook firm. The torturing conflict within Thomas, which
he endeavors to conceal by extremes of hard work and
exaggerated meticulousness of dress, finally breaks him. At
forty, he is burned out. His growing lack of self-confidence
is paralleled by the mounting losses of the firm. He sees that
his frail little son Hanno, who loves music and nothing else,
will never be a grain merchant. He realizes that his whole
life has been meaningless, his entire program of industry
artificial and forced, and one day, felled by a mortal stroke,
he collapses in the street, where his carefully groomed head
lies in a mud puddle. The tale of the decline of the Budden-

[8] Bud I, 265.

brook family comes to an end with the death of little Hanno, and the liquidation of the hundred-year-old business.

There are many interesting autobiographical associations in *Buddenbrooks*. Thomas Mann's own forbears were patrician bourgeoisie, grain merchants of Lübeck. As in the novel, Johann Mann built his own fine house, after moving from the large family dwelling. Like Hanno, young Thomas Mann hated school, loved music and the theatre, and the summer holidays at Travemünde.[9] Like Hanno too, Thomas Mann was meant to become a grain merchant, as his father had been, and to carry on the family business. But, also as in the novel, Johann Mann died prematurely, and the hundred-year-old firm was liquidated at a considerable loss. Another parallel is suggested by the contrasting characters of Mann's parents. Like Gerda, Frau Mann had beauty and musical talent. Like Thomas Buddenbrook, Johann Mann was a highly respected citizen, a Senator of the old Baltic town, careful, industrious, fastidious. However, similarity between the fictitious Senator and the real one must not be overdrawn. Even as the character of Hanno reflects the childhood hopes and fears of his youthful creator, the disintegrating tension within the person of Thomas Buddenbrook has its counterpart in Thomas Mann's own spiritual conflict—the struggle between the bourgeois conservative strain and the impulse to create.

Thomas Mann sketched diptychs of his contrasting parental influences again and again in his work. Even in the early tale "The Dilettante" (1897), there are portraits of a pretty, piano-playing mother, and a carefully groomed father, influential in civic affairs, who desired his son to become a merchant. There is a passage in this story which suggests the answer as to whether the final victory belongs to conformity

[9] Sk, 7.

or creation. The artist in the story tells how he, as a child, used to watch his father and mother:

"I sat in a corner loooking at my father and mother, and it was as though I would choose between them; whether I would spend my life in deeds of power or in dreamy musing. And always in the end my eyes would rest upon my mother's quiet face." [10]

In *Tonio Kröger* (1903), a tale to which we shall constantly return in this chapter, there are autobiographical overtones. Once more there is the grain-merchant father and the musical mother, as well as the author's self-confessed boyhood hatred of school. Of Tonio, we learn that:

As he wasted his time at home, was slow and absent-minded at school, and always had bad marks from the masters, he was in the habit of bringing home pitifully poor reports, which troubled and angered his father, a tall, fastidiously dressed man, with thoughtful blue eyes, and always a wild flower in his buttonhole. But for his mother, she cared nothing about the reports—Tonio's beautiful black-haired mother, whose name was Consuelo, and who was so absolutely different from the other ladies in town, because his father had brought her long ago from some place far down on the map.[11]

In *Royal Highness* (1905), Mann's second novel, which presents the industrial capitalist Spoelmann, the father of the lonely mathematical Imma, it is Spoelmann himself who has exotic traces in his blood. Speaking of the millionaire, a lady remarks, "He himself is a bit of a mixture, for his father married a woman from the South—Creole blood, the daughter of a German father and a native mother." [12] Then there is the parentage of Gustave von Aschenbach of *Death in Venice* (1911):

He [Aschenbach] was the son of an upper official in the judicature, and his forbears had all been officers, judges, departmental

---

[10] "The Dilettante," STD, p. 30.   [11] TK: STD, p. 87.   [12] RH, p. 140.

functionaires—men who had lived their strict, decent, sparing lives in the service of king and state. Only once before had a livelier mentality—in the quality of a clergyman—turned up among them; but swifter, more perceptive blood had in the generation before the poet's flowed into the stock from the mother's side, she being the daughter of a Bohemian musical conductor. It was from her that he had the foreign traits that betrayed themselves in his appearance. The union of dry, conscientious officialdom, and ardent, obscure impulse, produced an artist— and this particular artist.[13]

The bourgeois element in his character is at the root of Thomas Mann's searching inquiry into the relation of the artist to the world. Against a conservative background, non-artistic and disciplined, the problems of creative genius are thrown into high relief, thus facilitating the search of their origins. The German middle class, Mann tells us, had little understanding of the "prodigal sons of the class structure," [14] had, in fact, downright suspicion of the artist's profession, which seemed to the majority of the solid burghers no profession at all, but simply an irregular way of living. Thomas Buddenbrook is struck to the heart with pain as he comes to realize that his son Hanno will never be a merchant, but only a musician. Music! What had Gerda, his wife, said to him about music? "Thomas, once for all, you will never understand anything about music as an art, and intelligent as you are, you will never see that it is more than an after dinner pleasure and a feast for the ears." [15] It is not only this philistinism that stamps Thomas Buddenbrook as a bourgeois. He has all the qualities which Mann insists are characteristic of the class—personal fastidiousness, love of good living, passionate devotion to respectable work, morbid

[13] DV: STD, p. 382.
[14] "Standards and Values," N. Y. *Times*, Aug. 14, 1937; trans. Agnes Meyer from article "Mass und Wert" in *Mass und Wert*, Zürich, Summer, 1937.   [15] Bud, II, 118.

dread of the irregular and shiftless; even his tendency to melancholy and pessimism follows the nineteenth century bourgeois pattern. This last quality is brought to the surface in Thomas Buddenbrook by his accidental reading of Schopenhauer. But the resulting mystical joy and concomitant orientation toward death is short-lived. His more middle-class instincts "rose up against them—and his vanity too: the fear of being eccentric, of playing a laughable role." [16]

Tonio Kröger is the story of an artist whose middle-class heritage compels him to look upon his own vocation as irregular and suspect. This is the "bad conscience" theme, common in Mann's early stories, the result of much reflection on the relation of the creative instinct to the bourgeois inheritance. Even as a boy, he who bore the name of Tonio Kröger ("those syllables compact of the north and the south, that good middle-class name with the exotic twist to it")[17] felt a strange resentment struggle against his love for his pretty mandolin-playing mother, who never scolded him about the poor report cards he brought home from school:

. . . he found in his father's annoyance a more dignified and respectable attitude and despite his scoldings understood him very well, whereas his mother's blithe indifference always seemed just a little wanton. His thoughts at times would run something like this: "It is true enough that I am what I am and will not and cannot alter: heedless, self-willed, with my mind on things nobody else thinks about. And so it is right that they should scold me and punish me and not smother things all up with kisses and music. After all, we are not gypsies living in a green wagon: we're respectable people, the family of Consul Kröger." [18]

Later in the same tale, we are told that when Consul Kröger died his wife mourned bitterly for a while, then married an Italian musician and fled to the south. Her young artist son

---

[16] *Ibid.*, II, 221.   [17] TK: STD, p. 100.   [18] *Ibid.*, p. 88.

"found this a little irregular, but who was he to call her to order, he who wrote poetry himself . . . ?" [19] Tonio too moves away and in a southern land tries to find solace in adventures of the flesh. But these bring him only remorse. "It might have been his father in him," the author tells us, "that made him suffer so down there in the south." [20]

It is interesting to note that Consul Kröger's son, artist though he is, has nothing but distaste for the Bohemian sloppiness, the *je m'en fiche*, the eccentric posings, mannerisms and clothing which he finds so often affected by artistic people. When we observe that Tonio is punctiliously correct in his own demeanor, we realize that this is evidence of the bourgeois strain. "Mercy on you, Tonio Kröger! Don't be so formal," exclaims his friend Lisaveta, daughter of Russia, that most unbourgeois of countries. "Everybody knows that you were taught good manners in your nursery." [21] In protest against her jibes at his meticulous dress, Tonio Kröger says something which explains Thomas Mann's own personal preference for conservative, businesslike attire:

"Oh, leave my clothes alone, Lisaveta Ivanovna! Do you want me to go about in a ragged velveteen jacket or a red waistcoat? Every artist is as bohemian as the deuce, inside! Let him at least wear proper clothes and behave outwardly like a respectable being." [22]

Then he tells Lisaveta the whole story of his misgivings about the rectitude of his own calling, the guilty consciousness of being irregular, the instinctive suspicion of the artistic vocation:

"Now you see, Lisaveta, I cherish at the bottom of my soul all the scorn and suspicion of the artist gentry—translated into terms of the intellectual—that my upright old forbears there on the

---

[19] *Ibid.*, p. 98.   [20] *Ibid.*, p. 99.
[21] *Ibid.*, p. 100.   [22] *Ibid.*, p. 102.

Baltic would have felt for any juggler or mountebank that entered their houses." [23]

Says the Russian girl in an effort to find the nerve of Tonio's problem, "Now: the solution is that you, as you sit there, are, quite simply, a bourgeois. . . . You are a bourgeois on the wrong path (*ein verirrter Bürger*)." [24]

The motif of the youthful artist's bad conscience, the bourgeois suspicion of the artist's calling, is inseparable from the theme of *isolation* which runs through Thomas Mann's early work. This is the theme of the artist who is sensitive to his aloneness in the world, conscious of his difference from other men. All normal people instinctively feel this difference and are prompted to withdraw from the artist, leaving him to his solitude. Good folk of the middle class, whose ideal lies in hard, honest, respectable work, cannot but view the vocation of the artist as something deviating from the normal; they cannot help regarding an inhabitant of the strange realm of art as irresponsible and suspect. There is something about the artist, a sign on his brow perhaps, which denies him ordinary human companionship, even if he longs for it. This isolation, this consciousness of a gulf separating one from other men is doubly painful for an artist in whom the bourgeois element is inborn, in whom is ingrained by inheritance this very suspicion of the artist nature, of which he himself is an instance.

The isolation of the artist, the enforced solitude of the man of genius, is, of course, a subject thoroughly in the romantic tradition, and it is only individual artistry plus the emphasis on the bourgeois connection which makes Mann's treatment of the theme so highly individual. Byron's fondness for portraying the solitary genius is typical of the

[23] *Ibid.*, p. 105.   [24] *Ibid.*, p. 110.

attraction this motif had for European literary men of the romantic period. In *Manfred,* for example, the old abbot speaks to the self-oppressed hero of his past unhappy years. "Yet why not live and act with other men?" asks the monk. Manfred answers, "Because my nature was averse from life." [25] It is obvious that Byron intended the character of Manfred to be a symbol of the artist, the man of genius, in particular of Byron himself. In this poetic drama of his earlier years, the errant lord distilled in its most concentrated form the ichor of romantic gloom; the solitary genius broods over the vicissitudes of his lot, feels himself cut off from the ties that link other men to their fellows, knows himself a blighted being. This suffering brooding, this *Weltschmerz* is characteristic of the youthful Byron, of his work in the years immediately following his exile. His preoccupation with the theme lessens perceptibly in his later, better work; there is very little of it in *Don Juan.* But the people of Byron's own day liked to think of him always as "wearing his sables." The hero to whom the popular mind attached the tag "Byronic" was "the immedicable soul with heart-aches ever new," [26] who fled the mob and withdrew into himself, knowing that he was "a mark for blight and desolation." [27]

The literature of the eighteenth and nineteenth centuries was full of introspective solitary heroes—Atala, Rollo, René, Heinrich von Offterdingen, Alastor, Jean Sbogar, Axel, Maldoror, to name but a few of them. Their prototype was, of course, Werther. But Byron's treatment of the lonely self-contemplative hero is of special interest to us; in a century when dozens of blighted beings stalked through literature, it was the English poet lord who emphasized the *isolation*

---

[25] *Manfred,* Act II, scene 1.
[26] *Childe Harold's Pilgrimage,* Canto IV, cxxvi.   [27] *The Dream,* viii.

of the genius, his bitter withdrawal from the world of men, the separation from life and love enforced by his peculiar nature. The Byronic hero had early met the world—

> But soon he knew himself the most unfit
> Of men to herd with Man, with whom he held
> Little in common.[28]

This poetic sentiment is appropriate to Thomas Mann's early heroes; so many of his tales are portraits of young artists, newly fledged geniuses, who somberly reflect upon the penalty which the artist nature has brought down upon them, the punishment of the unbridgeable gap separating them from their fellow men. In Mann's work, however, we miss the Byronic shrillness; the German writer's heroes do not rail against humanity, nor do they flee their country to wander aimlessly about the world:

> Proud though in desolation, which could find
> A life within itself to breathe without mankind.[29]

Mann's young artists bewail their fate in gentler accents. Their feelings toward humanity, from which they are cut off, are ambivalent, a mixture of love and hostility. What is more, instead of swaggering about in the rakehellish style of Byron's heroes, they get down to hard work, the common refuge of the artist and the bourgeois.

The earliest explicit occurrence of the isolation motif in Mann's work is in the short tale "The Dilettante," which he wrote in his twenty-third year. This is one of the many early stories containing a portrait of a musical mother and a bourgeois father. The chief personage of this sketch is a young literary man whose "philosophic isolation" makes him wish to "hide in the dark like a bat or an owl and gaze with envy

---

[28] *Childe Harold's Pilgrimage*, Canto III, xii.　　　　[29] *Ibid.*

at the children of light." [30] The children of light? They are the normal, healthy, happy, ordinary people, one of whose number, Anna Rainer, attracts the love of the artist. He is soon given to know that his cause is hopeless. Happiness is barred to him, he can never be like those who are

. . . the favorites of the gods, it would seem, whose happiness is genius and their genius happiness; children of light, who move easily through life with the reflection and image of the sun in their eyes; easy, charming, amiable, while all the world surrounds them with praise, admiration, envy and love—for even envy is powerless to hate them. And they mingle in the world like children, capricious, arrogant, spoiled, friendly as the sunshine, as certain of their genius and their joy as though it were impossible things should be otherwise.[31]

The theme is also present in *Buddenbrooks*. Young Hanno's personality is so different from those of the other children of his class that his ordained merchant career is early despaired of. "Why was it," wonders his father, "that he cared so little for playmates of his own age and class." [32] And in *Tristan*, Detlev Spinell is a writer of sorts, who seems unsociable to others. He seeks nobody's company.[33] Ordinary, healthy life, symbolized by Klöterjahn's lusty baby, is positively repellent to him.

Mann's early story "The Hungry" (1902) contains a more explicit development of the isolation motif. In this piece, consisting for the most part of a monologue by a writer named Detleff, we see the artist on the way to a party. He wants to forget his all-absorbing work for a while in the midst of the gaiety of the young people; he wants to dance with a lovely lady for whom he nurses an unrequited affection. No use! Try as he may, he just cannot fit in. Standing

[30] "The Dilettante," STD, p. 41.   [31] *Ibid.*
[32] Bud, II, 226.   [33] *Tristan*, STD, p. 138.

apart from the dancers, he remembers something he has
written which runs:

"We lonely ones . . . we isolated dreamers, disinherited of life,
who spend our introspective days remote in an artificial icy air
and spread abroad a cold breath as from strange regions so soon
as we come among living human beings and they see our brows
marked with the sign of knowledge and of fear; we poor ghosts
of life, who are met with an embarrassed glance and left to
ourselves as quickly as possible that our hollow and knowledge-
able eye may not blight all joy . . . we cherish a hidden and
unappeased yearning for the harmless, simple and real in life;
for a little friendly, devoted, human happiness. That "life" from
which we are shut out—we do not envisage it as wild beauty
and cruel splendour, it is not as the extraordinary that we crave
it, we extraordinary ones. The kingdom of our longing is the
realm of the pleasant, the normal, and the respectable, it is life
in all its tempting banal everydayness that we want." [34]

This passage anticipates the lines from the later tale *Tonio
Kröger:*

"No, life as the eternal antinomy of mind and art does not represent itself to us as a vision of savage greatness and ruthless
beauty; we who are set apart and different do not conceive it
as, like us, unusual; it is the normal, respectable and admirable
that is the kingdom of our longing: life in all its seductive
banality." [35]

Both soliloquies recall the lonely Nietzsche's remark:

"It is we solitary ones that require love and companions in whose
presence we may be open and simple, and the eternal struggle
of silence and dissimulation can cease." [36]

Near the conclusion of "The Hungry" Detleff leaves the
party. He pauses to wait for a cab on the steps of the bril-

[34] "The Hungry," STD, p. 169.   [35] TK: STD, p. 108.
[36] Letter to his sister Elizabeth in *Selected Letters of Frederick Nietzsche,*
ed. Oscar Levy (London, 1924), p. 101.

liantly illuminated house; he hears the sound of music and gay voices inside. Suddenly he sees a ragged man staring at him enviously. The man, on whose face are the marks of hunger, has been looking in through the window at the bright, warm interior. The artist mentally addresses him:

". . . we are brothers. . . . Have you a weight here, my friend, a burning weight on your breast? How well I know it! And why did you come? Why did you not hug your misery in the shadow instead of taking your stand under the lighted windows behind which are music and laughter?" [37]

Royal Highness, written shortly after Mann's marriage to the daughter of the mathematician Pringsheim, is a rather long novel, whose cheerful tone was felt by the critics of 1905 to be "too light," coming as it did as the first big book after *Buddenbrooks.*[38] The tale concerns a young prince of a small European country which is in sad financial condition. Mann tells us that the story is an allegory of the artist and treats of the problem of "reconciling the claims of society and the solitary." [39] Applauded and admired by the crowd, Prince Klaus Heinrich feels fenced off from the rest of humanity. Indeed he cannot even speak to anyone without self-consciousness, in which hauteur and embarrassment are mixed. "The pleasures of a confidential intimacy are not for you," Dr. Überbein, his tutor, warns him. His Royal Highness is one of those "who are conscious of the dignity of their exceptional station, the marked men, those one can see are not as other men." [40] There is an undisguised artist in the novel, one Axel Martini, who descants on the loneliness of the artist, and his fated path of knowledge, so different from the path of love and life trod by ordinary people:

[37] "The Hungry," STD, p. 172.   [38] Sk, p. 34.
[39] *Ibid.*   [40] RH, p. 75.

"Enjoyment of life is forbidden to us, strictly forbidden, we have no illusions as to that—and by enjoyment of life I mean not only happiness, but also sorrow, passion, in short every tie with life. The representation of life claims all our forces, especially when those forces are not allotted to us in over-abundant measure. . . . Renunciation . . . is our compact with the Muse, in it reposes our strength, our value; and life is our forbidden garden, our great temptation, to which we yield sometimes, but never to our profit. . . . Everyone of us . . . knows what it is to make greedy excursions of that kind into the festival halls of life. But we return thence into our isolation humbled and sick at heart." [41]

The problem of the hero's isolation is brought to a unique and happy solution in *Royal Highness*. Klaus Heinrich's loneliness is put to flight by Imma Spoelmann, an American heiress, whose father's fabulous wealth has brought the curse of isolation on her too. Result—marriage; the State is refinanced by a benevolent father and all live happily ever after. *Royal Highness* is Thomas Mann's *Siegfried Idyll;* Mann himself tells us that it was "the first fruit of my married state . . . and it bears the marks of its origin." [42]

The most complete expression of the isolation theme is found in *Tonio Kröger*, which remains, says the author twenty-seven years after the first printing, "of all I have written perhaps still dearest to my heart today." [43] In this piece, synthesis of the lyric and the critical, Thomas Mann said once and for all, and said it exquisitely, all that he had to say concerning the isolation of the artist. In the story, Tonio is aware even in his boyhood of the cloud that is to darken his whole life. "Why is it I am different?" he wonders as a schoolboy. "Why am I at odds with the masters, and like a stranger among the other boys?" [44] Irresistibly drawn

[41] *Ibid.*, pp. 164-65.   [42] Sk, p. 34.
[43] *Ibid.*, p. 29.   [44] TK: STD, p. 88.

to his opposite, Hans Hansen, a merry, handsome lad who is interested above all things in horseback riding, Tonio knows that there is an impassable gulf between them. Tonio's beloved *Don Carlos* means nothing to Hans. And pretty, happy, commonplace Ingeborg Holm, who replaces Hans as Tonio's ideal, will have nothing to do with him, seems not even aware of him. Tonio soon comes to admit that "there was always something queer about him, whether he would or no, and he was alone, the regular and the usual would have none of him." [45]

The middle section of the story is set in the Munich studio of Lisaveta Ivanovna, the Russian artist friend. Tonio Kröger, now a writer of some eminence, discourses at length on the melancholy position of the artist. ("Lyric and prose essay in one," says Mann of this part of his tale, "the conversation with the entirely imaginary Russian friend cost me months." [46]) Art is no calling, mourns Tonio to Lisaveta, it is a curse:

"When does one begin to feel the curse? Early, horribly early. At a time when one ought by rights still to be living in peace and harmony with God and the world. It begins by your feeling yourself set apart, in a curious sort of opposition to the nice, sensible, regular people; there is a gulf of ironic sensibility, of knowledge, scepticism, disagreement between you and the others; it grows deeper and deeper; you realize that you are alone; and from then on any *rapprochement* is simply hopeless! What a fate; That is, if you still have enough heart, enough warmth of affections, to feel how frightful it is! . . . Your self-consciousness is kindled, because you among thousands feel the sign on your brow and know that everybody else sees it. . . . A genuine artist— not one who has taken up art as a profession like another, but an artist foreordained and damned—you can pick, without boasting very sharp perceptions, in a group of men. The sense of being

45 *Ibid.*, p. 91.
46 Sk, p. 29.

set apart, and not belonging, of being known and observed, something both regal and incongruous, shows in his face." [47]

The artist, says Thomas Mann, soon gets sick to death of knowledge. Let him attempt to mingle in the ranks of the living and the normal, and something pulls him back, saying as it did to Detleff of "The Hungry," "You may not live, you must create; you may not love, you must know." [48] Knowledge! What is this knowledge (*Erkenntnis*) which makes a man an artist and isolates him? It is insight; insight which pierces beyond the surface of human activity and penetrates to its core, insight which ruthlessly uses life for the purposes of art. That insight can be restrained neither by the bonds of intimacy nor the laws of morality. "Poets act shamelessly toward their experiences," says Nietzsche; "they exploit them." [49] Why is the artist isolated? Let us try to suggest an answer which will supplement what we find in *Tonio Kröger*. The artist is isolated because he must live and move in two worlds. He must be *in* life—living day by day beside his fellows, eating, sleeping, talking, loving, as must every human. And yet he is *apart* from life, standing off from it, over against it, transcribing it, seizing upon its most salient features and universalizing them. This distillation of life, this heightening and concentration of the human must be done without favor or partiality, without a trace of mere sentimental indulgence of one's good feelings.

The artist stands in a strange relation to normal humanity, almost as man himself stands to the animal. The animal lives and enjoys life, unconscious of the distinction between himself and nature, while man, moving through life as a part of nature, can nevertheless see himself as distinct from her; he can stand apart in his self-consciousness, he can place him-

[47] TK: STD, p. 104.   [48] "The Hungry," STD, p. 170.
[49] *Beyond Good and Evil*, Aph. 161.

self over against that very matrix which gave him birth and from which he can never completely dissever himself. Thus does the artist stand to humanity as a whole. While normal humans, happy or suffering, give little thought to their unique place in life, the artist—whose task it is to seize upon the raw material of human happiness and suffering and to mold it into a universal pattern—must stand apart from life, self-conscious and alone, in order to obtain his perspective. To be sure, the philosopher too is a self-conscious man, he too must take his stand apart from the world in order to see it in its most universal relations. But the philosopher is not bound to life as is the artist; his business is with mind, not with sense; he is occupied by a cosmic totality, not with the daily run of human things which are the artist's materials. Schopenhauer well knew the quality and effects of artist knowledge:

. . . genius lives essentially alone. It is too rare to find its like with ease, and too different from the rest of men to be their companion. With them it is will, with him it is knowledge that predominates.[50]

For this creative audacity, for this daring to stand apart from the human, ruthlessly scanning and noting down its every pulse and desire as material out of which to fashion something more universal than life, life itself takes revenge upon the artist. Regarding him as suspect, life withholds from him the warmth and joy freely granted to ordinary healthy folk with normal desires and respectable occupations. "Poetry," says Goethe, "isolates a man against his will . . . it is as inconvenient as a faithful mistress." [51] The artist is condemned to stand apart, as if he were on the edge of a

[50] "On Genius," WWI, III, xxxi.
[51] Letter 355, *Correspondence between Schiller and Goethe*, ed. Schmitz (London, 1877).

ballroom, wistfully watching the dancers go by, knowing full well that he can never have any share in their gaiety. Should he attempt an excursion into the realms of common good-fellowship, he is met with a suspicious glance, if he is not snubbed outright. He realizes then the meaning of Byron's words:

> They who know the most
> Must mourn the deepest o'er the fatal truth
> The Tree of Knowledge is not that of Life.[52]

The artist has the sign of Cain on his brow, says Thomas Mann; he is a marked man.[53] His "melancholy consciousness of aristocracy," [54] his conviction of an essential difference from the rest of humanity is made all the worse by his never-to-be-conquered desire to return to the life he has always loved, the life of familiar human happiness from which his artist's nature sets him apart. *Tonio Kröger* expresses this in a musically accented passage which is one of the highest points of lyric prose in all Thomas Mann's work. Tonio, mature and celebrated, has left Munich for Denmark, and stops at the Danish seaside hotel. There is a dance one night, and to it comes a young couple, who by virtue of their blond, blue-eyed, happy normality remind the artist irresistibly of the Hans and Ingeborg of his youth. Tonio muses to himself:

"Had I forgotten you? . . . No, never. Not you, Hans, not you, Inge the fair! It was always you I worked for; when I heard applause I always stole a look to see if you were there. . . . Did you read *Don Carlos*, Hans Hansen, as you promised me at the garden gate? No, don't read it! I do not ask it any more. What

[52] *Manfred*, Act I, scene 1.
[53] Mann uses the metaphor "marked man" or a variant of it when speaking of the artist in "The Hungry," STD, p. 169; TK: STD, p. 104; RH, p. 20. See Arthur Burkhard, "Thomas Mann's Treatment of the Marked Man," *Publications of the Modern Language Society*, XLIII, No. 2, June, 1926.   [54] Sk, p. 34.

have you to do with a king who weeps for loneliness? You must not cloud your clear eyes or make them dreary and dim by peering into melancholy poetry. . . . To be like you! To begin again, to grow up like you, regular like you, simple and normal and cheerful, in conformity and understanding with God and man, beloved of the innocent and happy. To take you, Ingeborg Holm, to wife, and have a son like you, Hans Hansen—to live free from the curse of knowledge and the torment of creation, live and praise God in blessed mediocrity! Begin again? But it would do no good. It would turn out the same—everything would turn out the same as it did before. For some go of necessity astray, because for them, there is no such thing as the right path." [55]

In his autobiographical sketch, Thomas Mann confesses that his early attitude towards his own art and fame included a "bad civic conscience." [56] This, of course, is the equivalent of Lisaveta's dictum that Tonio Kröger is a "bourgeois on the wrong path." Mann has always been self-conscious about his background, often to the extent of saying semiseriously that he really has no business in art. He has been overheard protesting that he is no artist at all, but simply "a good bourgeois drifted by chance into literature." [57] Now the connection between Mann's bourgeois heritage and the theme of isolation, which dominates the work of his early years, becomes clear. Every artist, especially every youthful artist, must be familiar with the isolation to which his task of knowledge and creation condemns him. But the artist who is at the same time a bourgeois—not merely a man with middle-class parents, but one to whom the bourgeois character is transmitted whole and entire—such a man must cope with inner tension as well as external isolation. In him, the demand for regularity and respectability must fight against the audacities of the creative urge. Like Hamlet, says Mann,

[55] TK: STD, p. 128.　　　[56] Sk, p. 15.　　　[57] *Three Essays*, p. 262.

the bourgeois artist knows what it means to be "called to knowledge without being born to it." [58] And in his solitary predicament he longs for the ordinary path of life, and the ordinary people who will have none of him.

"The artist is, and remains a gypsy," says Mann, "especially when he is a German artist of bourgeois culture." [59] The respectable and the conventional, the healthy and the normal are good bourgeois characters; it is for them and the people who embody them that Mann's young isolates yearn. These fledgling geniuses, all symbolic variants of their creator's youthful self, can never quite still the voice of the bourgeois conscience when it whispers to them that the artist's vocation is not quite aboveboard, is indeed suspect and subversive. Every artist must pay the price of differentiation from his fellow men. How true this is of the artist who is a German bourgeois, self-conscious and patrician as his class has always been! In addition to his awareness of the sign on his brow, such a man is fated to hanker after the untroubled conscience, the healthy metabolism of the good, solid, regular people from whose ranks he has sprung, and among whom he must always feel a stranger and an interloper. Tonio makes this clear in a letter to Lisaveta:

"My father, you know, had the temperament of the north: solid, reflective, puritanically correct, with a tendency to melancholia. My mother, of indeterminate foreign blood, was beautiful, sensuous, naïve, passionate and careless at once, and I think, irregular by instinct. The mixture was no doubt extraordinary and bore with it extraordinary dangers. The issue of it, a bourgeois who strayed off into art, a bohemian who feels a nostalgic yearning for respectability, an artist with a bad conscience. For surely it is

[58] "Freud," FGW, p. 9.
[59] *Reflections*, p. 402. References are made to the separately published edition (Fischer, Berlin, 1920), not to that of the *Sammlichte Werke*. Selections from this work in the text are translated from the German by the author.

my bourgeois conscience which makes me see in the artist's life, in all irregularity and all genius, something profoundly suspect, profoundly disreputable; that fills me with this lovelorn *faiblesse* for the simple and good, the comfortably normal, the average un-endowed respectable human being." [60]

Thomas Mann gives credit to the influence of his bour-geois heritage for the warm human sympathy in his own work, a sympathy for humanity perceptible beneath all his irony. "I ask myself," says Tonio Kröger to Lisaveta, "if you were aware how very close you came to the truth, how much my love of 'life' is one and the same thing as my being a bourgeois." [61] If we take Mann's word for it, the young bour-geois who strays into art must pay for his temerity by isola-tion; he must stand in two worlds and be at home in neither. But his art is the richer thereby, richer and deeper in the love and human warmth without which no art can be great or lasting.

In Mann's later work, the isolation motif retires to the background, giving place to other themes. To be sure, *Death in Venice* (1911) gives us an unforgettable picture of the tragic solitude of an artist. Aschenbach, the author informs us, "had grown up solitary, without companionship . . . his young days never knew the sweet idleness and blithe *laissez aller* of youth." [62] The last adventure of his life is begun and consummated in utter aloneness. But for all the emphasis on the solitude of Aschenbach, the earlier stress on the artist's longing for the normal and the commonplace is diminished; we are told of Aschenbach's youthful isolation only in pass-ing retrospect.

There is a faint echo of the isolation theme in *Disorder and Early Sorrow* (1925). This quiet little story of the days

[60] TK: STD, pp. 131-32.   [61] *Ibid.*, p. 131.   [62] DV: STD, p. 383.

darkened by the postwar inflation discloses one Professor Cornelius wistfully musing on the evening of a lively party given by his children. The house is filled with young people of student age, and the merry din of their dancing and laughter filters upstairs, where the professor sits uneasily in his room trying to work. He finds excuses to go down to the party. After all, he persuades himself, "it would be no more than friendly to go and contribute a box of cigarettes to the festivities." [63] But he feels an indefinable self-consciousness, he is not quite at home among the gay young folk, and he goes back to his study where he may sit alone with his nostalgia. His sadness deepens when one of the party—a cheerful, good-looking, but quite ordinary youth—so captivates the professor's baby daughter Ellie that later she pushes away her father, whom she ordinarily adores, and cries for her new idol.

In Thomas Mann's mature work the motif of the polarity between the bourgeois character and the creative instinct remains. The tension between order and irregularity, between bourgeois and genius is fundamental in the personalities of Gustave von Aschenbach and Hans Castorp. Aschenbach's spirit is the arena of an intense conflict between a fundamental conservatism and the artist's passion to beget in beauty. The blood of his ancestors, those respectable government officials, had up to the time of his Venetian sojourn stood the writer in good stead; his highly strung nature was held in a state of stability and control. Aschenbach had schooled himself in stern discipline, for "discipline, fortunately, was his native inheritance from his father's side." [64] But the apparent stability was only the result of the tension of equal and opposing forces. After the

[63] *Disorder and Early Sorrow*, STD, p. 516.   [64] DV: STD, p. 383.

first encounter with Tadzio, Aschenbach's soul becomes a veritable Armageddon; the disciplinary habits of a lifetime and the unleashed erotic-artistic drive have it out literally to the death. It is the former that crumbles. Order goes down before freedom, form wins over analysis, beauty triumphs over morality. Aschenbach is transformed from a reserved and dignified patrician into a berouged and leering satyr. But the victory over the bourgeois heritage is a Pyrrhic one. The feverish struggle shatters body as well as spirit—and the solitary dies in his beach chair.

The story of Hans Castorp is a projection on a larger scale of the same conflict, although the "bad conscience" note is missing. On a first reading of *The Magic Mountain* one may skip over an important little section near the beginning of the book, entitled "At Tienappels'." [65] Here, as Hans Castorp is described in his native Hamburg environment, Thomas Mann makes clear that the youth in his pre-sanatorium days was to all appearances a bourgeois to the manner born. He had all the earmarks of the *Bürger*. Overcareful of his personal appearance, he would be distressed by a rough spot on his shirt cuff. He was fond of good living, finishing off his ample meals with a finger bowl and a Russian cigarette. He reminds us in this respect of an earlier bourgeois hero, Wilhelm Meister. [66] To be sure, Hans had once executed a water color of a steamship, and someone who saw it remarked that the youth might develop into a good marine painter. But Hans's middle-class instincts had already prejudged the merits of an artist's career, so that when he heard the compliment, he "only laughed good-humoredly, and not for a

---

[65] MM, p. 37.

[66] Of Goethe's hero, we read: "Brought up in a substantial burgher's house, cleanliness and order were the element in which he breathed; and inheriting as he did a portion of his father's taste for finery, it had always been his care in boyhood to furbish up his chamber . . . in the stateliest fashion." *Wilhelm Meister's Apprenticeship* (Carlyle trans.), I, 84.

moment considered letting himself in for a career of being eccentric and not getting enough to eat." [67] Besides, he had chosen a solid bourgeois profession; his apprenticeship to the shipbuilding firm of Tunder and Wilms was only the first step, his neighbors knew, in a career which would in all probability reach its climax in his election to the Senate. (This was the apex of Thomas Buddenbrook's public life.) But here lay the weak spot. Hans Castorp assented readily, from force of habit, to the highest tenet in the whole bourgeois creed, namely, that in hard work lay the highest and most unimpeachable righteousness. But although his own work was all "very first rate, very solid, very important," Hans nevertheless admitted to himself that it was "confoundedly complicated and fatiguing." [68] In fact, although his bourgeois conscience would never have allowed him to admit it openly, Hans did not like work at all, liked it no more than his creator liked his own early drudgery in the Munich fire-insurance office. Indeed to Hans Castorp, work came to mean simply a rather disagreeable business that had to be got through in order that afterwards he might enjoy his dinner and his Maria Mancini cigar with a clear conscience.

Work was for him, in the nature of things, the most estimable attribute of life; when you came down to it, there was nothing else that was estimable. It was the principle by which one stood or fell, the Absolute of the time; it was, so to speak, its own justification. His regard for it was thus religious in character, and so far as he knew, unquestioning. But it was another matter whether he loved it; and that he could not do, however great his regard, the simple reason being that it did not agree with him. Exacting occupation dragged at his nerves, it wore him out; quite openly he confessed that he liked to have his time free, not weighted with the leaden load of effort; lying spacious before

[67] MM, p. 43.   [68] *Ibid.*

him, not divided up by obstacles one had to grit one's teeth and conquer, one after the other.[69]

All of this points to the conclusion that Hans Castorp was no simon-pure young burgher in his Hamburg days. Although from sheer inertia he professed loyalty to the bourgeois code of life, his deeper self at last rebelled against a smothering environment. The slight *malaise* which brought from his physician the advice to go vacationing was the first sign of revolt. Hans Castorp's unconscious—to put it in Freudian terms—weighed and found wanting the bourgeois world view in which his conscious self acquiesced. His rebellion took the form of disease. Castorp's illness was *antibourgeois*, a device to escape from a spiritually stifling atmosphere. And at the Berghof, where the air of freedom and laxness generated by the communal participation in illness prevailed, Hans's nonbourgeois impulses had full sway, culminating in his surrender to Clavdia on the carnival night. From that time on, his history is one of the gradual integration of his old conservative values with his new-found freedom. The final synthesis is prevented only by the coming of the Great War.

Ludovico Settembrini is the Banquo's ghost which arises in the sanatorium to remind Castorp that the life down below, which he has left for dead, still has its claims upon him. This Italian humanist is the pedagogic champion of international bourgeois ideals—progress, enlightenment and the rest. He is quick to praise Castorp's abandoned profession,[70] and his customary addressing of the youth as "Engineer" implies a reminder of duty forsaken. Settembrini fears the unleashing of antibourgeois drives in the young man; he twice advises Hans to flee the Circe's isle of shiftlessness

[69] *Ibid.*, p. 44.   [70] *Ibid.*, p. 77.

and degeneration. He detests Clavdia (the antipathy is mutual) for she represents to him the very demon of anti-rationality and irresponsibility; her equivocal charms, he feels in his bones, will enlist his pupil under the standard of Asia, the most unbourgeois of cultures.

In the mouth of Leo Naphta, however, the word "bour-geois" becomes a contemptuous epithet. The *verirrter* Jesuit reveals to Hans with cynical amusement that Settembrini is a Freemason, and that this society, which was once of hieratic character and spiritual aim, is now just "a god-forsaken bourgeoisiedom in the form of a club." [71] To Naphta, Set-tembrini's whole liberal morality is nothing but bourgeois sentimentality:

It was life-bound and thus entirely utilitarian; it was pathetically unheroic. Its aim was to make men grow old and happy, rich and comfortable—and that was all there was to it. And this Philistine philosophy, this gospel of work and reason, served Herr Settem-brini as an ethical system. As far as he, Naphta, was concerned, he would continue to deny that it was anything but the sheerest and flabbiest bourgeoisiedom.[72]

Naphta is, of course, represented as a Catholic, although his Jewish antecedents, his Marxist bent, and his terroristic nihilism make him a very strange one. Naphta's aristocratic bias is consistent with Thomas Mann's suggestions elsewhere that Catholicism represents the aristocratic principle, Protes-tantism the bourgeois. In Mann's eyes, Philip the Second of Spain—he of the high ruff and formal etiquette—is symbolic of the Catholic-aristocratic, his Counter-Reformation a fruit-less attempt to stem the rise of the Protestant middle class.[73]

Hans Castorp retains far more of the bourgeois character than he himself realizes. For all his professed abandonment

---

[71] *Ibid.*, p. 647.   [72] *Ibid.*, p. 586.
[73] *Ibid.*, p. 479. *Disorder and Early Sorrow*, STD, p. 511.

of traditional conservatism, Clavdia Chauchat sees through him. To her, Hans is in spite of himself a fitting representative of his country and class, he is at once "Bourgeois, humaniste, et poète." [74] On carnival night, the ardent youth tells Clavdia that humanism and progress may go to the devil, for he loves her. "Petit bourgeois!" she murmurs in reply. "Joli bourgeois à la petite tache humide." [75] Is this not an echo of Lisaveta's calling Tonio Kröger "ein verirrter Bürger"? Hans Castorp is simply another bourgeois on the wrong track, although he does not have as sore a conscience about it as had Tonio. Castorp is revealing when he confesses to Clavdia "I am hardly a very passionate man, though I have my passions, phlegmatic ones." [76] Only a bourgeois *à la petite tache humide* could confess to phlegmatic passions. In Hans, the bourgeois principle of order bows before the demands of antibourgeois *eros* and disease. But it bows *resiliently*, it is never quite downed.

"Yes, I am a bourgeois," said Thomas Mann long before the troubled times which brought his exile, "and in Germany that is a word whose meaning is as little foreign to spirit and art as it is to dignity, solidity and comfort." [77] Mann has always insisted that the bourgeois character in the Germany he loved has left its indelible stamp on German art. To be sure, the bourgeois character has its bad side: its philistinism, its hostility to the imaginative, its fetish of work as the be-all and end-all, its tendency to amalgamate with the shallow doctrines of Western Enlightenment, which makes of life an end in itself and considers humanitarian progress the highest good. It is this latter aspect of international bourgeois world view which Mann attacks in his *Reflections of a Non-Political Man*. But the bourgeois heritage includes

[74] MM, p. 425. [75] *Ibid.*, p. 432. [76] *Ibid.*, p. 749. [77] *Reflections*, p. 83.

blessings, too, that have left their mark on German art: a conservatism that checks overrefinement and hyperesthesia; the critical intuition, which develops keen self-scrutiny; the amenity to discipline, making possible the sheer hard work through which true art must be brought into being.

Goethe, Mann points out, is a happy example of a German artist who derived strength from his bourgeois inheritance. With explicit autobiographical reference in mind, Mann calls attention to the poet's tracing to his father the element of discipline—*des Lebens ernstes Führen*—in his own nature, and to his mother, the *Frohnatur,* the lively, sensuous, artistic impulse. In commemoration of the centenary of Goethe's death, Mann wrote an essay titled "Goethe as Representative of the Bourgeois Age." [78] This age, according to Mann, runs from the fifteenth century to the beginning of the twentieth. With Goethe in mind, he says:

The great sons of the bourgeois age, those whose capacity for spiritual growth raised them above the level of their class, are living proof of the fact that there are in the bourgeois nature infinite potentialities, unlimited potentialities for self-liberation and self-conquest.[79]

Mann finds in the man Goethe any number of typical bourgeois qualities—keen business instinct, love of order, patience, industry, tenacity—in short, "an element of care, of solicitude that may be regarded as bourgeois in its ethical aspects." [80] Goethe even had the bourgeois weakness for good living; he liked elegance and dressed fastidiously. Mann plays with this trait of the master in *The Beloved Returns,* in the scene where the poet is dressing for the day,

---

[78] *"Goethe als Repräsentant des bürgerlichen Zeitalters."* Reprinted as "Goethe," *Yale Review,* XXI (Summer, 1932).
[79] *Ibid.,* p. 735.   [80] *Ibid.,* p. 717.

enjoying the feel of his flannel gown, his cologne, his shave, and his hairgrooming.[81] But it was the bourgeois sense of discipline, Mann claims, that made possible the labor necessary for Goethe's vast artistic output. "Who knows," Mann asks, "whether *Faust*, infinite in its inner scope, would have reached even the stage of external completion that it has, if the bourgeois father had not implanted in the boy's mind the pedagogical imperative to finish things?"[82] It was Goethe who wrote *Hermann and Dorothea*, "that inspired poem of the German bourgeoisie." It was Goethe who wondered how the aristocrat Byron overcame the handicaps of a lofty social background—since a certain middle station seemed to Goethe best for the growth of talent.[83] It was Goethe's bourgeois quality, Mann tells us, that accounted for the poet's antirevolutionary sentiments.[84]

Richard Wagner stands out clearly in Thomas Mann's mind as another German artist who owes much to a similar heritage. He partially acknowledged this debt in *Die Meistersinger*, that musical tribute to *Bürgerlichkeit*. The composer's personality, says Mann, was an "indissoluble mingling of the daemonic and the bourgeois."[85] The latter shows up in Wagner's capacity for brutally hard, concentrated work. Who has ever sat through performances of the four parts of the *Ring* and has not wondered how a single human being, one mortal man, could have had the patience to cope with the tetralogy's technical side alone? Coupled with this mighty discipline is another bourgeois quality in Wagner— his well-known fastidiousness and love of good living. Wagner's taste for luxury has its decadent side, Mann thinks, and this actually carries over into his music. "Who would deny," he asks, "that there is a suggestion of satin dressing-

[81] *The Beloved Returns*, p. 320. Compare with "Goethe," *Yale Review*, XXI, 714. [82] "Goethe," *Yale Review*, XXI, 714.
[83] Eck, p. 89. [84] See p. 140, below. [85] "Wagner," FGW, p. 180.

gowns in Wagner's art?" [86] Taking the composer's career as a whole, from the days of 1848 to *Parsifal,* Mann believes that we can see how Wagner "went the way of the German bourgeoisie: from revolution to disillusionment, to pessimism and a sheltered, contemplative resignation." [87]

We have seen that the isolation theme tends to fade from Mann's later work, even though the motif of tension between the creative and bourgeois elements continues and is especially apparent in *The Magic Mountain.* It is only natural that maturity should bring about a diminution of the sorrows of the young artist, the "bad conscience," the feeling of isolation. "These are the pangs and anguishes of youth," says the artist of sixty years, "destined to be lightened and tranquilized as years flowed by and brought ripeness with them." [88] Or we can think of it in this way: as Mann's artistic personality matured, there came about—in a manner entirely natural in a great artist—a gradual reconciliation between the creative instinct and the bourgeois demands. The bourgeois element itself, though ever present, is canalized in Mann's later work. It is taken over into the discipline necessary to an artist maintaining his creative production over a long period of years—the discipline of intensive research, for example, that preceded the writing of the *Joseph* series. It is manifest in Mann's excursions into criticism, those carefully written essays scattered at intervals between his later creative works. It is apparent in his conservatism, his late emphasis on the category of democracy, his opposition to Fascism. In the democratic Mann, there emerges a bourgeois trait which comes to the defense of civic morality; the bourgeois conservative love of order rose to the challenge of antihumane reaction. Both artist and bourgeois in Mann were outraged by the anti-intellectual character of National

[86] *Ibid.,* p. 189.   [87] *Ibid.,* p. 198.   [88] "Freud," FGW, p. 9.

Socialism; in his passionate denunciation of this barbarism, artist and bourgeois were welded together in a final synthesis for which the ground was long prepared.

We shall return to an analysis of the political character of this "non-political" artist. But now we must examine one important reason why the artist cannot be constrained within the limits of the bourgeois pattern, however much that pattern may influence his character and his work. In Mann's words:

Genius, as we know, can never be normal in the banal, narrowly bourgeois sense; no matter how favored by nature, it cannot be natural, healthy, regular, in the sense of the philistine. Physically, there is always about it much that is delicate, irritable, precariously balanced; psychically, much that is uncanny, alien to the normal, and almost psychopathic.[89]

The artist's nature is fundamentally irregular. We have spoken of his creative insight, which isolates him from the ordinary. We must turn now to another aspect of his irregularity—his divergence from the norm of health, his bond with disease.

[89] "Goethe," *Yale Review*, XXI, 727.

2

DISEASE, ART, AND LIFE

IN THE PREFACE to his abridgment of Schopenhauer's *The World as Will and Idea*, Thomas Mann quotes Nietzsche's dictum to the effect that the position of a being in the hierarchy of reality is in direct proportion to its capacity to suffer, and adds: "Here Nietzsche betrays his ultimate dependence upon Schopenhauer's aristocratic theory of man's noble vocation to suffer. And in particular the highest type of man, the genius." [1] Not only Nietzsche, the knowing reader will interject, not only Schopenhauer, but Thomas Mann himself is at one with this aristocratic doctrine—especially that part of it which emphasizes the union of genius and suffering. No one who reads Mann for the first time can fail to be struck by his preoccupation with disease, his interest in suffering, his sympathetic concern with death. Indeed, the first reaction to Mann's books is often one of distaste, of positive repugnance at the highly technical descriptions of disease, the vivid deathbed photography, the minute attention to suffering, mental and physical. But deeper acquaintance with Mann's work proves, as we shall see, that his is no mere naturalistic interest in illness and physical dissolution, that in his creative products disease assumes an importance which we may justly call metaphysical, and that in certain cases, disease, the path to death, is

[1] *Schopenhauer Presented by Thomas Mann* (New York, 1939), pp. 23-24.

not just a process of organic destruction, but a quality which can heighten life and ennoble the sufferer.

No one familiar with currents in modern literature will deny that disease had been found a lively subject for literary treatment long before Thomas Mann's interest in it. Nineteenth century scientific progress in the isolation of germs and viruses had appealed strongly to the imagination of the reading public, and a wave of bacteriological-pathological interest was reflected in the literature of the times. Nor has this tendency yet disappeared. On the contrary, it has been augmented in our own day by popular interest in mental abnormality. Throughout the last century and thus far in the present one, a host of ailing characters have paraded through novels and dramas. Dumas brought tears to the eyes of the world by his portrayal of Marguerite's lingering death from consumption. Ibsen wrote the tragedy of inherited paresis in *Ghosts*. Dostoyevsky created unforgettable pictures of epilepsy in *The Brothers Karamazov* and *The Idiot*. In *Cousin Betty,* Balzac doomed his Valérie and Crevel to a mortal disease for which no cure was known. Gerhart Hauptmann even brought leprosy on the stage in his drama *Poor Henry*. The role of illness in English letters can be followed from sentimental beginnings in Dickens to Somerset Maugham's syphilitic Mildred. But that most of this purely random miscellany has little in common with Mann's treatment of disease becomes clear when we realize that each separate ailment, named above, is the result either of heredity, as in the case of Oscar Alving, or of simple infection, catching a germ, exposure to contagion. It is the psychic connotations of disease that Mann emphasizes, the intimate reaction upon the personality; he treats it as a way to self-realization rather than as simple bodily ailing.

Dostoyevsky is an exception. The Russian novelist, whose

books Mann read avidly in his youthful days, shows a certain affinity to the German writer in his conception of disease. Dostoyevsky's sympathy for infirmity, his faith in the power of suffering to redeem, is fundamental to his character. He was sick himself, and his portrayals of epileptics and "idiots" reveal a sympathy with disease which goes far deeper than mere concern with simple organic infection. Sickness of soul and of body go hand in hand in Dostoyevsky's work, and his reverence for suffering makes plain that he discerned a basic relation between illness and sanctity. Mann himself refers to *The Idiot* as "Dostoyevsky's attempt to present the purest and holiest in our humanity on the basis of the pathological." [2] We recall those words, so like Thomas Mann's, in which Dostoyevsky tells us of Myshkin:

. . . he often said to himself that all these gleams and flashes of the highest sensation of life and self-consciousness, and therefore also of the highest form of existence, were nothing but disease, the interruption of the normal condition; and if so, it was not at all the highest form of being, but on the contrary must be reckoned the lowest. And yet he came at last to an extremely paradoxical conclusion. "What if it is disease?" he decided at last. "What does it matter that it is an abnormal intensity, if the result, if the minute of sensation, remembered and analyzed afterwards in health, turns out to be the acme of harmony and beauty, and gives a feeling, unknown and undefined till then, of completeness, of proportion, of reconciliation, and of ecstatic devotion merging in the highest synthesis of life?" [3]

One group of literary men—the writers of the German romantic school—regarded disease sympathetically. Many of them thought of illness not as something ignoble and anti-human, but as a spiritual phenomenon, closely associated with intellectual and emotional awakening. "The idea of

[2] Review of Joseph Conrad's *The Secret Agent*, PM, p. 245.
[3] *The Idiot*, trans. Constance Garner (New York, 1928), pp. 224-25.

perfect health," Novalis proclaimed, "is interesting only from a scientific point of view. Sickness is necessary to individualization." [4] In his novel *Lucinde*, Friedrich Schlegel described illness as a spiritual force. E. T. A. Hoffmann composed a story of an artist whose disease was the source and condition of her art.[5] These are quite typical samples of the German romantic attitude toward illness, and it is worth remembering that these writers formed an important part of Mann's literary background.[6]

Thomas Mann's earliest work is represented by a group of short stories centering around "Little Herr Friedemann" (1897). Most of these stories concern individuals isolated from their fellows by some physical or mental deformity; descriptions of quivering suffering, mental cruelty and bitter death are common to them. The protagonist of "Little Herr Friedemann" is a pigeon-breasted dwarf, who is goaded by a lady of fashion into professing his love for her. She tortures him for a while, and when she throws his love back in his face, he drowns himself. "Tobias Mindernickel" (1897) tells of a sadistic recluse, who alternately caresses and mistreats a poor dog he has picked up, until he finally kills the animal with a bread knife. The hero of "Little Lizzy" (1897) is a pathologically obese lawyer, who is forced by his wife and her lover to appear at a garden party dressed as a little girl, and to sing an infantile song—which is cut short by his collapse and death. "The Way to the Churchyard" (1901) deals with the self-torture of an alcoholic, one Praisegod Piepsam, who screams himself into fatal apoplexy when a youthful cyclist rudely crowds him off the cemetery path.

[4] *Aphorisms*, Vol. IV of *The German Classics* (New York, 1914), p. 187.
[5] *Weird Tales*, trans J. T. Bealby (New York, 1923), p. 27.
[6] For a more detailed examination of the relation between the German romantic attitude toward illness and that of Thomas Mann, the reader is referred to the chapter "Disease" in Hermann Weigand's *Thomas Mann's Novel 'Der Zauberberg.'*

These stories were written in Mann's early twenties, and
it is interesting to observe in what contrast their harshness
and cynicism stands to the more mellow tone of his later and
larger works. In these first tales, there is no broad and
searching inquiry into the meaning of disease and death
such as marks the products of Mann's maturity. Yet in their
preoccupation with abnormality and suffering, the youthful
beginnings foreshadow what is to come. The cynicism of
the early stories may represent a reaction to the *Schwärmerei*
which prevailed in German household literature at the turn
of the century. But more than this, their pessimism reveals
the sensitiveness of a young artist who, in his "native tendency to idleness and dreams" [7] shrank from the harsh contact of the actual world, and developed toward life an
antipathy and distrust which he outgrew only many years
later.

In *Buddenbrooks*, Thomas Mann's first major work, there
is a certain flavor in the treatment of disease and death, as
well as in the appeal to the metaphysics of pessimism, which
goes far beyond the quality of the naturalistic novel. There
is, for example, the strange figure of Christian Buddenbrook,
sick of no ordinary illness, but of a psychophysiological
affliction marked by chorea and hallucinations. The discussion of Christian's illness conveys the implication, so characteristic of Mann, that a person may have a chronic disease,
not by accident, but by virtue of his own personality, so that
his ill-health is a necessary and inseparable aspect of himself. To his brother Thomas, Christian's nervous affliction
appears as part and parcel of the poor man's eccentric and
unbourgeois self. On the occasion of a quarrel between the
two brothers, Christian pleads his ill-health in excuse for his
shortcomings. To this, Thomas replies in a passion:

[7] Sk, p. 8.

"Don't you realize, you fool . . . that all these horrors are the consequence and effect of your vices, your idleness, and your self-tormenting? Go to work! Stop petting your condition and talking about it! If you go crazy—and I tell you plainly I don't think it at all unlikely—I shan't be able to shed a tear; for it will be entirely your own fault." [8]

The deaths of the Frau Consul and of Thomas Buddenbrook are handled with naturalistic attention to physiological details. But there is something more than naturalism in the account of the *aperçue* vouchsafed to Thomas, when shortly before his death he reads Schopenhauer by accident. The master's words on suffering give him comfort; the sense of futility, which is all that civic progress and honors have left him, is assuaged. Thomas Buddenbrook feels a nostalgia for death.

Only a few lines remained when the servant came through the garden at four o'clock to call him to dinner. He nodded, read the remaining sentences, closed the book, and looked about him. He felt that his whole being had unaccountably expanded, and at the same time there clung about his senses a profound intoxication, a strange, sweet, vague allurement which somehow resembled the feelings of early love and longing. [9]

Senator Buddenbrook dies of a bad tooth. At least, so it appears. The truth is, however, that his meticulously groomed exterior had for a long time covered up a morbid inner strain; antibourgeois inclinations to disorder, sternly suppressed, had set up in him a terrific tension which left him a burned-out shell at forty. When at last he admits to himself that his life is meaningless, his existence without purpose, death comes to him.

When we are introduced to Hanno, Thomas Buddenbrook's son, we discover the first of a long line of Mann's

<hr>

[8] Bud, II, 182.   [9] *Ibid.*, 256.

heroes who embody in themselves the combination of disease and genius. Hanno is a little artist, he plays the piano and composes; his musical gift he has inherited from his mother. Disappointing his father by his hatred of school and the practical things of life, Hanno is nervous and sickly from his infancy, a prey to *pavor nocturnus*. His boyhood is brightened only by the joy of listening to music, going to the opera, playing the piano and composing. In his adolescence, Hanno is struck down by typhoid fever. And just as Hans Castorp, a disease-ridden hero of a later day, finds that he must choose between life and death, so too in Hanno, during his final coma, the will-to-live struggles against the longing for death. Unlike Hans Castorp, whose love for life brings him out of his dream and safely back to the sanatorium, Hanno's desire to live struggles in vain against his shrinking from the harsh demands of life. And Hanno dies. Sometimes a dying man, Thomas Mann suggests, may live if he wills to:

But if he shudders when he hears life's voice, if the memory of that vanished scene and the sound of that lusty summons make him shake his head, make him put out his hand to ward it off as he flies forward in the way of escape that is open to him— then it is clear that the patient will die.[10]

In *Tristan*, one of the first stories Mann wrote after finishing *Buddenbrooks*, there is a further development of the theme of disease in a clinical setting curiously anticipating that of *The Magic Mountain*. The sanatorium of Einfried bears a sketchy resemblance to the Berghof at Davos. The two physicians of *Tristan*—Leander and Müller—stand to each other in something of the relation of Drs. Behrens and Krokowski. A careful obscurantism is practiced in both establishments when deaths occur among the patients.[11] A

[10] *Ibid.*, 354.   [11] *Tristan*, STD, p. 134.

love affair between a male patient and the consumptive wife of another man is treated both in the earlier and in the mature work. The analogies, however, between *Tristan* and *The Magic Mountain* must not be pushed too far, for the treatment of the disease motif in the slighter story is far more superficial than that of the later narrative, more superficial even than that of *Buddenbrooks*. Coming as it does immediately after the bourgeois novel, *Tristan* marks a brief return to the mocking cynicism of the first stories. But it is possible to discern in the somewhat ridiculous predicament of Spinell a portrait of the artist and his ambiguous relation to life, which is more delicately drawn in *Tonio Kröger*, written one year later.

The two principal characters of *Fiorenza* (1904), Mann's only drama, are both ill. The humanist Lorenzo de' Medici and the monk Savonarola are the protagonists; the former lies dying of an unknown disease in his Florentine pleasure palace, and the latter is consumed by fever even in his pulpit. "My life is tortured," the friar tells the dying Lorenzo. "Fever, dysentery and continuous mental labor for the weal of the city have so weakened all my internal organs that I can no longer bear the least hardship."[12] In this Renaissance drama, the humanistic attitude toward death—death is not opposed to life, but is rather a fulfillment of it—is represented by Lorenzo, who becomes in this respect the forerunner of Settembrini of *The Magic Mountain*. Lorenzo, however, forsakes this belief on his deathbed, realizing its insufficiency when facing the prospect of darkness. He cries to his friend, Pico Mirandola:

"Death is horrible, Pico. You cannot grasp it. No one here can grasp it save myself who must die. I have so dearly loved life that I held death to be the triumph of life. That was poetry and

[12] *Fiorenza*, STD, p. 264.

extravagance. It is gone, it fails one at a pinch. For I have seen dissolution unroll before me." [13]

Mann makes clear in his play that both ailing enemies, the Florentine voluptuary and the nihilistic zealot, are brother artists. Says Lorenzo to the Prior, "Brother you yourself—you too are an artist!" [14] And the monk admits the impeachment with the distinction that his art is holy, the art of the saint, which is knowledge and denial.

A little portrait of Friedrich Schiller, called "A Weary Hour" (1905), contains what is probably Mann's first explicit declaration that art and disease go hand in hand, that an artist's bodily affliction is part of the constitution which makes him an artist. In this sketch, which Mann admits is "highly subjective," [15] the poet is discovered tired and weak from his labor under the duress of his catarrhal infection. He rests a moment to reflect on the problem of the artist nature:

Pain . . . how his breast swelled at the word! He drew himself up and folded his arms; his gaze, beneath the close-set auburn brows, was kindled by the nobility of his suffering. No man was utterly wretched so long as he could still speak of his misery in high-sounding and noble words. One thing only was indispensable; the courage to call his life by large and fine names. Not to ascribe his sufferings to bad air and constipation; to be well enough to cherish emotions, to scorn and ignore the material. Just on this one point to be naïve, though in all else sophisticated. . . . But he *did* believe in it; so profoundly, so ardently, that nothing which came to pass with suffering could seem to him either useless or evil. His glance sought the manuscript, and his arms tightened across his chest. Talent itself—was that not suffering? [16]

[13] *Ibid.*, p. 239.
[14] *Ibid.*, p. 266.
[15] Sk, p. 17.
[16] "A Weary Hour," STD, p. 293.

Axel Martini, the poet of *Royal Highness*, makes the same point as does Mann's Schiller. Speaking to the prince, who questions him about his talent, Martini replies, "My health is delicate—I dare not say unfortunately, for I am convinced that my talent is inseparably connected with my bodily infirmity." [17]

As a work of art, *Death in Venice*, written three years before the outbreak of the first World War, probably marks the highest point achieved by Mann in his pieces of smaller scale, and it seems foolhardy to try to examine analytically this carefully wrought pattern, composed of the interweavings of so many threads, and to attempt to separate from them a single strand. This *Novelle* is, of course, an allegory of the artist, symbolically representing the dangers of his calling—his ambiguous relation to the moral realm, his carrying in himself by the very nature of his vocation the seeds of negation, of spiritual and physical destruction. Thomas Mann here presents a stage upon which are played off against each other, as warring elements in the person of Gustave von Aschenbach, the antithetical principles of form and analysis, art and judgment, nature and spirit. The theme of the tale is death and love—and their unity in one man. At the outset of the narrative, Aschenbach is seen pondering the headstone legends in a chapel graveyard, when the figure of a passer-by, dressed in hiking costume, calls up to his mind the associations of travel. (Is this mysterious hiker a human being of flesh and blood?) Yielding to an impulse to travel, to get away from the work which is consuming him physically and mentally, Aschenbach goes to Venice, where he may sit on the shore and gaze upon the sea which he loves.

Aschenbach's longing for the ocean is his nostalgia for

[17] RH, p. 163.

negation, for the unformed, for nothingness, a nostalgia which is buried beneath his professional preoccupation with form. Of the eminent man's love for the sea, the author of the tale tells us:

His love for the ocean had profound sources: the hard-worked artist's longing for rest, his yearning to seek refuge from the thronging manifold shapes of his fancy in the bosom of the simple and vast: and another yearning, opposed to his art, and perhaps for that very reason a lure, for the unorganized, the immeasurable, the eternal—in short, for nothingness.[18]

The artist and Nirvana! One thinks of Nietzsche, and a passage from his *Dawn of Day*, which is strikingly in key with the mood of Thomas Mann's tale:

Now everything is calm, wide, oppressive and dark like the lagoon in Venice. I wish for nothing, and draw a deep breath, and yet I feel inwardly indignant at this "wish for nothing"— so the waves rise and fall in the ocean of my melancholy.[19]

The sea is a symbol of death. We know that Aschenbach, having fallen in love with the beautiful Tadzio, refuses to leave Venice, even though well informed of the ever-spreading tropic plague. He dies in his beach chair, looking out to sea, in the direction of which his beloved seems at the moment of death to be pointing.

In the early pages of Aschenbach's story, Thomas Mann sketches the literary man's past life, with curiously autobiographical overtones. Describing the writer's personal appearance,[20] Mann talks of his tired eyes, and comments:

[18] DV: STD, p. 338.   [19] *Dawn of Day*, Aph. 492.
[20] The subjective aspect of Aschenbach reflects Mann's own feelings. Objectively, he is modelled after Gustave Mahler, the composer. The physical description of Aschenbach closely approximate's Mahler's. At the time of the composition of *Death in Venice*, Mann had wanted to do a story about Goethe, using as his theme the poet's love in his old age for the youthful Ulrike Levetzow. But Mann decided against a Goethe story, and his half-formed plan finally crystallized in the tale of an anonymous artist's love for

Art heightens life. She gives deeper joy, she consumes more swiftly. She engraves adventures of the spirit and the mind in the faces of her votaries; let them lead outwardly a life of the most cloistered calm, she will in the end produce in them a fastidiousness, an over-refinement, a nervous fever and exhaustion, such as a career of extravagant passions and pleasures can hardly show.[21]

Here is Mann's thesis of the inextricable union of disease and the artist nature. We know that in Mann's view—we shall consider this more fully later on—there are two types of illness. Most sickness degrades, lessens man's humanity, emphasizes his bodily part. But there is another kind of illness, a rarer phenomenon, which has its roots in the personality itself; this is fundamentally nonorganic in character. Inseparable from the nature of the sufferer, it is the corporeal manifestation of a disturbed psyche. Such sickness can ennoble, can heighten humanity, can indeed be the very condition of achievement. It is this form of illness to which the artist nature is most often subject. The creative personality, delicate and hypersensitive, is the locus of a spiritual tension which can carry over to the body in the form of ill-health. Artistic creation burns up with perilous swiftness not only psychical but physical energy. Art consumes, and in consuming, it may undermine the soundness of the body.

Artistic treatment of sickness and death is expanded to its widest development in *The Magic Mountain*, the product of a creative and speculative imagination of grand scope. The novel, which Thomas Mann published in 1924 after twelve years of intermittent labor, is a prose epic of disease and the coincident self-development of Hans Castorp, a

a young boy. Twenty-eight years later, Mann finally completed his Goethe story, *The Beloved Returns*, which does not, however, involve the aged writer's attraction to the maiden. (The author is indebted to Frau Dr. Mann for this information.)   [21] DV: STD, p. 338.

young student of engineering from Hamburg. In the clinical setting of an Alpine tuberculosis sanatorium, the ailing youth subjects himself to the tutelage of those around him. He derives powerful intellectual stimulation from Ludovico Settembrini, an Italian humanist, and from Leo Naphta, a nihilistic Jesuit mystagogue. He learns lessons other than those of the intellect from his military cousin, Joachim Ziemmsen; from an exotic Russian lady, Clavdia Chauchat; from a Dutch East Indian coffee king, Pieter Pieperkorn. While submitting himself to this battery of personalities, Hans Castorp nevertheless suffers none of them to govern completely the direction taken cautiously by his own gradually integrating self. *The Magic Mountain* deals with its hero's attainment of significant life values, of intellectual and spiritual fulfillment, through a pathway of disease, corruption, and death. It is the story of one to whom is barred the simple, honest, direct approach to life—of one who must take the other path, ambiguous, dangerous, shadowed.

Is *The Magic Mountain*, like its predecessors in Mann's work, an allegory of the artist nature? Hans Castorp does not write poems or compose music. He is not a novelist like Tonio Kröger or Gustave von Aschenbach. He cannot be called a painter, even though he once executed a sensitive water color of a ship. True enough, *literally* Hans Castorp is not an artist. Nevertheless, we see that in a certain sense, he may be considered an artist in symbol. *The Magic Mountain* has what we may call different levels of signification. In this it resembles other great art works. The groundling can see in Shakespeare's *Hamlet* a rousing good show with plenty of ghost, swordplay, and bloodshed. A less literal view reveals a play with an ethical problem. Abstracting still further, the man of perceptions discovers in the drama a deep psychological intuition of the problem of a solitary dreamer, a man who is called to action but not born to it. *The Magic Mountain*, literally read, tells a good story of a young man in a Swiss tuberculosis sanatorium. Taken on a higher level, the book presents a picture of the bourgeois society of pre-war Europe, and the antibourgeois instincts of a young German. Higher still, the work poses the problem of man's relation to humanity and nature. The humorous tone of the book can be regarded as good-natured fun, or as a subtle irony which shuttles back and forth between the various levels of meaning. In his *The Beloved Returns*, Mann makes Goethe decry frowning sublimity in art, saying:

"No, no, the depths must laugh! Profundity must smile, glide gently in, and smiling yield itself to the initiate alone—that is the esoteric of our art. For the people, gay pictures; for the *cognoscenti*, the mystery behind." [22]

One can think of Hans Castorp as an individual, as a German bourgeois, as a human being. The phrase "delicate child of life" is originally applied to the young engineer, later to the German people, later still to man himself in his relation to the cosmos.[23] Thus Hans Castorp is a representative of humanity, *homo dei*, a universal man. Now Thomas Mann has always believed that the artist is the most human of men. In his late maturity, he expresses it thus: "Always do we find in art the paradigm of things human, and in the artist the apogee of humanity—humanity viewed as such and in the abstract." [24] Mann here is at one with Schopenhauer, who avowed that the man of art was the human being *par excellence;* "the mirror of mankind," "the universal man," are the philosopher's words for the

[22] *The Beloved Returns*, p. 309.
[23] The phrase "delicate child of life" is applied to Hans on pp. 390 and 894, to the Germans on p. 425, and to man in general on p. 624.
[24] "Standards and Values."

artist.[25] The symbolism of *The Magic Mountain* is by no
means restricted to the artist's vocation. Yet it is possible
to see in Hans Castorp an artist, whose art work is his own
life.

Whether or not Hans Castorp is a genius is a question
which the author of *The Magic Mountain* skillfully avoids
answering. In this playful and deliberate reluctance to com-
mit himself Mann is of course consciously ironic. When we
first meet Hans we are told that he is a simple young man,
almost mediocre (*mittelmässig*).[26] But is the reader intended
to take this literally? If Castorp is indeed an ordinary youth,
it is difficult to understand how he develops with such suspicious rapidity into a student of the biological sciences, a
devotee of music, a dialectician and philosopher to whom is
vouchsafed a lofty vision of man's relation to death, love,
and life. On the occasion of a talk with Clavdia late in his
stay at the sanatorium, Hans speaks of his illness and its
quality in relation to genius, and of his love for Clavdia.
He cannot think of disloyalty to them ("Untreue gegen die
Krankheit und das Genie und gegen meine Liebe zu dir").[27]
During the course of the same conversation, Clavdia taunt-
ingly calls Hans "un homme de genie," and he denies it
("Ich bin natürlich von Hause aus kein homme de genie").[28]
But immediately he speaks of a quality he knew he had in
him even as a boy, something which his life at the sanatorium has brought to fruition. This quality is inseparable
from his familiarity with disease and death. His way to life
has led through death, it is the way of genius. For death,
says Hans, using the symbolism of medieval alchemy:

"death is the genius-principle [das geniale Prinzip], the *res
bina*, the *lapis philosophorum*, and the pedagogic principle too,
for love of it leads to love of life and love of humanity . . .

[25] WWI, III, 322.   [26] MM, p. 41.   [27] *Ibid.*, p. 751.   [28] *Ibid.*, p. 752.

There are two paths to life: one is the regular one, direct, honest. The other is bad, it leads through death—that is the path of genius [der geniale Weg]!" [29]

Although one cannot deny the continuity between Hans Castorp and Mann's earlier artist heroes, it is clear that in *The Magic Mountain,* Mann passes beyond preoccupation with purely artistic problems to broad considerations of the meaning of life and values. The highest level of signification of the Davos novel is its setting forth of man's relation to humanity and nature, but this is just as much metaphysical and ethical as it is aesthetic. It would be taking too narrow and one-sided a view to single out the aesthetic phase of the general problem and to make this the final category. The story of Hans Castorp may be best considered as one of development of genius consciously left abstract for the purpose of the epic novel's multiple symbolism.

We are told that from his childhood Hans Castorp was familiar with death. His mother died of an embolus when he was five years old. His father died shortly afterwards of inflammation of the lungs. His grandfather survived them a year and a half, and then he too passed away, leaving young Hans alone in the world. At the close of the scene of Grandfather Castorp's death, the author remarks "Thus for the third time in so short a space and in such young years did death play upon the spirit and senses—but chiefly on the senses of the lad." [30] Even as a boy, Hans knew that death had two aspects, noble and ignoble. He knew that:

In one aspect death was a holy, a pensive, a spiritual state, possessed of a certain mournful beauty. In another, it was quite different. It was precisely the opposite, it was very physical, it was material, it could not possibly be called either holy, or pensive, or beautiful—not even mournful. [31]

29 *Ibid.*   30 *Ibid.,* p. 34.   31 *Ibid.,* p. 35.

This dual aspect of disease and death, whose first statement in *The Magic Mountain* is given as Hans stands beside
the body of his dead grandfather, forms a methodological
key for the entire novel, whose way of analysis is consistently antithetical, ironic, or to put it in terms of music,
contrapuntal. Shortly after his arrival at the sanatorium,
Hans converses with Settembrini about Frau Stöhr, a particularly stupid and vulgar patient. "That seems strange to
me," Hans remarks, "diseased and stupid both . . . one always has the idea of a stupid man as perfectly healthy and
ordinary, and of illness as making one refined and clever
and unusual." [32] This thought, modestly expressed, calls
down upon Hans a long harangue from Settembrini, the
ambassador of reason:

"Disease has nothing refined about it, nothing dignified. Such a
conception is in itself pathological, or at least tends in that direction. Perhaps I may best arouse your distrust of it if I tell you
how ancient and ugly this conception is. It comes down to us
from a past seething with superstition, in which the idea of
humanity had degenerated into sheer caricature; a past full of
fears, in which well-being and harmony were regarded as suspect and emanating from the devil, whereas infirmity was equivalent to a free pass to heaven."

". . . disease, far from being something too refined, too worthy
of reverence to be associated with dullness, is, in itself a degradation of mankind, a degradation painful and offensive to conceive. It may, in the individual case, be treated with consideration; but to pay it homage is—mark my words—an aberration
and the beginning of intellectual confusion." [33]

Settembrini's opinion of disease is a common one. Most
people think of sickness—if they think about it at all, and
if it is somebody else's sickness—as an ugly and repulsive
business. Suffering, says Somerset Maugham, does not turn

[32] *Ibid.*, p. 126. [33] *Ibid.*, p. 127.

men into saints, but only into sick animals.[34] And to Mr. Cardan in Aldous Huxley's novel *Those Barren Leaves*, the passage from disease to death is so revolting that it shows up the whole play of the cosmos as a farce in the worst of bad taste:

The tragedy of bodily suffering has no catharsis. Punctually it runs its dull degrading course act by act to the conclusion. It ennobles neither the sufferer nor the contemplator. Only the tragedy of the spirit can liberate and uplift. But the greatest tragedy of the spirit is that sooner or later it succumbs to the flesh. Sooner or later every soul is stifled by the sick body, sooner or later there are no more thoughts, but only pain and vomiting and stupor.[35]

The discussion on the dual nature of disease in the first volume of *The Magic Mountain* finds its counterpart in the second in one of the acrimonious debates between Settembrini and Naphta. The unorthodox Jesuit, after crying down the Rousseauan element in Settembrini's philosophy, proceeds to exalt the spiritual aspect of disease far beyond the degree of Castorp's mild intuitions. After equating desire for health with bourgeois philistinism, Naphta pronounces bodily unsoundness to be the true way of the spirit. Quoting Naphta in the indirect discourse characteristic of *The Magic Mountain*, we are told that in the Jesuit's eyes:

The genius of disease was more human than the genius of health. How, then, could one who posed as a friend of man shut his eyes to these fundamental truths concerning man's humanity? Herr Settembrini had progress ever on his lips; was he aware that all progress, in so far as there was such a thing, was due to illness and to illness alone? In other words to genius, which was the same thing? Had not the normal, since time was, lived on the

---

[34] Maugham, *The Summing-Up* (New York, 1938), pp. 63-64.

[35] *Those Barren Leaves* (London, 1924), p. 334. See "The Intellectual as Ironist: Aldous Huxley and Thomas Mann," E. Kohn-Bramstedt, *Contemporary Review* (London), April, 1939.

achievements of the abnormal? Men consciously and voluntarily descended into disease and madness, in search of knowledge, which, acquired by fanaticism, would lead back to health.[36]

To this antihumanist thesis on illness, Settembrini replies with indignation that the Jesuit's proposition is tantamount to the monstrous assertion that the soul is disease. Even Hans Castorp, for all his sympathy with illness, is reluctant to go quite to this extreme, and at one point we find him momentarily inclining to Settembrini's doctrine as he runs the seemingly irresoluble antinomy over in his mind:

Say what you like—and there was a lot to be said for the idea that illness had something solemn and ennobling about it—yet, after all, you couldn't deny that illness was an accentuation of the physical, it did throw man back, so to speak, upon the flesh and to that extent was detrimental to human dignity.[37]

The argument concerning death, the climax of the disease process, is developed in similar dialectical fashion.[38] Hans Castorp regards death as a solemn and fascinating entity, and treats it with interest and respect. We have already mentioned his early contact with death, the ineradicable impression received at his grandfather's bier. During his term at the sanatorium, he often recalls this childhood scene. Hans speaks of his habitual ease in the presence of death, his admiration of coffins as pieces of furniture.[39] He remembers that as a child he thought death worthy of at least as much respect as life, that he pictured death as wearing a formal starched ruff—like those worn at the court of the Spanish Philip—while life, on the other hand, he imagined wearing an ordinary collar. Hans could not picture certain

[36] MM, pp. 587-88.   [37] *Ibid.*, p. 587.
[38] See *The Concept and Function of Death in the Work of Thomas Mann*, by Lydia Baer, University of Pennsylvania, 1932. See also Hans Kasdorff, *Der Todesgedanke im Werke Thomas Manns* (Leipzig, 1932).
[39] MM, p. 141.

people dead because they were ordinary and vulgar, unfit for the consecration of death.[40] On the mountain, Castorp carries his feelings of reverence for death into practice. The reader will recall his flower-accompanied visits to the *moribundi* of the establishment, his respectful excursion to the churchyard with the little girl who has necrosis of the finger tips—all in defiance of the official Berghof practice of screening the dying from the living.[41]

This pious reverence for death is briskly opposed by Settembrini. When he hears of Castorp's priestly visits to the dying, he shrugs: "Let the dead bury their dead." [42] The humanist's philosophy of enlightenment will not permit him to think of death other than as part and parcel of life. He rejects any view of death which sets it up as an entity distinct from life and makes of it an object of reverence. He counsels Hans thus:

"The only sane, noble—and, I will expressly add—the only religious way to think of death is as part and parcel of life; to regard it, with the understanding and with the emotions, as the inviolable condition of life. It is the very opposite of sane, noble, reasonable or religious to divorce it in any way from life, or to play it off against it. The ancients adorned their sarcophagi with the emblems of life and procreation, and even with obscene symbols: in the religions of antiquity the sacred and the obscene often lay very close together. For death is worthy of homage, as the cradle of life, as the womb of palingenesis. Severed from life, it becomes a spectre, a distortion, and worse. For death, as an independent power, is a lustful power, whose vicious attraction is strong indeed; to feel drawn to it, to feel sympathy with it, is without any doubt at all the most ghastly aberration to which the spirit of man is prone." [43]

Beneath all these fine words of Settembrini, it is easy to detect the same disgust for death that he has for disease. To him, death simply stands at the end of the process of

[40] *Ibid.*, p. 586.   [41] *Ibid.*, p. 370.   [42] *Ibid.*, p. 391.   [43] *Ibid.*, p. 256.

organic dissolution. It is the triumph of the physical over the spirit. It is painful to watch and repellent to the sensibilities. To Settembrini, death as such is not interesting. Something of this humanistic aversion to death and its accoutrements is apparent in the sentiment of Nathaniel Alden of Santayana's novel *The Last Puritan*. He remarks to his brother:

"Funeral services . . . funeral *services* are elevating, but actually to witness a burial in the ground can only be distressing to a person of feeling. That material duty should be left to the undertaker, who is hardened to it by custom and comforted by fees. The bereaved family shouldn't expose themselves to being morbidly harrowed by the ghastliness of physical death. Physical death is too unimportant." [44]

The same feeling is expressed more brutally by Buck Mulligan of James Joyce's *Ulysses* when he speaks to Stephen Dedalus of the death of the latter's mother:

And what is death, your mother's or my own? You saw only your mother die. I see them pop off every day in the *Mater* and Richmond and cut into tripes in the dissecting room. It's a beastly thing and nothing else. It simply doesn't matter. [45]

In *The Magic Mountain*, it is Naphta who denounces as irreligious materialism the humanistic refusal to pay homage to death. Without death, the Jesuit insists, "there would never have been either architecture nor painting, sculpture nor music, poetry or any other art"; [46] that—in the face of Settembrini to whom death is "the most dissolute of all powers," since, in his opinion, it delivers man over to the flesh. [47]

[44] *The Last Puritan* (Charles Scribner's Sons, New York, 1936), pp. 21-22. Reprinted by permission of the publishers.

[45] *Ulysses* (Random House, Inc., New York, 1934), p. 10. Reprinted by permission of the publishers.

[46] MM, p. 578.   [47] *Ibid.*, p. 522.

The whole antithetical movement of disease and death in *The Magic Mountain* is played out in the story's action and symbolism, quite apart from the formal debates in which Settembrini and Naphta are the chief participants. In the characters of the various patients who inhabit the Berghof, Thomas Mann has symbolized the dual nature of disease—its double effect of heightening humanity and degrading it. Hans, Joachim, Settembrini, Naphta, Clavdia, and Pieperkorn are all ill, but their illness has served to throw their characters into sharp focus, to develop in high degree the distinctive elements of their personalities. The majority of the patients at the sanatorium, however, are trivial irresponsible people, who think only of the next meal or the next love affair.

Hans Castorp has a tubercular infection. Mann's choice of this particular ailment for his modest hero is significant in that of all diseases tuberculosis is the one most commonly associated with genius. The peculiarly exciting effect of the illness upon the sufferer, the feverish racing of bodily and emotional processes which accompanies it, the glow of optimism (*spes phthisica*) that is characteristic of even the most advanced cases, the frequency of occurrence in talented people have all contributed to the well-nigh traditional suspicion that there is some ground of connection between the toxins of tuberculosis and creative energy. Lewis J. Moorman, in his *Tuberculosis and Genius*, has made a study·of several creative personalities who are either actually known to have been tubercular, or whose recorded symptoms point to the presence of the disease.[48] Moorman's study begins with Robert Louis Stevenson (whose engineering studies and later stay at Davos remind us at once of Hans Castorp) and includes essays on Schiller, Marie Bash-

[48] *Tuberculosis and Genius* (Chicago, 1940).

kirtseff, Katherine Mansfield, Voltaire, Molière, Francis Thompson, Shelley, Keats, and Francis of Assisi. To these essays, Moorman appends a random list of seventy people— drawn mostly from the field of literature—who either had tuberculosis, or, from the clinical evidence available, are suspected of having had it.[49] Moorman, himself a physician and director of a sanatorium, cites several medical opinions on the cause of the high incidence of tuberculosis in talented people. Two are especially interesting. Dr. Arthur Jacobson would admit a direct causal connection between tubercular infection and genius. "It is entirely conceivable," he says, "that the tuberculous by-products are capable of profoundly affecting the mechanism of creative minds in such a way as to influence markedly their creations."[50] Dr. J. A. Myers denies that the disease is a cause of genius, but admits it as a favorable condition: "Tuberculosis does not produce genius, but the life of physical inactivity which the tuberculous patient is frequently compelled to live may give him an opportunity to discover or to develop his native power."[51]

It is not unnatural then that Hans Castorp should meet *tuberculosis pulmonum* on the dark road to genius. But the young engineer's particular brand of tubercular infection has a strange character. We remember that he was never

[49] Moorman names Milton, Pope, Hood, Walt Whitman, Elizabeth Barrett Browning, Goethe, Schiller, Molière, Channing, Mérimée, Thoreau, Descartes, Locke, Kant, Spinoza, Beaumont, Samuel Johnson, Goldsmith, Sterne, De Quincy, Scott, Leigh Hunt, Jane Austen, Charlotte, Emily and Ann Brontë, Balzac, Rousseau, Washington Irving, Hawthorne, Gibbon, Kingsley, Ruskin, Emerson, Cardinal Manning, Lanier, Robert Southey, Westcott, Georges de Guérin, James Ryder Randall, N. P. Willis, John Addington Symonds, Stephen Crane, Paul Laurence Dunbar, Eugene O'Neill, Novalis, Klabund, Tchekov, Llewelyn Powys, W. E. Henley, William Cullen Bryant, John Greenleaf Whittier, Maxim Gorky, Feodor Dostoyevsky, Aubrey Beardsley, Eugene Albrecht, Beranger, Richard Lovelace, George Ripley, Blackmore, Joseph Rodman Drake, Kirke White, Adelaide Ann Proctor, Henry Timrod, H. C. Bunner, John Sterling, Havelock Ellis, and John Millington Synge.
[50] *Tuberculosis and Genius*, p. xv.   [51] *Ibid.*, p. xiv.

robust in his native Hamburg, that the indisposition which led Dr. Heidekind to prescribe a change of scene came just at the time the young man was about to enter upon his professional duties with the shipbuilding firm. We have already observed that his run-down condition was more than simple fatigue, that it was the result of his unconscious dissatisfaction with his life and environment. In a passage near the beginning of the story, Thomas Mann tells us that there was something ambiguous in his hero's chronic fatigue:

A man lives not only his personal life, as an individual, but also, consciously or unconsciously, the life of his epoch and his contemporaries. He may regard the general, impersonal foundations of his existence as definitely settled and taken for granted, and be as far from assuming a critical attitude toward them as our good friend Hans Castorp really was; yet it is quite conceivable that he may none the less be vaguely conscious of the deficiencies of his epoch and find them prejudicial to his own moral well-being. All sorts of personal aims, ends, hopes, prospects, hover before the eyes of the individual, and out of these he derives the impulse to ambition and achievement. Now, if the life about him, if his own time seem, however outwardly stimulating, to be at bottom empty of such food for his aspirations; if he privately recognize it to be hopeless, viewless, helpless, opposing only a hollow silence to all the questions man asks, consciously or unconsciously, yet somehow asks, as to the final, absolute, and abstract meaning in all his efforts and activities; then, in such a case, a certain laming of the personality is bound to occur, the more inevitable the more upright the character in question; a sort of palsy, as it were, which may even extend from his spiritual and moral over into his physical and organic part.[52]

In other words, as we have remarked before, Hans Castorp's illness was antibourgeois. Work, solid and respectable though he esteemed it, tired him out. He did not like it; it left him not nearly enough time to sit dreaming and smoking

[52] MM, pp. 41-42.

his Maria Mancini cigar.[53] Hence his first symptoms. Nietzsche says something in one of his letters which fits Hans Castorp's case astonishingly well:

The man who has only a few moments a day for what he regards as most important, and who has to spend the rest of his time and energy performing duties which others could carry out equally well—such a man is not a harmonious whole; he must be in conflict with himself and must ultimately fall ill.[54]

When overt pulmonary symptoms break out right at the beginning of his stay at the sanatorium, Castorp's disease reveals further entanglement with something else, and that something else is represented by Clavdia Chauchat. The Russian lady—whose "slackness" so annoys the Italian humanist—begins to occupy the mind of the young engineer, at first only teasingly, but later with an interest which grows in ever-increasing intensity. And the progress of Hans Castorp's disease is parallel to the growth of his love. Indeed the reader is soon convinced by a multitude of hints that the development of the two is not only coincident but joint. Not for nothing does the author seat Hans behind Clavdia at Dr. Krokowski's lecture—Hans, who still does not know that his fever and nosebleed come from affected lungs—while the psychoanalyst expounds the thesis: "Symptoms of disease are nothing but a disguised manifestation of the power of love; and all disease is only love transformed." [55]

Hans Castorp himself comes to realize during the long course of his silent love affair that his disease is no simple infection, no purely organic disorder consequent upon the catching of a germ, but a much deeper business, an external manifestation of something ingrained in his very nature.

[53] *Ibid.*, p. 44.
[54] Letter to Rohde, Selected Letters, ed. Oscar Levy (London, 1924), p. 114.   [55] MM, p. 165.

He knows at last that the disease is the organic accompani-
ment, the protective coloring of his passionate desire to be
near his beloved. He knows that even the old scars, which
Dr. Behrens discovered during the course of his first medical
examination, are the healed wounds left by a boyhood
erotic attraction to his schoolmate, Pribislav Hippe, who
with Clavdia shares the qualities of slant Asiatic eyes and
willingness to lend pencils.[56] The conviction that his disease
and his love are inseparable is insisted upon by Hans himself, during the incredibly intense address to Clavdia on the
night of the carnival, a scene conceived in the atmosphere
of and studded with allusions to the Walpurgis Night epi-
sode of *Faust*. Hans confesses to his beloved in French, the
irresponsible tongue of dreams:

"La fièvre de mon corps et le battement de mon coeur harassé
et le frissonnement de mes membres, c'est le contraire d'un inci-
dent, car ce n'est rien d'autre . . . rien d'autre que mon amour
pour toi." [57]

This passage is paralleled in the second volume by the following admission of Castorp to Pieperkorn just before the
conclusion of the *Brüderschaft*:

"For love of her, in defiance of Herr Settembrini, I declared myself for the principle of unreason, the genius-principle of disease,
under whose aegis I had already, in reality, stood for a long
time back." [58]

In the equivocal nature of Castorp's illness—the coincidence of his fever and his love for Clavdia, the connection
between the old healed scars and the almost forgotten boyhood love—the reader can readily detect the effects of
Thomas Mann's sympathy for the doctrines of Sigmund
Freud. Until about the time of the composition of *The*

[56] *Ibid.*, p. 158.   [57] *Ibid.*, p. 431.   [58] *Ibid.*, p. 769.

Magic Mountain, Mann had made no formal study of
Freud's teaching; yet parallels between the novelist's art
and the theories of the Viennese physician have been spied
out in his earlier work. The psychoanalysts, after reading
Death in Venice, claimed the author of the tale as their
own—and one can easily see why. The struggle between
Aschenbach's stern self-control and his erotic yearning, his
dreams of blood sacrifice, his yearning for nothingness, symbolized by the sea—all had their counterparts in the psychoanalytic concepts of the conflict between the Ego and the
Id, the dream symbolism, the relation between psychical
and organic aberrations, the death impulse, the desire for
the darkness of the womb. In *Death in Venice,* Tadzio acts
as a catalytic agent, changing the direction of the libido
from artistic creation to overt eroticism—an illustration of
Freud's postulate of the fundamental connection between
the artistic impulse and the erotic drive.[59] We remember
Aschenbach's creation of a page and a half of prose, which
the world soon afterwards acclaimed as a masterpiece. He
had done it with Tadzio before his eyes.[60]

Even in Thomas Mann's earliest stories, one can find passages which forecast the relation between his work and
psychoanalysis, a connection he later consciously admitted.
For a surprising parallel, compare Mann's story of the sadistic Tobias Mindernickel, who alternately caressed and
mistreated his dog, with the following case cited by A. A.
Brill, New York psychoanalyst and Freud's American translator:

A man, who was notorious as a great lover of animals, suffered
while riding his favorite pony from sudden attacks during which
he beat the animal mercilessly until he was exhausted, and then

---

[59] See Freud's monograph *Leonardo da Vinci,* trans. A. A. Brill (New
York, 1932).   [60] DV: STD, p. 414.

felt extreme remorse and pity for the beast. He would then dismount, pat the horse, appeasing him with lumps of sugar, and walk him home—sometimes a distance of three or four miles. We cannot here go into any analysis of this interesting case; all we can say is that the horse represented a mother symbol, and that the attacks, in which cruelty alternated with compassion, represented the ambivalent feeling of love and hatred which the patient unconsciously felt for his mother.[61]

Mann's story "The Blood of the Walsungs" (1905) uses incest symbolism, and the fragment "Felix Krull" (1911) hints of infantile sexuality.[62] Tonio Kröger's attachment to Hans Hansen, like that of Castorp to Pribislav Hippe, is consistent with the Freudian hypothesis that in adolescence the erotic drive may be directed toward one of the same sex in anticipation of the more mature heterosexual development. Mann declares that he was quite unaware of the existence or meaning of psychoanalysis in the days of *Tonio Kröger* or *Death in Venice*. "Indeed it would be too much," he writes in an essay on Freud, "to say that I came to psychoanalysis. It came to me." [63] While he was at work on *The Magic Mountain,* however, Mann became acquainted with the science; the existence of Dr. Krokowski bears witness. When Mann began the *Joseph* novels, he entered into a conscious alliance with Freud. In harmony with the psychoanalyst's intuitions, the *Joseph* saga embodies the double category of "myth" and "psychology," tracing as it does the parallel development of events buried, externally, in the dark coulisses of prehistory, and internally, in the depths of the unconscious.

Hans Castorp's disease is neurotic in character. That is, it is psychic not physical in origin. The young man falls in love with Clavdia, and his unconscious wish to be near her

61 Brill, *The Basic Works of Sigmund Freud* (New York, 1938), p. 19.
62 "Felix Krull," STD, p. 370.   63 "Freud," FGW, p. 12.

indefinitely—a condition which can only be fulfilled by a protracted stay at the sanatorium—produces the necessary symptoms. The Berghof's psychoanalyst, Dr. Krokowski, explicitly states that the conflict "between love and chastity" results ofttimes in illness, that symptoms of disease are disguised expressions of *eros,* that indeed all illness is only a transformation of love.[64] There is a distinct element of dramatic exaggeration in Krokowski's statements, and his equation of love and disease is oversimplified. Psychoanalysts know that the production of physical symptoms for a specific purpose can concern other things as well as love. As a matter of fact, Castorp's "run-down" condition in Hamburg came upon him before he knew anything at all about Clavdia; this early *malaise,* too, is neurotic in character, but it is produced—in part, at least—by the young man's unconscious dissatisfaction with his environment. So we must not take too literally—nor does the author intend that we should —Krokowski's dictum "All disease is only love transformed." [65] But the fact that Castorp's infirmity has a neurotic color, and that so many of Mann's ailing geniuses are victims of aberrations arising in the psyche, leads to the conclusion that Mann would corroborate Freud's belief that the artist does not have far to go to become a neurotic. We know that Mann does not suggest that the artist nature is related to all kinds of illness, but rather to a type arising from a susceptibility to disturbance of a delicate psychic mechanism, the stability of which is tenuous because of the feverish and consuming work it does.

Since the completion of *The Magic Mountain,* Thomas Mann has not returned to a major treatment of the themes of disease and death. There are, however, many allusions in his later work which reveal that these concepts are still im-

---

[64] See Krokowski's lecture, MM, pp. 160 *et seq.*   [65] *Ibid.,* p. 160.

portant to him. In the story *Disorder and Early Sorrow*, written in Mann's fiftieth year, there is Professor Cornelius, who thinks that "death is the root of all godliness and all abiding significance." [66] The scholar loves his tiny daughter dearly, but realizes that there is an ulterior motive in this love. He knows that "his devotion to this priceless little morsel of life and new growth has something to do with death as against life; and that is neither right nor beautiful—in a sense." [67]

As for the *Joseph* novels, unlike the line of Mann's protagonists from Hanno Buddenbrook to Hans Castorp, Joseph has no infirmity. His life becomes significant, however, only by his "dying," that is, his going down into the pit. And there is, in *Joseph in Egypt*, a very loving treatment of the death of Mont-Kaw, Potiphar's overseer. Joseph's ease and *savoir faire* in the presence of the dying, his poetic description of the charms of death as he sits beside the Egyptian's bed to whisper soothing words is reminiscent of certain characteristic traits of Hans Castorp.[68] Then too, in the first volume of the series, *Joseph and His Brothers*, there is an interesting suggestion of the power of the unconscious will to produce organic symptoms. This is the case of Isaac's blindness. It is hinted that Isaac subconsciously willed to be blind, so that he might give his blessing in good conscience to Jacob, crudely disguised as Esau. Isaac's desire to acquiesce in the hoax, Mann suggests, actually produced the needful symptoms.[69] Even in *The Beloved Returns*, the late novel about Goethe, Mann does not avoid the subject of the "pedagogic" principle of disease. His Goethe muses about the diseases of plants, and then observes, "Maybe the pathological teaches us most about the norm; it comes to

[66] *Disorder and Early Sorrow*, STD, p. 506.   [67] *Ibid.*, p. 507.
[68] *Joseph in Egypt*, I, 350.   [69] *Joseph and His Brothers*, p. 216.

me sometimes that by setting out boldly on the track of disease we might best pierce the darkness of living forms." [70]

It must be admitted, though, that Thomas Mann's preoccupation with disease and death as artistic concepts seems to be quite distinctly a major concern of those years of his life which were brought to a close by the completion of *The Magic Mountain*. In his late maturity, Mann's energies turned toward two different channels—the development of the mythological-psychological in the *Joseph* series, and the antifascist polemics. Why is the emphasis on disease and death diminished? As a young artist, Mann's attitude toward life was one of suspicion and hostility. He felt his isolation all the more keenly because he was a "bourgeois on the wrong track." His first stories, those grouped around "Little Herr Friedemann," are concerned with suffering of the cruelest sort. These tales form the artist's vindication of his youthful enmity to the world, his revenge on the life from which he feels himself cut off. Hostility to life leads to thoughts of death. Schopenhauer's pessimistic metaphysic, with its flavor of "The Cross, Death and the Tomb," [71] was made to order for the youthful literary philosopher. Thus we have *Buddenbrooks*, a story of the meaninglessness of life, of decline and death.

Psychoanalysts say that preoccupation with symptoms of disease can be a substitute for curiosity about death, since the former can be observed and talked about, whereas the latter is a mystery of which no one living has had experience. Perhaps this is applicable to Thomas Mann's case, for his literary interest in death is paralleled by his absorption with the details of illness. In the very fact that *The Magic Mountain*—that pandemonium of disease and death—

[70] *The Beloved Returns*, p. 334.
[71] See Nietzsche, *Selected Letters*, p. 46.

was written, one can discern the reason for the considerable lessening of emphasis on these themes in Mann's later work. The novel took twelve years to write, and one cannot escape the conclusion that in it the author is writing about himself. That is to say, *The Magic Mountain* represents Mann's final and complete raising to the level of consciousness the painful roots of his preoccupation with disease and death, exposing them to the play of dialectical movement and all-embracing irony. Not for nothing does the epic novel concern itself with the doctrines of Sigmund Freud. At some time during the composition of the work, Mann had experience with psychoanalytic treatment. The novel itself can be conceived as self-administered analysis, in which the author brings to the surface of consciousness the roots of the disease and death concepts, objectifying in a work of art what had for long years weighed on his mind. In short, *The Magic Mountain* can be regarded as a dissolving of Mann's own personal bond to disease and death. In dislodging an incubus, Mann produced his greatest work.

The results of the catharsis are already apparent in the Davos novel itself. Thomas Buddenbrook was forced to acknowledge the futility of life; he gave himself over to a melancholy resignation to his fate. Aschenbach became enamored of death, and death came to claim him. But what is the final conclusion of *The Magic Mountain?* It is that Hans Castorp has found life and fulfillment through illness and death, that these dark powers—despite what humanistic enlightenment may say to the contrary—are worthy of reverence and homage. Inseparable from this conclusion, however, is the injunction that disease and death should not be exalted over life, and life's highest quality, love. Lordship over mind and action should never be surrendered to death. In his dream during the snowstorm, Hans Castorp states his final determination, as he hovers in body and spirit between life and death:

"It is love, not reason, that is stronger than death. . . . I will keep faith with death in my heart, yet well remember that faith with death and the dead is evil, is hostile to humankind, so soon as we give it power over thought and action. *For the sake of goodness and love, man shall let death have no sovereignty over his thoughts.*" [72]

The transition from *The Magic Mountain* to the *Joseph* novels can be summed up in this way: Thomas Mann has had intimate personal contact with illness and death.[73] By maturity, by experience with psychoanalysis, by artistic objectification and fulfillment, he emerged after completing the Davos novel on a plane where he had left illness and death behind, and thus became free to make a different employment of the instruments of his own therapy by setting to work on myth-psychology.

During the composition of *The Magic Mountain*, Mann wrote a longish essay, *Goethe and Tolstoy* (1922), which he called a supplement to the epic novel. This critique is a detailed examination of the artist nature, pairing off Goethe and Tolstoy against Schiller and Dostoyevsky. Mann considers the relation in which these artists stood to illness and health, and he ponders over the double effect of illness on the human spirit. Here is an excursion into the philosophy of disease, taken from the essay:

Disease has two faces and a double relation to man and his human dignity. On one hand it is hostile: by overstressing the

[72] MM, p. 626.

[73] Reflections on death absorbed Thomas Mann in his youthful days. He told the writer of this study, that as a young man, he thought he would die at forty. In the early years of his marriage, when his suspicion of life had been softened (see *Royal Highness*), death broke in upon him violently. His sister Carla took poison, and died in agony, pathetic and terrible. (Sk, pp. 35-38.)

physical, by throwing man back upon the body, it has a de-humanizing effect. On the other hand, it is possible to think and feel about illness as a highly dignified human phenomenon. It may be going too far to say that disease *is* spirit, or, what would sound very tendentious, that spirit is disease. Still, the two conceptions do have very much in common. For spirit is pride; it is wilful denial and contradiction of nature; it is detachment, withdrawal, estrangement from her. Spirit is that which distinguishes from all other forms of organic life this creature man, this being which is to such a high degree independent of her and hostile to her. And the question, the aristocratic problem, is this: is he not by just so much the more man, the more detached he is from nature—that is to say the more diseased he is? For what can disease be, if not disjunction from nature? . . . in spirit, then, in disease, resides the dignity of man; and the genius of disease is more human than the genius of health.[74]

Schiller was a consumptive, Dostoyevsky an epileptic. "Do we not feel," asks Mann, "that their illness was rooted in the very being of the two of them, an essential and typical trait of the kind of men they were?"[75] Mann's essay postulates a fundamental dualism that is cosmic in character, pervading all things, the antithesis of nature and spirit. We shall consider the significance of this dualism in another place; suffice it to say here that in Mann's view there are two kinds of artistic nobility, the natural and the spiritual. To artists like Schiller and Dostoyevsky—men who live fevered, tortured lives, and write books about suffering humanity—there is accorded nobility of spirit. To artists like Goethe and Tolstoy—giant men and godlike, whose art is rooted in sense and marked by power and tranquillity—there is given nobility of nature. In the personalities of Schiller and Dostoyevsky, Mann suggests, there was an element essentially hostile to nature, bound to the principle of spirit; conse-

[74] G-T (*Three Essays*), p. 29.   [75] *Ibid.*, p. 28.

quently, they met early deaths. Goethe and Tolstoy, on the other hand, were allied to nature, and hence lived to venerable ages. But even these godlike men were no strangers to illness, even these earthy sons of nature had their moments of infirmity. Tolstoy was afflicted with a strange nervous disorder, which coincided with his interest in religion, during the years 1880-81. Goethe was a victim of physical and mental exhaustion before his fortieth year. True, both recovered, one by fleeing to the steppes, the other to Italy. But the fact remains, Mann points out, that they had been ill. "To be a man of letters," Goethe complains, "is an incurable disease, and so the best one can do is to come to terms with it." [76]

In speaking of those artists to whom he is bound in cultural sympathy, Thomas Mann likes to emphasize their contact with illness. Not only in *Goethe and Tolstoy,* but in other places through his works, Mann points to the precarious health of his chief literary hero. In *The Beloved Returns,* Mann describes an interview in which Goethe's son August tells Lotte about the master's afflictions:

"Did you know that four of his brothers and sisters died in infancy? He [Goethe] survived, he lives—one might almost say he lives in the highest degree. But several times since his childhood he has been close to death—momentarily or during a given period . . . the haemorrhage in his youth, the serious illness in his fifties, besides the attacks of gout and stone, that made him when still so young begin to visit the Bohemian spas. Then there have been times when, without anything definite ailing, everything was at sixes and sevens with him, and society would not have been surprised to hear any day of his death." [77]

There is also Wagner. Thomas Mann has written an essay entitled *The Sufferings and Greatness of Richard Wagner,*

[76] Mann quotes this in "Goethe," FGW, p. 54.
[77] *The Beloved Returns,* p. 229.

in which he insists that the composer's sufferings were indispensable to his greatness. Wagner, says Mann, was intermittently ill with "one of those organically intangible illnesses which make a fool of a man years on end and without being actually dangerous cause life to be a burden to him." [78] Wagner, as we know, was chronically nervous. He too thought death was near when he was not yet forty. He even went to a hydropathic establishment for treatment. Mann comments on this latter step, remarking, "He looks to have cold water cure him of his art; that is, from the constitution which makes him an artist." [79]

A classic example of the union of disease and genius is Thomas Mann's spiritual friend, Friedrich Nietzsche, who was tormented by a plethora of ills—an infected breast wound, chronic nervousness, stomach trouble, screaming headaches, semiblindness, and finally madness. Nietzsche was well aware that his fantastically evil health was in some way the condition of his genius. He knew that his illness was the means of release from academic duties, and the means of devoting himself to writing. Thomas Mann says of him:

He well knew what he owed to his morbid state, and on every page he seems to instruct us that there is no deeper knowledge without experience of disease, and that all heightened healthiness must be achieved by the route of illness.[80]

Mann is doubtless thinking of such statements of Nietzsche as "To an intrinsically sound nature, illness may even constitute a powerful stimulus to life, to a surplus of life" [81] and "It was *illness* which first brought me to reason." [82] We remember from the pages of *The Magic Mountain* an

---

[78] "Wagner," FGW, p. 144.
[80] "Freud," FGW, p. 10.
[82] *Ibid.*, p. 35.

[79] *Ibid.*, pp. 146-147.
[81] *Nietzsche*, Ecce Homo, p. 12.

occasion upon which Dr. Krokowski expresses to Hans Castorp his "doubt whether the two conceptions, man and perfect health, were after all consistent with one another." [83] This is very similar to Nietzsche's "Man, no question whatever, is sicker, less secure, more changeable, more unfixed than any other animal—he is *the* sick animal." [84] In Thomas Mann's opinion, Nietzsche's mental destruction, whatever organic basis there may have been for it, was fated by a conflict in his own character, by a hopelessly irreconcilable antithesis deep in his nature. For throughout his life the man was tortured by an internal struggle in which his intellectual hostility to romanticism was pitted against his instinctive attraction to the romantic, to music, to Wagner. It is hard to see how Nietzsche could have avoided some kind of breakdown.

Forty-five years ago, the art lovers of two continents were rudely shocked by the appearance of Max Nordau's *Degeneration.*[85] This bulky volume maintained that the art and literature of the nineteenth century was a product of sickness, that the artists who created this work were diseased. Modern art, said Nordau, is a pathological symptom. Modern artists are decadents, blasted by the nervous exhaustion of the race. Consider the morbidity of their themes and techniques! Count their bodily and mental ailments! They are, in a word, degenerates. No one of importance escapes Nordau's denunciation. Ibsen, Wagner, the Symbolist poets, the Impressionist painters, the pre-Raphaelites, Tolstoy, Nietzsche, Zola, and many others are separately judged and condemned. It does not seem to have occurred to Nordau that a fundamental point at issue in any such discussion is whether or not art, by its very nature, has something to do with disease. He assumes that an artist who bears the marks

[83] MM, p. 245.   [84] *Genealogy of Morals,* II, 13.   [85] New York, 1895.

of illness is on that account open to suspicion of degeneracy. Whereas, from the point of view we have been describing, the artist's familiarity with disease may prove only that he possesses the usual concomitant of genius. In reference to an essay written in refutation of Nordau's thesis,[86] Bernard Shaw touches on this question begging: "Though I think this essay of mine did dispose of Dr. Nordau's special pleadings, neither the pleadings nor the criticism dispose of the main question as to how far genius is a morbid symptom." [87]

In a sense, however, Thomas Mann is not completely at odds with Nordau. Despite his admiration of the greatness and power of nineteenth century art, Mann is quick to admit its decadent tendencies. For the nineteenth century saw the triumph of romantic art, and in Mann's eyes the romantic genius, for all its surface freshness and delight, is extremely liable to decay. It is but a short step, says Mann, from the romantic to the decadent, for the sympathies of romantic art lie not with life but with death. In short romantic art, and particularly German romantic art, has a compact with disease.[88] We remember that Goethe made this equation explicit when he remarked to Eckermann:

I have thought of a new phrase which states not too badly the relation between the classic and the romantic. The classic, I call

[86] The Sanity of Art (London, 1908).   [87] Ibid., p. 10.

[88] Sigrid Undset, in understandable bitterness toward all things German after her flight from Norway in 1940, says: "Psychopaths, suicides, fanatic ego-worshippers, wild dreamers, and tuberculosis patients, with the heightened self-absorption of sickness, were the majority of the great poets whose names are synonymous with German romanticism's artistic conquests; for it is true that the threat of destruction of personality in insanity or death very often stimulates gifted individuals to heightened productivity. It literally looks as if such a threat, of early death or madness, is necessary before German talents can produce something above sheer mediocrity; while, for example, English genius as often seems to be the fruit of health and normality, intensified to the highest degree." Return to the Future (New York, 1942), pp. 236-37.

the healthy, the romantic, the diseased. If we distinguish classic and romantic on this basis, we shall soon clarify the situation.[89]

But in talking about romanticism, we are anticipating the subject of our next inquiry—the romantic category and its bearing on Thomas Mann's art.

[89] Eck, p. 305.

3

MUSIC AND THE ROMANTIC

RICHARD WAGNER is to Thomas Mann at once arch-musician and arch-romantic. For all Wagner's spiritual and artistic shortcomings—and these Mann has pointed out over and over again—the hold the composer's music gained over the youthful writer was not to be loosed even in the years of critical maturity. And Mann is at one with Nietzsche in emphasizing the romantic element in Wagner. "Our present German music—" Nietzsche exclaimed with Wagner in mind, "Romanticism through and through!" [1] Thomas Mann sees in Wagner the culmination of a century of German art, the most complete expression of the romantic movement. As far as romantic art is concerned, for Mann, Wagner is its destined goal, its summing up.

The romantic character, says Mann, is fundamentally equivocal. Romanticism has alliances both with light and darkness; beneath its surface freshness and vigor is a *rapport* with sickness and death. Mann asks, in an essay on Nietzsche,

is not the romantic the sweetest and wholesomest thing in the world, goodness itself, born as it is in the deepest depth of the folk-soul? Yes, no doubt. But it is a fruit, splendidly fresh and sound for its moment, and yet extraordinarily prone to decay; the purest refreshment to the spirit if enjoyed at the right moment, yet at the next, the wrong moment, spreading rottenness and

[1] *The Birth of Tragedy,* p. 12.

corruption among men. It is a fruit of life, conceived of death, pregnant of dissolution.[2]

Now Mann speaks of Wagner's music as "magnificently equivocal."[3] What does he mean by that? There are two aspects of Wagner, which, for want of better words, we may call his "bright" and "dark" sides. The brightness we find in the joyous springtime atmosphere of *Siegfried*, the lyricism of *Lohengrin*, the foursquare, bourgeois straightforwardness of *Die Meistersinger*, the calm serenity of the *Siegfried Idyll*. Then the dark side: the composer plays with the forbidden in *Die Walküre;* under the bright song of the first act lies the theme of incest. In *Tristan*, the death motif is never long separated from the hymn of love. *Parsifal* combines the odor of incense with that of decay and death; a lofty Christianity, a refined asceticism blends with mystic sensuality. In the person of Kundry a saint and a harlot are joined. This hieratic music drama, with its Amfortas of the eternal wound, is full of sickness and suffering. The whole of *Parsifal* is an extrapolation of the pain-choked third act of *Tristan*. The music itself is sick, and exhales an odor of dissolution. Nietzsche remarks of Wagner, "He is one of the late French romanticists—sick and incurable."[4]

Or consider a very different aspect of the composer's work. Why does it appeal to the few and the masses alike? Wagner's music has captivated such differing personalities as Baudelaire, Nietzsche, Bernard Shaw and the mad King Ludwig of Bavaria. Yet this music has conquered the common people, it is beloved by the man in the street. All-Wagner concerts consistently draw crowds, and Wagnerian music dramas invariably fill the opera houses. This quality of double appeal in Wagner is an ambiguity of which

[2] "Nietzsche and Music," PM, p. 144.   [3] "Wagner," FGW, p. 172.
[4] Ecce Homo, p. 11.

Thomas Mann is well aware and which he considers a fundamentally *romantic* attribute:

Only in the romantic can popular appeal unite with the extreme of subtlety, with a "heinous self-indulgence" in means and effects —and it alone can make possible that "double optic" of which Nietzsche speaks with reference to Wagner, that knows how to cater to the coarsest and the finest—unconsciously, of course, for it would be stupid to introduce the element of calculation—whose *Lohengrin* can enrapture spirits like the author of the "Fleurs du Mal" and at the same time serve to elevate the masses; that leads a Kundryish double life as a Sunday afternoon opera and as the idol of initiative and suffering and supersensitive souls.[5]

Indeed Wagner's music knows how to "cater to the coarsest"! Sinister irony attended Mann's discovery that his beloved Wagner was the idol of Adolf Hitler, that the composer had become apotheosized by the National Socialists into a symbol of party ideals. Hitler himself is said to have heard more than two hundred performances of *Die Meistersinger;* he ordered it played on the Berlin stage that day in 1933 when he seized power. After the fall of France, seven years later, *Götterdämmerung* was heard by Hitler at the Bayreuth festival—soldiers admitted free—the same opera that was performed when the German armies were mobilizing for the attack on Poland.[6]

Thomas Mann has called attention to certain points of affinity between the spirit of Wagner and that of the Hitler party. In November and December, 1939, Peter Viereck wrote two articles for the magazine *Common Sense,* in which he traced in Wagner's life and writings the anticipation of National Socialism.[7] Wagner's antisemitism, his rela-

[5] "Wagner," FGW, p. 172.
[6] N. Y. Times, July 28, 1940, Editorial section, p. 2.
[7] The question of Wagner's relation to National Socialism, as well as that of the whole German romantic movement to the same is treated by Viereck in his *Metapolitics; from the Romantics to Hitler* (New York, 1941).

tions with his son-in-law, Houston Stewart Chamberlain, his plan for a classless society and an army of civilian elite are sketched by Viereck, who concludes that there was a strong and quite natural bond between Wagner's revolutionary nationalism and Hitler's National Socialism. The editor of the magazine sent the articles to Thomas Mann, thinking that he, as a Wagner partisan, might welcome opportunity to dispute this thesis. To his surprise, Mann communicated his thorough agreement with Viereck's articles, only stating that in his opinion they did not go far enough. Here is a portion of Mann's letter to the editor:

You see, I go further than Mr. Viereck. I find an element of Nazism not only in Wagner's questionable literature; I find it also in his work, similarly questionable, though in a loftier sense— albeit I have so loved that work that even today I am deeply stirred whenever a few bars of music from this world impinges upon my ear. The enthusiasm it engenders, the sense of grandeur that so often seizes us in its presence can be compared only to the feelings excited in us by Nature at her noblest, by evening sunshine on mountain peaks, by the turmoil of the sea. Yet this must not make us forget that this work, created and directed "against civilization," against the entire culture and society dominant since the Renaissance, emerges from the bourgeois-humanist epoch in the same manner as does Hitlerism. With its *Wagalaweia* and its alliteration, its mixture of roots-in-the-soil and eyes-to- ward-the-future, its appeal for a classless society, its mythical- reactionary revolutionism—with all these, it is the exact spiritual forerunner of the "metapolitical" movement today terrorizing the world.[8]

Such is the equivocal character of Wagner's art. "To call him romantic," Mann says in an essay on the composer, "is probably the most apt characterization of his nature." [9] Only a romantic genius could join religion and erotics in

[8] *Common Sense*, January, 1940, p. 13.   [9] "Wagner," FGW, p. 172.

an opera, only he could appeal at once to the artistically initiate and the crowd. But, to Mann, what stamps Wagner with an even more individual mark of romanticism is his cult of night, the affinity of his music for the cover of darkness. The music of *Tristan* is *Nachtmusik*. In the second act, the lovers are united under shelter of night. The torch is the signal that burns through the darkness to tell Tristan that Isolde is waiting, while King Mark's hunting horns sound in the shadowy forest. The lovers call themselves "night-consecrate," in their love duet they hymn the praises of the night. To Thomas Mann, this worship of the night is "arch-romantic." He says in his Wagner essay:

Its cult of the night, its execration of the day, are what stamps the *Tristan* as romantic, as fundamentally affiliated with all the romantic aspects of emotion and thought. . . . Night is the kingdom and home of all romanticism, its own discovery, always it has played it off against the empty vanities of the day, as the kingdom of the sensibilities against reason. . . . This deliberate stress upon the night, the lovelier half of day, is arch-romantic; and its romanticism is bound up with the whole mother- and moon-cult which since the dawn of human time and human sun-worship has stood opposed to the male- and father-religion of the light. Wagner's *Tristan* belongs, generally speaking, to this world.[10]

We know that German romantic literature is full of this worship of the night. In the books of the romantic writers, the moon shines down on all love affairs, the heroes and heroines dream in a world of shadows. Tieck's William Lovell berates the day, and longs for night. Novalis claims the realm of darkness for his own, and writes in his *Hymns to Night:*

I turn to thee, holy, ineffable, mysterious night! . . . How poor, how childish seems the day, how joyful and blessed its departing!

10 *Ibid.,* p. 166.

. . . Praised be the Queen of the Earth, the august revealer of holy worlds, the guardian of blessed love! She sends me thee, my beloved, sweet son of the night. Now I wake, for I am thine and mine. Thou hast proclaimed to me the life-giving gospel of Night, hast made of me a human being. Consume my body with the glowing flame of the spirit, that I may mingle yet more ethereally yet more closely with thee, and the bridal-night be eternal.[11]

In Friedrich Schlegel's *Lucinde,* that curious little novel once thought so wicked by the world, the praises of night, *heimatliche Nacht,* are sung by the lovers: "O infinite longing! But a time is coming when fruitless desire and vain delusions of the day will die away and disappear, and the great night of love will bring eternal peace." [12] As a youthful and ardent Wagnerian, Thomas Mann read these words of *Lucinde,* and was amazed by the parallel they suggested. "It was nothing more nor less than a literary discovery that I made," he says, "when already as a young man I underlined the ecstatic passage between Julius and Lucinde . . . and wrote in the margin: *Tristan.*[13]

In a little essay called "Sleep, Sweet Sleep," Thomas Mann confesses that he himself has always cherished a warm and intimate love of night and sleep. One thinks immediately of the day, with its stress upon activity and the deed, as the symbol of intellect and enlightenment—and Mann's own early suspicion of what he called "the shallow and outworn idealistic optimism of the daylight cult of Apollo." [14] We remember that during his stay at Davos, Hans Castorp once mused on the difference in his feelings toward Settembrini, the humanistic pedagogue of the West, and Clavdia Chauchat, whose image Hans always associated with Asia. He then recalled a boat ride on a lake he once took at the hour

[11] The German Classics, IV, 189-90.   [12] *Ibid.,* p. 172.
[13] "Wagner," FGW, p. 166.
[14] "Freud's Position in the History of Modern Thought," PM, p. 174.

of dusk when he looked "with dazzled eyes from the glassy daylight of the western shore to the mist and moonbeams that wrapped the eastern heavens." [15] "Sleep, Sweet Sleep" closes with these lines:

Surely that man is the greatest who keeps faith with and yearns for the night, the while he performs the mightiest tasks of the day. And so it is that I love best that work which was born out of "yearning after the holy night," and as it were in spite of itself stands today glorious both in slumber and in strength of will—I mean Richard Wagner's "Tristan und Isolde." [16]

A kindred spirit of Mann claimed that the whole realm of music belonged to the kingdom of shadows. In an aphorism called *Night and Music,* Friedrich Nietzsche says:

It was only at night time, and in the semi-obscurity of dark forests and caverns, that the ear, the organ of fear, was able to develop itself so well. . . . When it is clear daylight the ear is less necessary. Hence the character of music, which is an art of night and twilight. [17]

What is the nature of the romantic? Precise definition is not easy. [18] Thomas Mann avows that "the concept *romantic* is so complex and changeable that it seems to be less a category than the abandonment of categories." [19] One may safely remark, however, that an element common to all phases of the romantic character is emphasis on feeling. The romantics found in the nonrational side of human experience something to be valued and cultivated; they raised sensibility from its traditional place of inferiority to intellect to a relative independence of its own. In the romantic hero we find a man whose individuality lies in the quality of his feelings,

---

[15] MM, p. 205.   [16] PM, p. 276.   [17] *Dawn of Day,* Aph. 250.
[18] For an excellent monograph on Thomas Mann's relation to the romantic, see Käte Hamburger's *Thomas Mann and die Romantik* (Berlin, 1932).
[19] "Wagner," FGW, p. 172.

whose life story is not so much a history of intellectual convictions as an adventure of emotions. Of course, there was
in the romantic movement a definite intellectual content of
which the usual oversimplified view fails to take account.
Most of the German romantics were highly intelligent men,
the "intellectuals" of their day. Their work was a reaction
less against intellect as such than against the rationalistic
refusal to value anything other than the pure cold light of
reason. The peculiar vitality of the romantic movement was
nevertheless inseparable from its fixing on "life" as an ideal
rather than "mind."

We all know how the poets and novelists of the German
romantic school fell in love with feeling and sensibility. But
the tide of romanticism flowed beyond the precise bounds
of what we call "the Romantic School." A broad stress on
the primacy of instinct, a fundamental attention to the whole
realm of what we may call the *infra-rational,* filters through
the length of the nineteenth century in Germany. That is
why Thomas Mann calls this period the *romantic* century.
Speaking of the German contribution to the epoch, he says:

Backwards, is the cry: back into the night, the sacred primitive,
the foreknown, the life-bearing; backwards into the romantical,
prehistorical mother-womb. . . . No matter what the field of
intellectual activity—whether history, where Arndt, Görres, and
Grimm set up the idea of the primitive folk against that of
humanity; or cultural critique, where Carus exalts the unconsciously shaping life-principle at the expense of the spirit, and
Schopenhauer humbles the intellect far below the will, before
prescribing to it a means of moral conversion and self-regenera-
tion; or archaeology, where from Zoega, Creuzer and Müller to
Bachofen the legalist of matriarchy, all sympathy goes out to the
chthonic and the daemonic, to night and death—in short, to a
pre-Olympic, primeval and earth-born religion, in significant antagonism to the classical cult of reason.[20]

[20] "Freud's Position in the History of Modern Thought," PM, p. 173.

What is the common denominator present in the work of those men whom Mann considers the giants of the nineteenth century, those men in whom culminated the most powerful elements of the German romantic movement—Schopenhauer, Nietzsche, Wagner, and Freud? It is exploration in the realm of the infra-rational. Reversing a philosophic tradition dating back to Anaxagoras, Schopenhauer makes Will, not Intellect, the prime cosmological factor. His philosophy insisted, says Mann, that "in a world entirely the work of the will, of absolute, unmotivated, causeless and unvaluated life-urge, intellect had of course only second place." [21] As for Nietzsche, we know how passionately he defended "Life" against the encroachments of "Reason," how he denounced the Socratic enmity toward instinct in hot words:

The most blinding light of day: reason at any price; life made clear, cold, cautious, conscious, without instincts, opposed to the instincts, was in itself only a disease—and by no means a return to "virtue," to "health," and to happiness. To be obliged to fight the instincts—this is the formula of degeneration: as long as life is in the ascending line, happiness is the same as instinct.[22]

Wagner is representative extraordinary of the kingdom of the emotional and the nonverbal, over which music, of all the arts, holds the completest sway. Even if we were to allow that some composers have appealed to the cerebral, in so far as their art would permit, certainly we cannot list among them Wagner, whose music captures by sheer weight of its assault upon the feelings. What fascinates Thomas Mann is that Wagner's tremendous impact on the sub-rational sensibilities has its counterpart in the composer's going back to origins, to dark primeval sources, his working from "Siegfried's Death" all the way back to that aural sym-

[21] *Schopenhauer Presented by Thomas Mann*, p. 8.
[22] *Twilight of the Idols*, p. 16.

bol of the beginning of things, the long E-flat bass note with which *Rheingold* opens.[23] With Wagner in mind, Nietzsche speaks of the reaction of his own century to the Enlightenment's esteem of reason:

The cult of feeling took the place of the cult of reason, and the German musicians as the best exponents of all that is invisible, enthusiastic, legendary and passionate, showed themselves more successful in building up the new temple than all the other artists in words and thoughts.[24]

Sigmund Freud lived his latter days in the twentieth century, but his roots are in the nineteenth. His subject matter perhaps most clearly deserves the adjective infra-rational. Knowing Freud's emphasis on the dynamic drives lying below the level of the conscious reason, with his discovery of hidden meanings in the dusk of primeval time, we can readily concede to Mann that the psychoanalyst's work is unique in "its emphasis on the daemonic in nature, its passion for investigating the night-side of the soul." [25]

In the essay just quoted, called "Freud's Position in the History of Modern Thought," Mann talks at length of this devotion to the infra-rational in nineteenth century Germany, and explicitly links it to romanticism:

The nineteenth century was "romantic" not only in its first half but throughout, through all its decades; its pride of science was balanced, yes, outweighed by its pessimism, its musical bond with night and death, for the sake of which we love it and defend it against the contempt of a present not half its size.[26]

This essay—dated 1928—is interesting for more than one reason. Mann wrote it with the rising tide of German fascism before his eyes. He was anxious to distinguish between the spirit of German romanticism and that of National Socialism. He warns his readers not to confuse the political theories

[23] "Wagner," FGW, p. 133.   [24] *Dawn of Day*, Aph. 197.
[25] PM, p. 191.   [26] *Ibid.*, pp. 176-77.

and racial philosophies of the twentieth century with its predecessor's work on will, emotion, instinct and the primeval, even though these theories and philosophies strive to ally themselves with the genuine results of older tasks. Recent doctrines of blood and race myth, Mann warns, are nothing but sterile hoary ideas.[27] The work of the men of the romantic century, he insists, was no retreat to the past for the sake of the past. In their reëmphasis on the dark bourne below reason, in their readjusting the bounds of intellect by surveying the vast stretches of the subrational, there was genuine revolution, real progress. For in correcting the excesses of the Enlightenment, which had held back from instinct its just due, there was promise of a new advance, this time over solid ground. German romanticism is revolutionary, German fascism is just what it appears to be—the blackest reaction. In Mann's words of 1928:

It would be a rash critic who would give the name of romanticism to this temper of the time, which prevails today nearly everywhere, but most of all in Germany. No, for love of the intellect, passionate utopianism, orientation toward the future, conscious revolutionary spirit, are all far too distinctive characteristics of the German romantic movement to let its name be applicable here.[28]

Schopenhauer demonstrated the extent of the Will's domain, but only to end by proposing a means of reconciliation with the Idea. Nietzsche's anti-Socratism was inseparable from hopes of humanity's future evolution to greatness. Freud's investigation of instinct and the primitive was tied to the vision of mankind freed from the incubi which saddle it from the cradle. This, says Mann, was revolution through reaction, progress through retreat.[29]

The passing years brought events and reflections which shook Mann's faith in the distinction, set forth in the 1928

[27] *Ibid.*, pp. 189-90.   [28] *Ibid.*, p. 182.   [29] *Ibid.*, p. 198.

Freud essay, between the romantic elements in nineteenth century Germany and the spirit of German fascism. He came to admit the thesis (at present widely held) that certain ancestral lines can be drawn from romanticism to National Socialism. We have noted that shortly after the start of the second World War, Mann pronounced the arch-romantic Wagner's work a spiritual forerunner of "meta-politics." Is this distrust of the romantic character a suspicion which occurred to Mann only after the sorrow of exile? No: despite all the loyal words in the essay on Freud, Mann had long before this become convinced that there were equivocal and harmful elements latent in the romantic. In the darkness and melancholy beloved of romanticism he detected more than a mere affection for twilight. He felt that the romantic has a bond with death. Its longing for what Schiller called Ossianic gloom and chaos betrayed to Mann its tendency to dissolution, its nostalgia for negation—in a word, its decadence. We memember that song in *The Magic Mountain* which Hans Castorp loved—Schubert's *The Linden Tree*. This lovely melody, oddly enough, made Hans think of death. Why? Because the spirit of that song, we are told in the novel, was

a fruit, sound and splendid enough for the instant or so, yet extraordinarily prone to decay; the purest refreshment of the spirit, if enjoyed at the right moment, but the next, capable of spreading decay and corruption among men. It was the fruit of life, conceived of death, pregnant of dissolution.[30]

This is a familiar passage. We recognize in it the identical words from Mann's essay on Nietzsche, quoted earlier. But in that instance, Thomas Mann is not talking about *Der Lindenbaum*, but of the romantic character itself.[31]

---

[30] MM, p. 821.
[31] For further discussion of the theme of decadence, see Gerhard Jacob's *Thomas Mann und Nietzsche zum Problem der Decadence* (Leipzig, 1926).

He was to use harsher words. As he watched the shadows descend on Europe and the world for the second time in his life, Mann reluctantly acknowledged that the fruit of the romantic century's preoccupation with the dark realms below reason was indeed capable of spreading decay and corruption among men. In a wartime denunciation of the nineteenth century percursors of Hitler's Germany,[32] he names Fichte, who maintained "the metaphysical right of Germany to subjugate the world." He names Wagner and his disciple Houston Stewart Chamberlain. He names Nietzsche, whose "hatred for Bismarck and power politics" does not excuse his "anti-Christian, anti-social and anti-democratic" ideas. He names Schopenhauer "in whom elements of an abysmally black reaction are alloyed with those of lofty humanism in an inseparable amalgam." In sum, Mann sees Nazi Germany sucking life from the ideals of romanticism:

What we call National Socialism is the virulent perversion of ideas that always bore within themselves the seeds of murderous degeneracy and that were very much at home in the old Germany of culture and learning. There these ideas eked out a life in the grand style—they were labelled "Romanticism" and exerted a good deal of fascination on the entire civilized world. It is not too much to say that they have now gone to the dogs, and that they were destined to go to the dogs, since they were to go to Hitler.[33]

The span of Thomas Mann's creative work is marked by varying degrees of emphasis on what we have called the infra-rational. His early antipathy for the humanistic adoration of the intellect, an antipathy of which he was conscious as a quality both personal and German, is analyzed by himself in painful detail in his *Reflections of a Non-Political*

[32] "Germany's Guilt and Mission," *Decision*, July, 1941.
[33] *Ibid.*, p. 12. This passage is reproduced almost *verbatim* in "How to Win the Peace," *Atlantic Monthly*, February, 1942.

Man, from the point of view that German culture has always been characteristically "musical" rather than rationalist. *Death in Venice* is an allegory of the triumph of the senses over reason. In the person of Aschenbach are united in tenuous stability the critico-moral-analytic principle and the artist's love of beauty, which is at bottom foreign to the moral sphere, and has nothing to do with rationality. In the catastrophe, it is the latter which conquers the former.

The Magic Mountain projects the antithesis on a huge scale. Castorp's thought "It is love, not reason, that is stronger than death" [34] might well be the motto of the book. Settembrini, of course, stands for reason, criticism and analysis, while Clavdia represents *eros,* the formless and the anti-analytic. The issue is decided on the night of the carnival, when Hans Castorp, after expressing his gratitude for Settembrini's wordy pedagogy, defiantly throws in his lot with Clavdia—who had in a year's time spoke to him little more than a casual "*merci.*" In the second volume, it is Pieter Pieperkorn who can hardly speak three consecutive sentences, and yet he overshadows the "cerebral" Settembrini and Naphta by the sheer weight of his mighty personality. "Good Lord, what a personality!" we say with Hans Castorp.[35] The monster coffee king is the Dionysian preceptor of feeling. "For feeling, young man," he contrives to say to Hans Castorp, "is godlike. Man is godlike in that he feels." [36] Taking the Davos novel as a whole, we must not forget the dominant role played in it by disease, the most antirational principle of all.

In Thomas Mann's later creative work, the infra-rational is still to the fore, with emphasis fixed on myth and the unconscious. The *Joseph* story shows kinship with the work of the nineteenth century historians, archaeologists, and cul-

[34] MM, p. 626.   [35] *Ibid.,* p. 715.   [36] *Ibid.,* p. 760.

tural critics, in its sympathy for "primeval and earth-born religion in significant antagonism to the classical cult of reason." The Biblical saga is an ambitious attempt to drive backwards into the past, to get to the beginning of things, to plumb the depths of the "Well of Time." This orientation has a romantic character. It recalls the spirit of those men whom Mann visioned reaching "back into the night, the sacred primitive . . . backwards into the romantical, pre-historical mother-womb."

As his creative work matures, Mann becomes increasingly sensitive to the importance of intellect, without denying the fruitfulness that lies in the realm below reason. Like his own Settembrini, Mann reverences the "Word." The very fact that Hans Castorp receives the Italian humanist's tutelage with gratitude, that he himself learns to reason analytically, that he comes to rue his neglect of the newspapers, is evidence that in his creator's view the realm of intellect has its own autonomy, provided that its boundary lines are not pushed back to enclose more than its rightful territory.

We note in Thomas Mann's maturest work that, side by side with a novelistic treatment of the infra-rational sphere of myth-psychology, there is the intellectual's passionate denunciation of the denial of intellect, the twentieth century sin against the Holy Ghost which would willingly surrender all the frontier that human reason has so painfully pushed back, to the greatest irrationality of all—war. In the work of his latest period, Mann is quick to come to the defense of intellect. Let philosophy be impugned, let the Word be slighted—even if by one of his own admired friends—he swiftly demands correction. In his Vienna speech in honor of the eightieth birthday of Sigmund Freud, Mann did not hesitate to rebuke the master himself on a certain excess of anti-intellectualism. His words on that occasion were:

Perhaps this is the moment, my friends, to indulge on this festive occasion in a little polemic against Freud himself. He does not esteem philosophy very highly. His scientific exactitude does not permit him to regard it as a science. He reproaches it with imagining that it can present a continuous and consistent picture of the world; with over-estimating the objective value of logical operations; with believing in intuitions as a source of knowledge and indulging in positively animistic tendencies, in that it believes in the magic of words and the influence of thought upon reality. But would philosophy really be thinking too highly of itself on these assumptions? Has the world ever been changed by anything save by thought and its magic vehicle the word? I believe that in actual fact philosophy ranks before and above the natural sciences and that all method and exactness serve its intuitions and its intellectual and historical will.[37]

However critical of romantic excess Thomas Mann may be, we must not lose sight of his own affinities to romanticism. His isolation theme, his *Sympathie mit dem Tod,* his stress on feeling and the inarticulate side of man, his fondness of twilight and night, his eventual interest in the world of myth and the primitive—all are strongly romantic qualities, as indeed Mann himself defines them. To these, we must add his love for music. The genius of music is intimately allied to the romantic spirit and touches Thomas Mann's own art in a peculiar and personal way.

Mann's attraction to music is completely consistent with the character of the romantic tradition in Germany. To German novelists and poets of the first half of the nineteenth century, music was the most complete expression of human feeling, and they strove to make their works as nearly like music as possible. Their books are full of the praises of music. To Tieck, only in instrumental music was art completely free, relieved from all the restraint of the outer world. "Do you not think," he asks, "many thoughts so deli-

[37] "Freud," FGW, p. 22.

cate, so spiritual that in despair they take refuge in music, there at last to find rest?" [38] "Music takes the very being of art to itself," says Novalis, "not the slightest suspicion of imitation can touch it." [39] The saintly Wackenroder, to whom the art was as a gift from heaven, declares, "The art of music seems to me always the first and most perfect, your whole life must be a music." [40] "Is not music," queries E. T. A. Hoffmann, "the mysterious language of a higher spirit-realm, where wondrous accents make their way into our souls, awakening in them a higher intensity of life?" [41] Hoffmann, who himself composed music, insisted that poetry was inseparable from that art. His fantastic stories are peopled with musical personages and strewn with long harangues about music. Even his Kreisler talks of stabbing himself with a gigantic Fifth! Some of the romantics sought to carry the technique of music into their own writing. Tieck worked musical alliteration into the ground in his poetry; [42] Goethe remarked that a better title for *Franz von Sternbald* would be "Musical Wanderings." [43] Novalis's addresses to the night were well named "hymns," and in these pieces he tried to capture the tonal atmosphere with words which occur again and again as musical themes—"Licht," "Tag," "Nacht," and so forth.

In a famous passage of his essay on Giorgione, Walter Pater proclaims that "All art constantly aspires to the condition of music." [44] The English musical critic, Cecil Gray,

[38] "Overture" to *Die verkehrte Welt*, trans. Georg Brandes; see Brandes, *The Romantic School in Germany*, Vol. II of *Main Currents in Nineteenth Century Literature* (New York, 1924), p. 123.

[39] *Schriften* 2 S 228. (Author's translation.) See Werner Flörcke's monograph, *Novalis und die Musik* (Marburg, 1928).

[40] "Phantasien über die Kunst," in *Wackenroders Werke und Briefe*, ed. Eugene Diederich (Jena, 1910), p. 172. (Author's translation.)

[41] "Herzensergiessungen," *op. cit.*, p. 131.

[42] Brandes, *The Romantic School in Germany*, p. 119.

[43] *Ibid.*, p. 134.   [44] *The Renaissance* (New York, 1925), p. 135.

insists that the celebrated dictum should be revised to read "All *romantic* art constantly aspires to the condition of music." [45] This is in complete accord with the convictions of the German romantics. They saw in music the art of arts, the romantic art, the medium *par excellence* for the artistic expression of the emotions, of sensibility, of the secrets of the soul. The power of music to transfigure the language and moods of love was unrivaled by any other art. The romantics felt that music, of all the arts, was at home in the kingdom of the night, that music alone could blend with the moonbeams and shadows they loved so much. "It is only in the realm of the Romantic," says Hoffmann, "that music is at home." [46]

The tradition of German romantic enthusiasm for music lived on in Schopenhauer and Nietzsche. No one who has read the third book of Schopenhauer's *The World as Will and Idea* will doubt the philosopher's love of music and his extraordinary intuitive grasp of the art. To Schopenhauer, who linked music directly with the cosmic principle of the Will, the art of music is highest in the metaphysical scale. It is not, says the philosopher, like the other arts which are mere copies of Ideas; music is the objectification of the Will itself. Schopenhauer's insistence that music "stands alone, quite cut off from all the other arts" [47] and that it possesses reality far beyond that of the phenomenal world is the philosophic counterpart of the less critical rapture of Tieck and Novalis. When he says that music is "the material in which all the movements of the human heart can be portrayed," [48] he is agreeing with Hoffmann on the interdependence of music and the romantic.

Nietzsche's passion for music is familiar. "He loved music,"

[45] *A Survey of Contemporary Composers* (New York, 1928), p. 24.
[46] *The Serapion Brethren,* trans. Alexander Ewing (London, 1886), I, 84.
[47] WWI, I, 330.   [48] *Ibid.,* III, 236.

says Thomas Mann, "as no one else has loved it." [49] Nietzsche thought of music as the Dionysian art, the embodiment of the Heraclitean principle of flux. In his early writings, he opposed the genius of music to shallow European rationalism, and was convinced that victory over this bloodless intellectualism would be won by a "music-loving Socrates." [50] Nietzsche's relations with music were his relations with Wagner writ large. For he loved, yet came to distrust them both. His later life was torn by conflict over them. All his instincts urged him toward music and toward Wagner, who represented to him the boldest development of the art. But Nietzsche's intellectual conviction that in the romantic art of Wagner—even in music generally—lay the danger of spiritual narcosis, made him deny his sometime friend of Triebschen and the art he stood for. Thomas Mann remarks of Nietzsche:

In a word, his relation to music was one of passion. But passion —the word, of course, derives from suffering; and what part, and wherefore, does an element of suffering play in the conception? What is it that makes lovers suffer? It is doubt. Nietzsche once said that the love of a philosopher for life is like the love of a man for a woman he does not trust. The same, precisely, might have been said for his love of music. [51]

Nietzsche is quite explicit about the connection between music and the romantic: "I am afraid," he writes in a letter to Georg Brandes, "I am too much of a musician not to be a romanticist." [52] Nietzsche's own language, with its fluidity, its tonal color, its brilliant crescendos, its rhythmic rise and fall, belongs more to music than to philosophy. Speaking again of the composer's torturing doubts about music, Thomas Mann says:

[49] "Nietzsche and Music," PM, p. 142.   [50] The Birth of Tragedy, p. 169.
[51] "Nietzsche and Music," PM, p. 143.   [52] Selected Letters, p. 334.

If I may guess, they arose because he—in this a very German—placed music on the same level with the romantic, and it was his lot, his mission and heroic destiny, to put himself to the touch upon that so seductive master-complex of the soul, the musical-romantic and the romantic-musical—and thus almost the German complex.[53]

Thomas Mann's deep sympathy for music cannot fail to strike even the most casual reader of his books. It is more than sympathy, it is outright assimilation of the spirit of music which marks Mann's art. Even his early stories are full of hints of the importance music is to assume later in his life and work. And in these youthful tales, music is synonymous with Wagner. The deformed protagonist of "Little Herr Friedemann" [54] falls deeper into love while listening to the strains of *Lohengrin*. In *Buddenbrooks*, the boy, Hanno, is a musician; he plays the piano and composes. His mother is a Wagnerian, and she wins over to the master's cause her son's music teacher. Old Pfühl's first reaction to the music of Wagner is typical of the critical blasts launched at the composer in his day:

I cannot play that, my dear lady. I am your most devoted servant —but I cannot. That is not music—believe me! I have always flattered myself that I knew something about music—but this is chaos. This is demagogy, blasphemy, insanity, madness! It is a perfumed fog, shot through with lightening! It is the end of all honesty in art.[55]

Mann's story *Tristan*, of course, betrays by its title that the youthful author had surrendered to the spell of master of

[53] "Nietzsche and Music," PM, p. 143.

[54] Mann has told how Oskar Bie, editor of the *Neue Deutsche Rundschau*, and musical connoisseur as well, accepted "Little Herr Friedemann" for publication: "Perhaps more than chance willed it that it was a musician and connoisseur of music who performed this decisive function in my life, bringing to light a writer whose work was from the first marked by a deep inward affinity to the art and a tendency to apply its technique in his own field." STD, Introduction, v.   [55] Bud, II, 108.

Bayreuth. To Mann, as to many another, the highest and
most personal achievement of Wagner—despite the poly-
phonic grandeur of *Die Meistersinger* and the mighty archi-
tectonics of the *Ring*—is his music drama *Tristan und Isolde*.
In the story *Tristan*, Detlev Spinell sits beside his loved one
at the piano while she plays the *Vorspiel*. Mann strives to
capture the mood of the music in the language of his description:

The *Sehnsuchtmotiv*, roving lost and forlorn like a voice in the
night, lifted its trembling question. Then silence, a waiting. And
lo, an answer: the same timorous lonely note, only clearer, only
tenderer. Silence again. And then with that marvellously muted
sforzando, like mounting passion, the love-motif came in; reared
and soared and yearned ecstatically upward to the consummation, sank back, was resolved; the 'cellos taking up the melody to
carry it on with their deep heavy notes of rapture and despair.

Not unsuccessfully did the player seek to suggest the orchestral
effects upon the poor instrument at her command. The violin
runs of the great climax rang out with a brilliant precision. She
played with a fastidious reverence, lingering on each figure,
bringing out each detail, with the self-forgotten concentration of
the priest who lifts the Host above his head. Here two forces, two
beings, strove toward each other, in transports of joy and pain;
here they embraced and became one in delirious yearning after
eternity and the absolute. . . . The prelude flamed up and died
away.[56]

In "The Infant Prodigy" (1903) Mann sketches a little
Greek child playing his own compositions on the piano
before an adult audience, with just the same loving care with
which Hanno Buddenbrook played his. Emphasis returns to
Wagnerian symbolism in "The Blood of the Walsungs"
(1905), this time in the mood of *Die Walküre*. The mature
Death in Venice, like Wagner's *Tristan*, tells of a love that
leads to death, a love that is inseparable from death. Venice

[56] *Tristan*, STD, p. 153.

is the city "where musicians were moved to accords so weirdly lulling and lascivious," [57] and it is the city where Wagner died on what Nietzsche calls "that sacred day." The beloved Tadzio's speech, in a language of which Aschenbach understands not a word, becomes mingled harmonies in his ear. The boy's name, as the writer hears it called out on the beach by the other children, becomes a sweet and wild musical cadence; and in Aschenbach's fevered dream, a few days before his death, this call becomes the bewitching low notes of a flute. The whole tale is a prose composition in which the elements of love and death are introduced, developed, and woven together as musical themes.

Hans Castorp has five musical favorites, all very different.[58] Three of these endear themselves to him perhaps as much by the characters and action in the background as by the music itself. The recordings of scenes from Verdi's *Aïda* attract the young patient who listens to the grim story they tell of Rhadames, who, because of love has forsaken the post to which honor bound him and is punished by death in a walled-up crypt, where the faithful Aïda joins him. Hans also likes the records of the scenes between the gipsy heroine and Don Jose in Bizet's opera *Carmen*. Here once more, the story behind the music is that of a soldier forced to choose between honor and his heart's deepest desire, and, here again, the gratification of love leads to death. Both by his philosophizing on the meaning of honor and loyalty and by his own yielding once to what Settembrini thought of as shame, Hans Castorp could well sympathize with deserters of causes. In a third selection from the sanatorium's gramaphone library—Valentine's song from *Faust* by Gounod—a

[57] DV: STD, p. 421.
[58] Hermann Weigand discusses Hans Castorp's favorite selections in his commentary on *The Magic Mountain*. See his *Thomas Mann's Novel 'Der Zauberberg,'* p. 113.

question of honor again hovers in the words, but this time it is honor upheld by a soldier brother. The music makes Hans think of his dead cousin Joachim, whose loyalty to duty compelled him to break away from the Venusberg of Davos to join his regiment, only to return to die. Valentine too died for honor. So intimately does Hans associate this song with the personality of his cousin that the recording of it later evokes the physical manifestation of Joachim in Dr. Krokowski's seance.

Debussy's prelude to Mallarmé's eclogue *L'Après-Midi d'un Faune* takes the music-loving Castorp far from honor and duty. This music, fluid and formless, this unparalleled distillation of mood and nuance into ten minutes of time, is in a certain sense—and not in an entirely honorable sense— the purest music. It has nothing to do with honor or duty. To Hans Castorp,

No "Justify thyself," was here; no challenge, no priestly court-martial upon one who strayed away and was forgotten of honor. Forgetfulness held sway, a blessed hush, the innocence of those places where time is not; "slackness" with the best conscience in the world, the very apotheosis of rebuff to the Western world and that world's insensate ardor for the "deed." [59]

Schubert's *Der Lindenbaum* was the last of the five favorites of Hans Castorp, and his reaction to it was the most subjective. It sung to him, as we have noted before, not of honor or of forgetfulness, but of death. It was this song, *The Linden Tree*, whose notes awoke in Hans Castorp his old nostalgia for death. There was something about the simple melodic line, something in the way it affected him, that called up lovely but perverse suggestions of dissolution and death. The self-critical Hans realized this consciously. He acknowledged the illicit element in his love, for he had

[59] MM, p. 814.

sworn on the day of his snow vision to let death have no
power over his thoughts. Long afterwards, on the day he
advances along the battle line in Flanders, Hans sings this
song to himself.

But why is there no recording of Wagner's music among
Hans Castorp's favorites? To begin with, four of the records
represent, in symbol, aspects of a single problem of all-
embracing importance to him. They attract the young man
because of the honor-abandonment antithesis (personified
in Joachim and Clavdia) which is constantly present to him.
The *Aïda* and *Carmen* recordings are symbols of honor forsaken, the *Faust* of honor vindicated. The prelude to
L'Après-Midi d'un Faune fascinates simply because it has
nothing whatever to do with honor; it is abandonment with
no bad conscience. Well then, what about the fifth record,
the one which stands for death? The shadow of Wagner *is*
cast here, it stands behind the Schubert song. Without men-
tioning the composer by name, Thomas Mann interpolates
an author's comment into Hans's musings on *The Linden
Tree*. "One need have no more genius," so reads the end of
the chapter "Fullness of Harmony," "only much more talent,
than the author of *Der Lindenbaum*, to be such an artist of
soul-enchantment as should give to the song a giant volume
by which it should subjugate the world." [60]

If no explicit reference to the music of Wagner is made in
The Magic Mountain, a methodological device characteristic
of the composer is definitely employed there. It is the *Leitmotiv*.[61] We use the term *mutatis mutandis*, of course, since
the purely musical invention is transferred to a literary
medium. In *Buddenbrooks*, to be sure, an attempt has been
made at something of the sort. Each character in that work

[60] *Ibid.*, p. 822.
[61] Ronald Peacock examines Mann's use of this device in his *Das Leitmotiv bei Thomas Mann* (Berne, 1934).

has his descriptive tag by which we may identify him. Christian rubs his left side upon almost every appearance. Grünlich has his "gold-colored whiskers," Cousin Clara's leanness is alluded to whenever she makes an entrance, and so on. In *Tonio Kröger,* and later in *The Magic Mountain,* Mann's use of the leitmotiv goes far beyond a mere constant recurrence of characteristic adjectives or verbs joined to the name of somebody, and develops into a subtle musical synechdoche. Mann himself tells us of his experience with the leitmotiv:

Here [in *Tonio Kröger*] I first learned to employ music as a shaping influence in my art. The conception of epic prose-composition as a weaving of themes, as a musical complex of associations, I later on largely employed in *The Magic Mountain.* Only that there the verbal leitmotiv is no longer as in *Buddenbrooks* employed in the representation of form alone, but has taken on a less mechanical, more musical character, and endeavors to mirror the emotion and the idea.[62]

Throughout *Tonio Kröger,* the boy's father is never mentioned without "the field-flower in his buttonhole." [63] But there is much more subtle use of the leitmotiv in the tale. Take for instance the phrase "blue-eyed." It is mentioned first in connection with Hans Hansen and Ingeborg Holm, who are blond young people and have blue eyes. The phrase occurs again and again in the story to suggest everything these two stand for—simple, normal, healthy life, untroubled by the vexations of the body and mind to which the artist is prey. When near the end of the story Tonio says to Lisaveta "But my deepest and secretest love belongs to the blond and the blue-eyed," [64] the entire mood of the piece is suggested in musical recapitulation—the isolation to which this bourgeois artist is fated, and his vain longing for friendly inter-

---

[62] Introduction, STD, p. vi.   [63] TK: STD, pp. 87, 98, 99, 115.
[64] *Ibid.,* p. 132.

course with young and healthy and handsome ordinary folk, from whose society he is forever banned because of his calling. Or, read the lines describing Tonio's leave-taking from Hans Hansen as the latter promises to read Tonio's beloved *Don Carlos:*

His heart beat wildly: longing was in it, and a gentle
envy; a faint contempt, and no little innocent bliss.[65]

Now at the story's end, the same nuance is evoked when the mature and famous Tonio tells Lisaveta of his love for the commonplace, the happiness of ordinary people untroubled by artistic instincts:

"Do not chide this love, Lisaveta; it is good and fruitful.
There is a longing in it, and a gentle envy; a touch of
contempt and no little innocent bliss." [66]

Throughout *The Magic Mountain,* one finds side by side both varieties of this artistic stratagem. The naturalistic character tag is worked to the limit, and is one of the important factors responsible for the vividness and sharp outline with which the personages of the novel stand out. Frau Stöhr is almost invariably presented affectedly drawing back her lips over her teeth. Settembrini always prefaces his speeches with his "crisp" smile. Behrens has his purple face and goggling eyes. But then we find the naturalistic shading over into the musical. The phrase "Kirghiz eyes"—used in connection with Clavdia—suggests not only Hans Castorp's boyhood friend Hippe, but also by association the illimitable stretches of the continent of Asia, and in its subtlest overtones, the whole culture of the East, of which Clavdia is a symbol— lethargy, passivity, sensuousness, anti-intellectualism, compassion and all the rest of it.

Again, from the Davos novel, take the leitmotiv *"fanati-*

[65] *Ibid.,* p. 92.   [66] *Ibid.,* p. 132.

cal" which is intoned so often when Joachim is on the scene. Many times did Hans Castorp reflect, we are told in the course of the story, on a certain spiritual-military aspect of human culture, which stands opposed to the enlightened philosophy of humanism, yet has its own dignity and validity. The atmosphere of this culture is suggested by Catholic formalism, which insists upon the importance of death as an independent spiritual principle, and pays it homage with befitting ceremony. It is found in the manners of the court of the Spanish Philip the Second, typified by the stiff formality of the ruff and solemn black of the period.[67] It is present too in Joachim's vocation—"profession" would be too bourgeois and civilian a word—the vocation of the soldier who blends unreasoning faith and obedience in a cause. The epitome of this tradition, Hans Castorp thinks, is the act of the soldier being sworn to the colors, as Joachim must be before taking his commission. ("'What fanatical customs,' the civilian remarked.")[68] Yes, there is something fanatical in the singleminded, unquestioning faith of the priestly calling and of the soldierly life, which Settembrinian rationalism can neither understand nor condone. St. Ignatius Loyola is not a hero to humanists. "Well, get along and take your fanatical oath," says Hans Castorp to his cousin when the latter deserts the sanatorium for the colors.[69] This leit-motiv is again sounded when Joachim has paid the penalty of death for his desertion of the stern service of the cure to join his regiment in the "flat-land." The word "fanatical" is used with seeming carelessness, yet the effect is poignant in the highest degree; the single word by itself calls up the whole spirit of the honor-loving Joachim, all that is loyal and kind in him, all that is noble and valid in the principle of life to which, by the nature of his calling, he has been sworn:

[67] MM, p. 373.   [68] *Ibid.*, p. 535.   [69] *Ibid.*, p. 537.

We let the curtain fall for the last time but one. While it rustles down, let us take our stand in spirit with Hans Castorp on his lonely height, and gaze down with him upon a damp burial-ground in the flat-land; see the flash of a sword as it rises and falls, hear the word of command rapped out, and three salvoes, three fanatical salutes reverberating over Joachim Ziemssen's root-pierced grave.[70]

The leitmotiv in Thomas Mann's work is but one aspect of his method of mingling themes into a "musical" synthesis. This technique, elusive in the face of analysis, reaches its highest point of development in *The Magic Mountain*, which Mann himself describes as a "thought-texture woven of different themes, as a musically related complex." [71] We come first upon the simple motifs of the personages in the sanatorium. But these are soon discovered to be simplifications, crystallizations of larger and broader themes which emerge from the background and are played off against each other in a sort of musical counterpoint. The themes of Joachim and Clavdia, for instance, are presented and developed until we begin to realize that they are just the abridged and sharply outlined forms of the generic themes of what we may call "Honor" and "Abandonment." Now these main themes have their associated motifs, their own related bars of literary music which, when sounded, bring to the mind of the "hearer" the main theme and its attendant music. Thus "fanatical" for Joachim brings up the "Honor" theme, and its related "Spanish-Aristocratic" harmony. The chord "Kirghiz eyes" for Clavdia calls back the "Abandonment" theme as well as recollections of Pribislav Hippe and Asia. The motifs of Settembrini and Naphta are similarly played off against each other, merging into the generic themes of the "liberal-humanistic-bourgeois" and the "mystic-Catholic-

---

[70] *Ibid.*, p. 680.   [71] Sk, p. 30.

communal." In Thomas Mann's own words: "To me, the novel is like a symphony. There are the themes, first presented in simple form. These are the characters. The themes are then woven together and developed contrapuntally in ever-increasing complexity." [72] The whole technique is a matter of associations. "I love that word 'associations,'" Mann confesses; "For me, and in however relative a sense, that which is full of associations is, quite precisely, that which is significant." [73] Here we have music linked with psychology. The psychoanalyst suggests that dreams and waking fantasies connect with associations, that the dream or persistent image in waking thoughts is a condensation of the various associations of a person's experience. Thus Hans Castorp, day-dreaming of Asiatic eyes and borrowed lead pencils, is experiencing musical-psychological compressions of his boyhood love for Hippe and his passion for Clavdia, which are themselves connected.

Finally there is the question of the "political" significance of music. Settembrini of The Magic Mountain and Socrates of Plato's Republic have much in common in their opinion of the art. Plato insists, as we know, that in addition to poetry and painting, music must be subjected to keen scrutiny before it may be permitted to enter the ideal State. No soft and effeminate compositions, such as those of the Ionian or Lydian modes—termed as they were "relaxed" [74]— would the philosopher suffer to play upon the plastic souls of the youths of his commune. Only the strains of courage and temperance, couched in the austere harmonies of the Dorian and the Phrygian would be permitted to pass the censorship of the philosopher kings. Nor would instruments of beguiling range or seductive timbre be admitted—no flutes

---

[72] Author's interview with Thomas Mann, January 27, 1941.
[73] Sk, p. 41.   [74] Republic, Book III, p. 399.

at any cost, for in its tonal comparability with forbidden harmonies, the flute is the worst offender among instruments.[75] Moral categories are decidedly admissible to art, thinks Plato, and in the ideal State, the tendency of music to weaken the moral fibre, to envelop the soul in the narcotic fumes of sensuous sweetness, must not be tolerated. Some music might remain, but only that which is conducive to uplifting and stimulating the soul. For, he says through the mouth of Socrates in the *Republic:*

"When a man allows music to play upon him and to pour into his soul through the funnel of his ears, those sweet and soft and melancholy airs of which we were just now speaking, and his whole life is passed in warbling and song; in the first stage of the process the passion or spirit which is in him is tempered like iron, and made useful, instead of brittle and useless. But if he carries on the softening and soothing process, in the next stage he begins to melt and waste, until he has wasted away his spirit and cut out the sinews of his soul; and he becomes a feeble warrior." [76]

This might almost be Settembrini speaking. Plato's Socrates looks askance at music, as he does at all art, because it is an imitation twice over of the ideal world. Mann's Settembrini suspects the art because his literary and humanistic heart is chronically suspicious of the formless and the inarticulate. But both agree that music unsupervised is a menace to good politics. Of course, to Socrates of the *Republic* a certain amount of music is tolerable provided that it is accompanied by moral direction; and to Settembrini music could indeed fulfill a function *dignum et justum,* as a humanistic incitement to the souls of men, a handmaid to the Word. Preceded by literature, the Italian admits, music could even serve the cause of rebellion, freedom and en-

[75] *Ibid.*   [76] *Ibid.*, p. 411.

lightenment, as (we venture to supply him with examples) in the case of the *Marseillaise* or the *Rakoczy* March. But alone, music is a danger. Settembrini warns Hans Castorp:

"Music? It is the half-inarticulate art, the dubious, the irresponsible, the insensible. Perhaps you will object that she can be clear when she likes. But so can nature, so can a brook—what good is that to us? That is not true clarity, it is a dreamy, inexpressive, irresponsible clarity, without consequences, and therefore dangerous, because it betrays one into soft complacence. Let music play her loftiest role, she will thereby kindle the emotions, whereas what concerns us is to awaken the reason. Music is to all appearance movement itself—yet, for all that, I suspect her of quietism. Let me state my point by the method of exaggeration; my aversion to music rests upon political grounds." [77]

Settembrini's hostility to music reflects Nietzsche's mixed feelings toward the art. Nietzsche loved music, he wrote that beautiful phrase "Music and tears—I can scarcely tell them apart." [78] But the philosopher saw in music—and it took his Wagner experience to bring this home to him—a danger to Germany, the danger of preferring the wordless mood of music to the extent of neglecting the intellectual, analytical, nonmusical element which he insisted must be included in her culture if she were to participate in the future Europe. In the popular total capitulation to Wagner, who represented to him at once the most powerful and the most harmful elements in music, Nietzsche perceived what he thought of as "the German hostility to Enlightenment." [79] He therefore warned against the tendency to narcotic use of music by Germans who "wish to be transported by the artist into a state of dreamy passion." [80] Settembrini speaks with the tongue of Nietzsche when on one occasion he comes upon the cousins smoking, drinking beer and listening to a

[77] MM, p. 146.   [78] *Ecce Homo*, p. 45.
[79] *Dawn of Day*, p. 199.   [80] *Ibid.*, Aph. 217.

band concert: "Beer, tobacco, music—behold the Fatherland!" [81] In Nietzsche's mind, future hope of the revolutionary march of intellect in synthesis with feeling was not
compatible with dalliance in present love, no matter how
personally dear music might be. That is why he said " 'Cave
musicam' is to this day my advice to all who are men enough
to insist on cleanliness in matters of spirit." [82]

Settembrini of *The Magic Mountain* is in many ways a
sounding board for Thomas Mann's self-criticism. In his
book of essays written during the first World War, Mann
maintains as a fundamental thesis that Germany, of all countries, is the "musical" nation, and that the failure of other
nations to understand her can be explained on this basis.
While the nations of Western Europe have placed their faith
in the Word, in the critico-analytic tradition of letters, Germany's characteristic arts have been music and poetry. This
musical character of the Fatherland is puzzling to the more
vocal Western Europeans; in their fondness for words, for
rationalizing, they do not realize that Germany is "das unliterarische Land." [83] Thus the 1918 *Reflections*. Now in *The
Magic Mountain*, Settembrini is cast in the role of ambassa-
dor-representative of Western liberalism, and he holds music
in deep suspicion. "I shall not be going too far," remarks the
Italian, "in saying at once that she [music] is politically
suspect." [84] He insists that this overweening love for music
is a dangerous weakness in the character of Hans Castorp
and in the soul of Germany. Settembrini's warnings were not
without foundation. Already during the writing of *The
Magic Mountain* Thomas Mann had misgivings about
"music," and later came to admit the realization of Nietzsche's fears, to confess that Germany's refusal to permit her

[81] MM, p. 145.   [82] *Human, All Too Human,* II, 3.
[83] See below, p. 136.   [84] MM, p. 148.

"musical" nonpolitical culture to be mixed with the literary, analytic, and political elements she might have received from the West, made her prey to the great anticultural reaction which was to plunge her, before she had recovered from the effects of 1914-18, into another war.[85]

Discussion of the moral and political implications of music leads to questions concerning the moral and political significance of art generally, in connection with Thomas Mann's work. To these two inquiries we may now proceed, with some confidence that we have not neglected "the romantic—in league of course with music, toward which it continually aspires, without which it can have no fulfillment." [86]

[85] "Culture and Politics," *Survey Graphic*, LXXV (Feb., 1939), 96.
[86] "Wagner," FGW, p. 172.

4

MORALITY AND THE ARTIST

IMMANUEL KANT, in his *Critique of Judgment*, outlined a position which set precedent for the aesthetic pronouncements of later Germans who were interested in problems of art. With characteristic fondness for nice, symmetrical deductions, Kant declared that there is in man a faculty mediating between the theoretic understanding and the ethical, practical reason. This is the faculty of judgment, a bond between sense and spirit, the locus of man's aesthetic cultivation. And, added Kant, just as the ethical Ought, the categorical imperative of practical reason, has no justification other than its own sweet self, Beauty too has her autonomy. The aesthetic state is one of disinterested contemplation; faced with a thing of beauty, the aesthetic attitude is "pleasure without interest" (*interesselos Wohlgefallen*).[1] Kant did not mean, however, that art is cut off from morality by a hatchet. The faculty of judgment undergirds the transition from understanding (whose object is nature) to practical reason (whose object is the willing self) and thus aesthetic perception has roots in both knowing and moral man. He did mean that judgment has a relative, but none the less real, autonomy; that a work of art does not and should not be expected to illustrate directly the moral law.

Friedrich Schiller spent years studying Kant—thereby, according to Goethe, wasting that much of his time—and he

---

[1] *Critique of Judgment*, trans. J. C. Meredith (New York, 1911), p. 42.

incorporated something of the philosopher's doctrine into his own aesthetic theory. The autonomy of art is emphasized in Schiller's *Simple and Sentimental Poetry*. In that essay, Schiller takes pains to deny that art should strive for moral ends. Although it is generally true, he remarks, that art is conducive to the moral progress of humanity, the artist should not create with this in mind; for the "ideal of moral ennoblement tends to draw the poet away from real Nature to the realm of the ideal—wherein reason will abstract itself too much from experience." [2]

The artist, Schiller declares, is in something of the position of man prior to the loss of his moral blamelessness, before the onset of corrupting civilization and the concomitant growth of the moral sense. "The laws of decency are strangers to innocent nature," [3] Schiller reminds his reader; and as for the poet, "All that is permitted to innocent nature is equally permitted to him." [4] Schiller, however, had a strong personal moral bent, and was fond of rendering explicit Kant's suggestion that art, though autonomous, was nevertheless a bridge between nature and morality. The poet liked to bring out so emphatically the spontaneous assistance to morality provided by the beautiful that his emphasis at times verged on inconsistency with his "disinterested" position. One thinks of the essay *The Stage as a Moral Institution*—the very title of which betrays Schiller's bias—and of certain strange pronouncements included in it, such as, "The uncertain nature of political events, rendering religion a necessity, also demands the stage as a moral force." [5] We can find a more general preachment in one of the poet's letters to Goethe:

It is truly worth remarking that laxity in aesthetic matters always

---

[2] *Essays Aesthetical and Philosophical* (London, 1910), p. 332.
[3] *Ibid.*, p. 310.   [4] *Ibid.*   [5] *Ibid.*, p. 333.

shows itself connected with moral laxity, and that the pure, strict striving after what is highly beautiful . . . will lead to rigoressness in moral matters.[6]

Goethe had fewer scruples about the moral significance of art than had his friend. He believed that art had little business with moral welfare, and any claims to the contrary always angered him. "Art itself gives laws," [7] he would say, "we should take care not to be always looking for culture only in that which is decidedly pure and moral." [8] Goethe was continually exasperated by moral-seeking philistines—those, for example, who declared that no virtuous lady could read *Wilhelm Meister* [9]—and he liked to retort that no work of art could have an influence nearly as pernicious as life itself, which daily displays the most scandalous scenes in abundance.[10] Art, he felt, has little to do with what good people call "morality" and (he would only hint this) it has more than a bit to do with what good people call "sin." After all, when you come right down to it, "To poetize is wantonness." [11] Yet Goethe would admit that art has a kind of indirect moral significance, that art can be measured by the norm of humanity. The poet was a son of the eighteenth century, and the ideal of that epoch was humanity. While the German literary men were protesting against narrow moralizing, the Enlightenment's noble conception of *Humanität* influenced them all as a broad moral doctrine.

Beside Goethe and Schiller, three other artist philosophers dear to Thomas Mann—Schopenhauer, Nietzsche, and Tolstoy—have expressed themselves on the relation of art and morality. The first of these made it plain in *The World as Will and Idea* that, since the artist is the mirror of mankind

[6] Letter 440. *Correspondence between Schiller and Goethe* (London, 1890).
[7] *Goethe's Literary Essays,* ed. Spingarn (New York, 1921), p. 71.
[8] Eck, p. 358.   [9] *Ibid.,* p. 337.   [10] *Ibid.,* p. 465.
[11] *West-Eastern Divan,* trans. Alex Rogers (London, 1890), p. 211.

whose task it is to make men aware of what they feel and do, he may sing of voluptuousness or of mysticism with equal right. "No one has the right," says Schopenhauer, "to prescribe to the poet what he ought to be—noble and sublime, moral, pious, Christian, one thing or another, still less to reproach him because he is one thing and not another." [12]

Nietzsche's doctrine is more difficult to isolate. He was, after all, a clergyman's son, and he always retained a fondness for reading a moral lecture, although his concept of what was moral hardly squared with the traditional one. Nietzsche betrays the moralist in him by the very shrillness of his railing against Christian morality, and by the enormous amount of space he devotes to invective against it in his books. Thomas Mann is aware of this inclination in Nietzsche. Speaking of his early attraction to the philosopher, he says, "My youth . . . did not prevent me from recognizing the moralist in Nietzsche—at a time when he meant little to the public save a childish misinterpretation of the superman idea." [13] When Nietzsche recoils from Wagner with the query "Who will dare to utter the word, the right word for the *ardeurs* of the *Tristan*-music?" Mann asserts that the question betrays the "old-maidishness" of Nietzsche, the "arch-moralist." [14] When we come to Nietzsche's own words as to whether art should have a normal purpose or not, we find that while he admits that art and morality are two different things, he insists upon some important qualifications:

If art is deprived of the purpose of teaching morality and of improving mankind, it does not by any means follow that art is absolutely pointless, purposeless, senseless, in short *l'art pour l'art* —a snake which bites its own tail . . . what does all art do? does it not praise? does it not glorify? does it not select? does it not

[12] WWI, III, 332.   [13] "Dürer," PM, p. 150.
[14] "Wagner," FGW, p. 175.

bring things into prominence? In all this it strengthens or weakens certain valuations. . . . Is his [the artist's] most fundamental instinct concerned with art? Is it not rather concerned with the purpose of art, with life? with a certain desirable kind of life? Art is the great stimulus to life; how can it be regarded as purposeless, as pointless, as *l'art pour l'art?* [15]

As for Tolstoy, one thinks immediately of those pages of *What Is Art?* in which the Russian novelist indicts in scathing language the vogue of what seems to him the dreadful sensuality in the art and literature of the nineteenth century. He adduces instance after instance of art used as a vehicle for vice, and points to this corruption as a serious and sinister forerunner of what may happen if people cannot come to the realization that art, far from being purposeless, has a definite and ordained aim, this goal being the brotherhood of man. Music can inflame the senses, cries Tolstoy in *The Kreutzer Sonata*,[16] sweet and sensuous tones can make man plunge into the most utter abandon. Painting has degenerated into a mere titillation of the flesh—that art which should act as a communal force to bind man to his fellow in a union high and austere. Modern art is used only as an instrument to debase, for:

From Boccaccio to Marcel Prevost, novels, poems and verses, invariably transmit the feeling of sexual love in its various forms. Adultery is not only the favorite, but almost the only theme of all the novels. A performance is not a performance unless under some pretext women appear with naked busts and limbs. Songs and romances—all are expressions of lust idealized in varying degrees.[17]

[15] *Twilight of the Idols*, pp. 79-80.
[16] Oddly enough, *The Kreutzer Sonata*, intended as an indictment of modern art as conducive to immorality, was itself once officially condemned as immoral in the United States. John Wanamaker, Postmaster General, found Tolstoy's book indecent and suppressed it in 1890.
[17] Tolstoy, *What Is Art?* (New York, 1930), p. 154.

Thomas Mann knows this moralizing Tolstoy, and asks us to take him with a grain of salt. To Mann, the Russian is a son of "Nature" and consequently has no business moralizing. Morality is the concern of men of "Spirit"—artists like Schiller and Dostoyevsky—not of the godlike ones, the beloved of nature. Occasionally though, Mann admits, the sons of nature are apt to be ridden temporarily by a yearning for spirit. Tolstoy is a prime example of this seizure, and that period of his life which brought illness, asceticism, and self-renunciation, was only a passing nostalgia for spirit.[18] Passages culled from Tolstoy—such as the foregoing—are evidences only, Mann insists, of "the shattering, involuntary impulse spiritwards of the wild son of nature."[19]

Now what is Thomas Mann's own attitude toward the problem? In discussing what he has written on art and morality, we must observe that he nearly always approaches the general problem through emphasis on one of its more tangible aspects, namely, the morality of the artist. Mann is not interested in the formula "art for art's sake," nor does he claim that art is hostile to morality. What he does claim is that the sources of art, that is, those depths in the artist from which creative power wells up, are frequently ambiguous in character; that art arises from elements in the artist nature which are connected with the forbidden and the harmful, and that consequently the artist has his own special morality.

Early in his artistic career, Mann had concluded that artistic creation was not seldom rooted in equivocal sources, even in the unclean and evil. Tonio Kröger speaks of the praise his writings receive from good honest souls, and confesses, "I positively blush at the thought of how these good people would freeze up if they were to get a look behind the scenes."[20] Ordinary folk, Tonio remarks, think that an artist's

[18] G-T, p. 40.   [19] "Goethe, Novelist," PM, p. 110.   [20] TK: STD, p. 103.

talent is a "gift" and thereby labor under a misapprehension which is perhaps just as well for all concerned: "Because in their innocence they assume that beautiful and uplifting results must have beautiful and uplifting causes, they never realize that the 'gift' in question is an extremely dubious affair." [21] Years after *Tonio Kröger* was written, the same warning as to the equivocal origins of the beautiful is echoed in *Death in Venice*. One remembers that Aschenbach wrote a little essay which was "so chaste, so lofty, so poignant with feeling" that the world afterwards acclaimed it as a masterpiece. But Aschenbach fashioned his essay out of his illicit love for Tadzio; he watched the boy playing on the beach as he wrote it. And the author comments:

Verily it is well for the world that it sees only the beauty of the completed work and not its origins nor the conditions whence it sprang; since knowledge of the artist's inspiration might often but confuse and alarm and so prevent the full effect of its excellence. [22]

In a late essay on Goethe, Thomas Mann quotes an aphorism of the French painter Degas to the effect that a picture must be painted with the same feeling as that with which a criminal commits a crime. Mann finds this a "beautiful, disturbing saying." [23] With reason: for the statement is in accord with Mann's own feeling that the artist's talent rests on such ambiguous grounds that there is something not far from criminal about it. One of the characters in his story

---

[21] TK: STD, p. 105. Compare this with the following comment by Moorman in his *Tuberculosis and Genius*, p. xxv: "How unhappy many pious prohibiting souls might be if they really knew through what questionable avenues the most beautiful and significant creations of genius have travelled. . . . How surprised these same prohibiting individuals might be if they knew what a frightful price has been paid for many of the literary, artistic and scientific treasures in which we are permitted to revel without thought of their laborious birth."

[22] DV: STD, p. 414.   [23] "Goethe," FGW, p. 85.

"At the Prophet's" (1904) lists, as a necessary condition of genius, "approximation to crime." [24]

Tonio Kröger tells Lisaveta of a banker he once knew who was sent to jail for a serious offense and there discovered the talent in himself which later brought forth literary pieces of undisputed excellence. "Can you escape the suspicion," Tonio asks his friend, "that the source and essence of his being an artist had less to do with his life in prison than they had with the reason that *brought him there?*" [25] The suggestion of a relation between the artist and the criminal is delicately symbolized in the same story. Tonio, after taking a holiday from his artistic labors in Munich, goes north to visit his native city which he has not seen since he left it in his youth. While stopping at a hotel there, under the watchful eye of the proprietor, he is questioned by a police officer who suspects that the writer is none other than a certain Munich swindler wanted by the police. The suspicion of the hotel manager and the policeman does not make Tonio angry. In fact "He even agreed with them—up to a point." [26] We can see that Tonio Kröger's conviction that artistic talent has something irregular about it is inseparable from his "bad conscience." His misgivings about his divergence from bourgeois morality is an element in his consciousness of isolation. The artist departs from the normal, not only in health but in morals. Thomas Mann once put his serious thoughts on the matter in jest when he drew this little self-portrait for a German magazine:

Those who have turned the pages of my books will recall that I have always regarded the artist's or the poet's life with extreme distrust. Indeed, my astonishment at the honors which society bestows upon this species will never cease. I know what a poet is,

[24] "At the Prophets," STD, p. 289.   [25] TK: STD, p. 105.
[26] *Ibid.*, p. 118.

since, according to all accounts, I am one myself. A poet, in short, is a fellow who is thoroughly useless in every domain of serious activity, who wastes his time on trivialities, one who is not only not useful to the state, but actually rebelliously inclined towards it. He need not even possess distinguished mental gifts, but may be as slow and dull as I have always been. Moreover, inwardly childish, inclined toward dissoluteness, he is in every respect a disreputable charlatan who should expect nothing from society—and actually expects nothing else—but silent contempt. But the fact is that society gives this type of humanity the opportunity to achieve in its midst prestige and a life of luxury. That suits me; I profit by it. But it should not be so. It only encourages vice and enrages virtue.[27]

This interest in the interrelation of criminal and artistic elements is carried into "Felix Krull," the idea of which was suggested to Mann by the memoirs of a Rumanian adventurer named Manolescu. The tale, a fragment which was never completed, is according to its author "in essense the story of an artist; in it the element of the unreal and the illusional passes frankly over into the criminal." [28] The equivocal nature of the sources of art is symbolized here by the dual character of the actor Müller-Rose. Little Felix is taken by his father to the theatre, where across the footlights he sees the actor, elegantly dressed and shiningly handsome, give a masterful performance which brings forth storms of applause. Afterwards the boy accompanies his father to Müller-Rose's dressing room where he discovers a man removing his make-up, a leering pasty-faced man whose body is covered with pimples. A thought strikes Felix: the actor—in fact, any artist—is like a glowworm. His art is bright and beautiful, but may not his own inner character more often resemble the crawling thing the insect is when it gives no light? [29] Grandfather Maggotson's words to Felix

[27] The English translation is in "Goethe," *Yale Review*, XXI (Summer, 1932), p. 711.   [28] Preface, STD, p. vii.   [29] "Felix Krull," STD, p. 359.

are of interest in this connection. The old man, who was himself once forced to flee from a criminal investigation, tells the boy who is to become a forger, a story about the Greek artist Phidias. The sculptor, says Maggotson, stole some of the gold given him for the statue of Athena. He was imprisoned. Upon his release, by order of Pericles, Phidias stole again, this time gold and ivory entrusted to him for the chryselephantine statue of Zeus. Whereupon the artist went to jail once more, and died in the prison at Olympia. The moral of this tale is pointed out by Grandfather Maggotson in these words.

"But that is the way people are. They want people to be talented —which is something out of the ordinary. But when it comes to the other qualities which go with the talents—and perhaps are essential to them—oh, no, they don't care for them at all, they refuse to have any understanding of them." [30]

Society excludes the criminal and tolerates the artist. But the latter must accustom himself to an atmosphere of suspicion. Thomas Mann thinks that the prejudice which causes normal folk to look askance at the artist's calling is not entirely baseless. The traditional bourgeois suspicion of the artist's life, he feels, rests upon an intuition which is at least half-sound. For in the abandonment of the genius there is something of the abandonment of the criminal.

Abandonment? The morality of the artist lies in this rather than in discipline and self-restraint. The artist has ties to the Platonic *Unlimited,* that wayward, nonintellectual, conscienceless principle which is so opposed to check of any kind, which demands freedom even at the price of disorder. The artist is not "immoral," but he has his own peculiar morality. This lies in abandonment, in surrender to experience, in yielding to the forbidden, even if it lead him to

[30] *Ibid.,* p. 352.

destruction. Thomas Mann explicitly formulates this concept of artist morality in the early Schiller study. The poet is seated at work, weary and ill. He rests to muse:

And the moral laws? . . . Why was it that precisely sin, surrender to the harmful and the consuming, actually seemed to him more moral than any amount of wisdom and frigid self-discipline? Not that constituted morality: not the contemptible knack of keeping a good conscience—rather the struggle and compulsion, the passion and pain.[31]

In the *Reflections*, Mann reiterates his conviction that the morality of genius consists in abandonment, and he revaluates certain ethical concepts in the light of this. "Virtue" he calls the good conscience of the bourgeois, and to it opposes the "morality" of the artist, who must yield to the hurtful and the forbidden. This surrendering to danger, when it presents itself, Mann calls "sin," but he insists that the word should not be confused with "immorality." In his own words:

We speak of . . . the psychical species "artist" and his relation to virtue,—it would be better to say at once that there is no relation at all, or, at most, a tempting and precarious one . . . the moralist differs from the man of virtue in that he is open to the dangerous and the harmful; in that he "resists not evil" in the words of the Evangelist—what concerns the man of virtue is respectable results. But what is the dangerous and the harmful? Pastors call it sin. But this severe and frightening word is only a word, and has several meanings. There is sin in the sense of the Church, and sin in the sense of humanism, humanity, science, emancipation, "mankind." But in our meaning, "sin" is doubt, the urge to the forbidden, the impulse to adventure, to lose oneself to experience, to explore, to know—it is temptation and seduction. . . . Only philistines will hasten to call this impulse immoral; that it is sinful, no one will deny.[32]

The revaluation of "sin" is suggested again in "Sleep, Sweet Sleep." In this little essay, the traditional opposition between

[31] "A Weary Hour," STD, p. 409.   [32] *Reflections*, p. 399.

sin and morality is flatly denied in the very words of the
earlier Schiller sketch:

Only the Philistine considers that sin and morality are opposed
ideas; they are one, for without knowledge of sin, without yielding to harm and destruction, all morality is nothing but sheer
flabby virtuousness. It is not purity and innocence which are
morally desirable, not cautious egoism and a contemptible knack
at keeping a good conscience, but the struggle and compulsion,
the pain and the passion that make up morality.[33]

And in the same half-whimsical, half-serious essay, Mann
relates this revolutionary notion of morality as abandonment
specifically to the artist. It is he who must find morality by
yielding to what experience may bring, so that he may not
stultify himself in reasoned judgment and conscious calculation:

. . . all work born of an artist's cold, calculated and correct
resolve is bad, ignoble, bloodless, repellent. His true morality
lies in abandonment, devotion, in surrender and error; in struggle
and compulsion, experience, knowledge, passion.[34]

A further parable of this morality of abandonment is to be
found in the story of Hans Castorp. Not for nothing does
the youth make Settembrini's Petrarchan motto "Placet Ex-
periri" his own, albeit in a somewhat antihumanistic sense.
The whole force of *The Magic Mountain* is directed to con-
vince us that by turning his back on that love of order, that
loyalty to the regular and upright—the legacy of his ancestors and his bourgeois environment—and by yielding to guilt
and the forbidden, Hans Castorp attains spiritual maturity
and self-realization. Clavdia Chauchat symbolizes the realm
of the equivocal and the forbidden. Settembrini, in his
attempt to keep Castorp from succumbing to her allures,

[33] PM, p. 274.   [34] *Ibid.*, pp. 274-75.

represents the traditional bourgeois humanist morality. And on the carnival night, when Hans flings reason aside to approach his beloved, the Italian is left like a mother hen watching in dismay her adopted duckling take to the water, a dangerous and alien element. Surrender to Clavdia represents to Settembrini a bond with the world of darkness, and it is with calculated classical allusion to the shadowy world of Hades that his first address to Hans after that fatal interview is: "Well, Engineer, and how have you enjoyed the pomegranate?" [35] Hans Castorp cheerfully violated the code of his fathers when he went to Clavdia's room to return her pencil on the night of the carnival, but the author of the story leaves us to compare the merits of this guilty liaison with those of a once possible marriage to some "healthy little goose" down in the Flatland. Hans Castorp might have said with Faust:

> Yes, let me dare those gates to fling asunder
> Which every man would fain go shrinking by! [36]

It is not Hans Castorp, but Clavdia Chauchat who is articulate on the problem of morality in *The Magic Mountain*. She puts into words her lover's own silent convictions on the carnival night, just before Hans bursts into his remarkable address in French. When he questions her as to the details of her discussion on morality with a visitor from her own country, she replies:

"Morality? That interests you? Well, it seems to us that one must seek morality not in virtue, that is, in reason, discipline, good manners, uprightness, but on the contrary, I mean in sin, in abandoning oneself to danger, to that which is harmful, to that which consumes us. It seems to us that it is more moral to lose oneself, even to let oneself perish, than to save oneself." [37]

[35] MM., p. 449.
[36] Goethe, *Faust*, trans. Bayard Taylor (New York, 1930), p. 30.
[37] MM, p. 430. The author has translated from the original French.

Just as sin belongs to the world of spirit rather than that of nature, so, paradoxical as it is, sin is spiritual; it has no place in the sphere of innocent nature. This thought is echoed in the *Joseph* story on an occasion when Mann comments, "Yes, at bottom, all spirit is nothing else than understanding of sin." [38] In his capitulation to disease and sin, Hans Castorp finds life and fulfillment. It is even hinted that ill-health and sin may not be two disparate things, but in some cases two differently viewed aspects of one and the same principle. Herr Settembrini is quick to unite disease with perversity, death with the dissolute. While yet in his first day at the sanatarium, Hans Castorp's fever and palpitation is joined to a reckless wonder "how it must feel to be finally relieved of the burden of a respectable life and made free of the infinite realms of shame." [39] Castorp and Aschenbach are both ridden by fever, and both surrender to the forbidden. The difference is that the abyss engulfs Aschenbach, while Castorp manages to override it. While the eminent man of letters gives himself up to destruction only after a tortured struggle with himself, the sometime engineer on the carnival night is blithe in his resolve:

> To take this step with cheerful resolution
> Though Nothingness should be the certain, swift conclusion. [40]

There are really two distinct crises in the life of Hans Castorp at the sanatorium in each of which he is forced to a choice between the straight and the primrose paths. The first volume of his story is brought to a climax with his surrender to Clavdia. But he is compelled to another decision much later in his stay at Davos. This occurs in the second volume, in the chapter "Highly Questionable." Here Hans is called upon to decide whether or not he shall cooperate with

---

[38] *Joseph in Egypt*, II, 518.   [39] MM, p. 104.   [40] *Faust*, p. 31.

the powers of darkness in summoning the phantom presence of his dead cousin Joachim. Once again it is Settembrini, on the side of law and order, who pleads with his protégé to keep his hands from the world of the dark and the irrational. With honest passion the humanist begs Hans to "hold in abhorrence these luxations of the brain, these miasmas of the spirit." [41] But Hans had already reached other conclusions:

By little and little his morality and his curiosity approached and overlapped, or had probably always done so; the pure curiosity of inquiring youth on his travels, which had already brought him close to the forbidden field, that time he had tasted the mystery of personality, and for which he had even claimed the justification that it too was almost military in character in that it did not weakly avoid the forbidden when it presented itself.[42]

So on the evening of that memorable scene, presided over by Dr. Krokowski with the youthful Ellen Brand as medium, Hans Castorp, who by now has the boldness to say "It is more moral to lose your life than to save it," [43] calls up before the horrified company the phantom of Joachim Ziemssen, wearing the field helmet of the German soldier of the World War.

Does it follow from Mann's postulates that the truly moral man is one who himself has known sin? "The great moralists," remarks Clavdia Chauchat, "are not at all virtuous men, but adventurers in evil, men of vices, great sinners." [44] In his preface to the Epicon edition of Goethe's *Elective Affinities*, Mann tells how the master's public was shocked at the "sinfulness" of the novel; he adds, "As though Christianity the world over has to do with anything but sin, as though sainthood could ever spring from any soil but just

41 MM, p. 839.   42 *Ibid.*, p. 828.   43 *Ibid.*, p. 704.
44 *Ibid.*, p. 430. The author has translated from the original French.

that." [45] This is in key with a saying of Novalis, "He who understands sin, understands virtue and Christianity." [46]

Mann had presented this paradox in symbolic form as early as 1904 in his Renaissance drama *Fiorenza*. In the play, the monk Savonarola is portrayed as an ascetic of great personal magnetism, who draws all Florence to hear him thunder at the erotic vanities of the shameless city. Especially does Fiore, the lovely mistress of Lorenzo de' Medici, draw down the cleric's wrath. But a somewhat equivocal light is thrown on Fra Girolamo's saintliness when Fiore discloses to her lord that this awesome friar was once but an ugly youth in Ferrara, who years ago begged her with the blackest passion in his eyes to yield herself to him. Scornfully repulsed by her, he had fled to a cloister, whence he soon emerged to preach repentance and the Judgment of the Lord. [47] Delicately it is suggested in the course of *Fiorenza* that Lorenzo, the magnificent voluptuary, and the monk, inflamed with holy anger, are brothers under the skin, that there is in both the identical dynamic drive with a difference only in its direction. The same theme is presented in less developed fashion in Mann's story "*Gladius Dei*," written two years before *Fiorenza*. This is the tale of a young religious fanatic who demands of a Munich art dealer that he remove from his show window a Madonna, done by a famous painter whose mistress was the model for the work. "This picture had its origin in sensual lust and is enjoyed in the same!" [48] shrieks the unhappy youth in whose feeling for the picture fascination and repulsion are mixed. [49]

The oblique implication in Fiorenza that the nature of

---

[45] "Goethe, Novelist," PM, p. 111.
[46] Novalis, *Aphorisms*, Vol. IV of *The German Classics*, p. 186.
[47] *Fiorenza*, STD, pp. 254-55.   [48] "Gladius Dei," STD, p. 190.
[49] A later reference to the ascetic's equivocal nature may be found in the speech of the hermit of *The Transposed Heads*, pp. 137 *et seq*.

artist and saint rest on a common foundation is rather similar
to some points of Freud's theory of art—although at the time
of the play's composition Mann had not come in contact
with the psychoanalyst's doctrine. Freud holds that a man's
libido, forbidden free expression by the inner censor, often
wells back in upon the organism to wreak havoc in the form
of neuroses. Now the man of art is especially ripe for this
derangement. "The artist has . . . an introverted disposition," says Freud, "and has not far to go to become a neurotic." [50] But the artist, adds the psychoanalyst, also has a
distinct advantage over his less gifted fellow man. He can—
unconsciously, of course—universalize the wish fantasies that
only bedevil his ordinary brother and can alter them so
that their origin in forbidden sources cannot be perceived.
The result of this sublimation of the erotic drive is art. The
coincidence of Mann's doctrine with that of Freud on this
point is best observed in some mature remarks in the writer's
preface to his Schopenhauer selections. The philosopher,
says Mann, made a mistake when in his hatred of sex as a
diabolical distraction from contemplation, he postulated art
as something far and safely removed from the realm of the
erotic, something which is, indeed, the only salvation—
apart from consecration—for the human spirit tortured by
the cravings of the Will. But right there, Mann insists, lies
the philosopher's error; for he does not see that this dichot-
omy between art and the erotic is impossible:

Suppose he had understood that genius does not at all consist in
sensuality put out of action and will unhinged, that art is not
mere objectification of spirit, but the fruitful union and interpenetration of both spheres, immensely heightening to life and
more fascinating than either by itself! That the essence of the
creative artist is nothing else—and in Schopenhauer himself was

[50] A General Introduction to Psychoanalysis (New York, 1930), p. 326.

nothing else—than sensuality spiritualized, than spirit informed and made creative by sex.[51]

What is the nature of the abandonment, the yielding to the forbidden which Thomas Mann submits is the essence of artist morality? Abandonment is the common element in the artist and the criminal. Neither the artist nor the criminal can be bound by ordinary laws; both surrender to the forbidden, both lay themselves open to the harmful. They share a feverish tension, liable to disintegration. They possess a common sensitivity. The artist is quickened by every stimulus life presents, the criminal nature is seldom found to be without some trait of exaggerated sentimentality. They share a common ruthlessness. The artist cannot let mere good feeling stand in the way of his task of seizing on life and using it to his purpose; mere consideration for others can mean nothing to him. To the criminal's cruder arrogance, also, the rights of others have no meaning. Both artist and criminal are isolated from society, marked men, shunned by honest people. Both are completely free to make what they can of life, both are absolutely at liberty to choose their subject matter. As Somerset Maugham remarks:

The artist can within certain limits make what he likes of his life. In other callings, in medicine, for instance, or the law, you are free to choose whether you will adopt them or not, but having chosen you are free no longer. You are bound by the rules of your profession; a standard of conduct is imposed upon you. The pattern is predetermined. It is only the artist, and maybe the criminal, who can make his own.[52]

The artist's abandonment, in which there are suggestions of the criminal, is simply Faustian morality. The original sin,

[51] *Schopenhauer Presented by Thomas Mann* (Longmans Green and Company, New York, 1939), p. 26. Reprinted by permission of the publishers.

[52] *The Summing Up* (Doubleday, Doran and Company, Inc., New York, 1938), p. 50. Reprinted by permission of the publishers.

for which the first man was expelled from Paradise, was
his yielding to the thirst for knowledge, to a desire to know
the forbidden. Goethe's hero commits this primordial sin.
Faust had to learn, to know through experience, be that
experience honorable or guilty. How could he obtain complete discernment without welcoming all joys and passions,
innocent and forbidden alike? Faust learns through complete surrender to whatever offers itself, even to outright
crime, for his betrayal of Gretchen was nothing but that.
The pragmatic morality of Goethe's hero represents something quite opposed to Schiller's sensibilities. Take, for example, the latter's poem "The Veiled Image of Sais." It tells
of a truth-seeking youth who is shown a veiled statue by an
Egyptian hierophant, and told that he who lifts the veil
shall know Truth, but that only sacerdotal hands may un-
cover the image. Returning in the night, the youth lifts the
veil and dies, leaving the message "Woe unto him who seeks
the Truth through Guilt." Nietzsche was a moralist, but he
insisted on the morality of abandonment. Though he denies
that art has nothing to do with morality, he insists that
morality does not mean avoidance of the harmful. "Live
dangerously," he cries. "Resist ye not evil." He points out
that the man who died on the Cross showed by his example
how one ought to live—"to refrain from resisting even the
Evil One." [53] The primordial sin was knowledge, the philosopher claims, and in the interdict against it, traditional morality was born.

"Resist ye not evil." These words might have been written
at the head of *Death in Venice*. For Aschenbach knows at
the outset of his adventure that it will lead him into the
realms of danger and the forbidden. His inborn discipline,
his bourgeois conscience makes him flee Tadzio at once. But
when his baggage goes astray, forcing him back to the hotel

[53] *Antichrist*, no. 35.

once more, he makes "a gesture of welcome, a calm and deliberate acceptance of what might come." [54] Intoxicated by the Polish boy's beauty, the eminent literary man is well aware of the possible consequences. "This was utter frenzy— and without a scruple, nay, eagerly, the aging artist bade it come." [55] Aschenbach pays for years of stern self-discipline when his artist's nature at last finds him out and exacts from him a final and terrible tribute, concentrating in a moment of passionate consummation the abandonment from which his conscience had for a lifetime held him back. "Who shall unriddle the puzzle of the artist's nature?" asks Aschenbach's creator. "Who understands the mingling of discipline and license in which it stands so deeply rooted?" [56] In *Death in Venice*, Mann tells us that the artist's task has two aspects— Knowledge and Form. Knowledge is that painful, isolating scrutiny of life which, in Aschenbach's words, is "all-knowing, understanding, forgiving; it takes up no position, sets no store by form. It is compassion with the abyss—it *is* the abyss." [57] Such knowledge is fraught with peril, its effect upon spiritual fibre is weakening, disintegrating. Now Form is the artist's creative discipline, the stern strength which fashions, molds, limits. It welds spirit to sense, the universal to the particular. It stands opposed to discernment, it integrates, it checks the sapping of spiritual strength by Knowledge. But this control of Knowledge by Form sets up a dangerous tension, feverish and unstable. Creative asceticism may make an artist prey to spiritual dissolution. Disciplined detachment and preoccupation with Form may "lead to intoxication and desire, they may lead the noblest among us to frightful emotional excesses." [58] Form itself is equivocal, for, as Mann puts the question:

[54] DV: STD, p. 409. [55] *Ibid.*, p. 412. [56] *Ibid.*, p. 414.
[57] *Ibid.*, p. 435. [58] *Ibid.*

And has not form two aspects? Is it not moral and immoral at once: moral in so far as it is the expression and result of discipline, immoral—yes, actually hostile to morality—in that of its very essence it is indifferent to good and evil, and deliberately concerned to make the moral world stoop beneath its undivided sceptre? [59]

We must remember that *Death in Venice* is a parable, an allegory. The story of Aschenbach's downfall is a recognition of certain potentially tragic elements in the artist nature. Mann takes the spiritual tension of that nature, its ambiguities, its inclination to feverish excess, and heightens them in symbolism far above the literal. These are deep waters and bode no little peril for one who would act lightly upon the author's reflections. Plato says in one of his letters that there are profound truths which should not be made explicit before the general public, since they are liable to cause only misunderstanding and confusion.[60] Thomas Mann has not disobeyed this warning, for his artistic ethic is so cunningly embedded in his works that the majority into whose hands they fall pass over the doctrine without thought. The morality of genius is for the few, even though the products of genius are beloved of the many. Mann seems fully conscious of the grave responsibilities which must accompany the privilege of genius. He has always held aloof from Bohemianism. Anyone who would find in his statement of artist morality an incitement to general moral anarchy would thereby betray a total misunderstanding of the man and his work. The morality of the artist, Mann warns, must not be confused with cheap libertinism:

Not that we would be foolish enough to recommend the fashionable bourgeois view of the artist's life form as an immoral "amoral" life form. The measure of personal ethic, even of social

[59] *Ibid.*, p. 386.   [60] Epistle VII, 343.

love, which inhabits a productive artistic life, is under all circumstances a reasonable measure—let it stand at that.[61]

Hans Castorp does not go as far as Faust. He does not hurt anyone. If there is an element of danger in his surrender to whatever may come, it threatens only himself, never another. Nor is abandonment to be taken for pusillanimity. On the contrary, it is "military" in character in that it does not "weakly avoid the forbidden" when it presents itself.[62] In his ethic, the artist resembles the soldier who by his vocation must lay himself open to the hurtful and the destructive, and yet does not do so from mere spiritual flabbiness. Reiterating his belief in the validity of this doctrine of the artist morality of abandonment, Thomas Mann declares in 1941:

"This is a *pessimistic* view of the artist-nature. Standing opposed to the notion that artistic production is simply a matter of sheer joy and sheer loveliness, it is an emphasis on the dark side of creation. Even today, I would hold this moral doctrine universal and valid in the realm of art." [63]

At the outset of our discussion, we observed that Thomas Mann treats of the relation of art and morality almost exclusively from the standpoint of the morality of the artist. The question now arises as to what Mann thinks of the relation of the two categories apart from the personality of the artist. Does it follow from his doctrine of the morality of abandonment that art is hostile to morality? It does not. The artist is not "immoral," but has his own special morality; to him it is *moral* to be open to the harmful. To postulate that the artist has an individual morality certainly does not imply that art has no ground in common with morality.

---

[61] *Reflections*, p. 399.   [62] MM, p. 828.
[63] Author's interview with Thomas Mann, Princeton, Jan. 27, 1941.

But what is the common ground, according to Thomas Mann?

Art and morals have their origin in the human, one cannot be separated from humanity any more than can the other. As Nietzsche remarks, art, as the stimulus to life, cannot be pointless. Goethe defended the freedom of art, denied that its purpose was to sermonize, but insisted that the final test of the artist—as well as of any man—was what he weighed in the scale of humanity.[64] Friedrich Schlegel is at one with Goethe when he says "The morality of a book lies not in its theme or in the relation of the writer to his public, but in the spirit of the treatment. If this breathe the full abundance of humanity, it is moral." [65] Now it is in the sphere of the human too that Thomas Mann finds the connection between art and morality. Art "intensely human, intensely humane," [66] cannot ignore human values. The goal to which humanity strives is truth, and it is in truth that art and morals meet. Art cannot be indifferent to truth, the artist cannot tolerate falsehood. He must be sincere, and his art a product of that sincerity. In Mann's words:

Sincerity—therein art and morality have a common ground. We are not aesthetes nor vainglorious immoralists. The word "good" when applied to a work of art never has a merely aesthetic significance; nothing is "good," certainly not today, unless it has weight "in the scale of humanity," and everything barbaric is not only aesthetically but morally inferior and despicable. It is above all in their supreme contempt for falsehood that the artist and the moralist are united.[67]

Coincident with the rise of National Socialism, Thomas Mann began to emphasize his belief in the interrelation of art and morals. He became convinced more and more

[64] Eck, p. 347.
[66] "Standards and Values."

[65] *The German Classics*, IV, 179.
[67] *Ibid.*

strongly that when the fundamentals of human relations are challenged, no man can stand indifferent; no artist can remain aloof, nor his art unaffected. Mann himself left Germany, not only because his moral instincts were outraged, but because he was convinced that his art would have suffered had he remained. Art has connections that reach beyond itself:

Art is the determining, the critical scale upon which it is dangerous to be weighed, for soon that scale or standard becomes more than a measure of taste; it decides values that go far beyond those which precede and constitute the basis of aesthetics; it decides value itself in the most substantial and fundamental meaning of the word.[68]

Art and morals have *value* in common, they both concern themselves with what is good. That is why Santayana says:

I can draw no distinction—save for academic programs—between moral and aesthetic values: beauty, being a good, is a moral good; and the practice and enjoyment of art, like all practice and all enjoyment, fall within the sphere of morals—at least if by morals we understand moral economy and not moral superstition.[69]

Thomas Mann follows Schiller in defining art as play, but insists that it is "a strangely serious play," which is in some way related to the idea of good itself.[70] In words which parallel Santayana's, Mann states:

The word "good" covers much; it is common to the aesthetic and the moral sphere. What is good aesthetically, what is skillfully done and perfect, must not necessarily be good from a moral point of view, but the infinite effort for what is good artistically

[68] *Ibid.*

[69] *Contemporary American Philosophy,* ed. Adams and Montague (The Macmillan Company, New York, 1930), II, 256. Reprinted by permission of the publishers.

[70] "How to Win the Peace," *Atlantic Monthly* (Feb., 1942), p. 177.

has the same root as the endeavor for what religion and morality call "good." [71]

Morality is both personal and civic. A question of the former we call ethical, of the latter, political. The Greek philosophers emphasized this juncture, for they considered morals as falling within the sphere of politics. Since the state was man writ large, they thought of the science of politics as continuous with and embracing the study of ethics. Thus our own study passes from the question of the artist's relation to morals to his relation to politics. We must record Thomas Mann's adventures in this sphere, his transition from a "non-political man" to an active and articulate political apologist.

[71] *Ibid.*

5

ART AND POLITICS

1939. AFTER TWENTY YEARS of uneasy peace, war again spreads darkness over the world. Reason, enlightenment, culture are out—reaction, force and the irrational have become top dogs. Is this the time for aesthetic idealism, can art ignore problems upon the solution of which may depend the future course of humanity? That question challenged men of art. It is a question which Thomas Mann found to be of the utmost personal significance.

To Mann in his late maturity came the realization that art and politics cannot be completely separated. Germany fell to the Nazis, he says, largely because in the past her men of culture stood contemptuously aloof from the political sphere. By their scorn of politics they brought about what Mann calls "the unfortunate schism between authority and intellect which characterizes the tragic aloofness of the German state from German culture." [1] But it was Thomas Mann himself who wrote the *Reflections of a Non-Political Man* in which he equated politics with all that was foreign and hostile to German culture.

At the outset, it is well to take with a grain of salt Mann's early claim to a non-political character. While he denounced politics as un-German, and insisted that he was an "Unpolitische"—nevertheless he could not conceal his keen, if hostile, interest in things political. His incisive political sense and historical instinct were first tried immediately after the

[1] "Standards and Values."

outbreak of the first World War. He was convinced that Germany had been forced into the war by the Entente powers, and he passionately defended his country's course of action with the best his pen could produce. In 1914, he wrote an essay called *Frederick the Great and the Grand Coalition*,[2] in which he drew an ingenious parallel between the Prussia of the eighteenth century and the Germany of the twentieth. The point of the study was that the coalition of European powers, engineered by the wily Kaunitz, was actually responsible for the war which began in 1756, and that Frederick had to assume the technical guilt—by striking the first blow—in order to bring the real guilt home to his enemies, where it belonged. Although never explicit, Mann's implied parallel between the two wars is obvious enough. Especially does his description of the shrieks of indignation all Europe sent up when Frederick invaded "neutral" Saxony recall the cries of horror that arose when Belgium was invaded in 1914.

Throughout the World War of 1914-1918, Thomas Mann worked on a series of political essays, finally published under the title *Betrachtungen eines Unpolitischen* (*Reflections of a Non-Political Man*). This book is the only major work of Mann which has not been translated into English. What was the thesis put forward in the *Reflections?* Mann himself asks this question and answers it in a later essay:

What, then, was the fundamental idea of the book, the axiom which formed its point of departure? It was the identity of politics and democracy, and the essential un-Germanness of the combination; in other words, the native strangeness of the German spirit towards the world of politics or democracy, against which it sets up, as its own peculiar concept, the unpolitical, aristocratic one of *Kultur*.[3]

[2] This appears in English in *Three Essays*.
[3] "Culture and Socialism," PM, pp. 204-5.

Or, to go to the words of the *Reflections* itself, we have Mann's remarks in the preface of that bulky work:

If, in the following discussion, the identity of the concepts "political" and "democracy" is defended or treated as self-evident, it is with an unusually perceptible and clearly distinct right. One is not a "democratic" or a "conservative" political man. One is political, or he is not. And if one is political, then he is a "democrat." [4]

There we have it! German culture is defined as hostile by nature to the political. "I am non-political," Mann states in his War book, "but I am non-political after the fashion of Germany, the bourgeois culture, and the romantic." [5] The culture of Germany, says Mann, is her tradition of music and metaphysics. It includes a pessimistic ethic, inseparable from the bourgeois heritage (cf. *Buddenbrooks*) and a melancholy sympathy with the romantic night-side of reality, with sickness and death. *Zivilisation,* as opposed to *Kultur,* stands for reason, morality and enlightenment—for shallow, wordy, optimistic, humanitarian idealism. Germany, *das unliterarische Land,* essentially musical by nature, seems awkward, fumbling and inarticulate before the *Zivilisationsliterats* voluble command of language which could so easily turn—as it did in the War—into self-righteous abuse. Germany's long history of political disunion, continues the *Reflections,* together with the lofty aloofness in which her great artists have stood apart from the sphere of the political, is proof enough that neither politics nor "democracy" is any of her business. The political is the concern of the humanistic democrats of the Western Enlightenment whose wartime screams of denunciation might bewilder Germany, but could never frighten her into submission. For the Germans are a

[4] *Reflections,* p. xxxi. [5] *Ibid.,* p. 84.

people of "the Middle"; their culture is essentially bourgeois
—that is, middle class—and Germany is set apart from the
uncomprehending nations of Western Europe, destined to
be the middle ground, the synthesizing medium between
East and West.[6] Her geographical position, her place between Western Europe and Asia—represented by Russia—
makes plain her role as cultural mediator.

What made the introspective task of the *Reflections* more
bitter for Thomas Mann was the fact that his own brother
Heinrich was the *Zivilisationsliterat* constantly before his
eyes as he wrote. Heinrich Mann's love and deepest interests
have always been with the Mediterranean countries; Italy
and France have had extensive claims on his life and art.
Heinrich always had a holy horror of chauvinism, and his
savage hostility toward German nationalism is easily observed in his pre-war novel *The Patrioteer*, originally titled
das Untertan ("The Subject"). The hero of this novel, one
Diederich Hessling, goes about yelling "I shall smash!" in
imitation of the Kaiser, whom Diederich has heard proclaim
"Intellectual weapons are no use today. National deeds will
win the future!"[7] Heinrich Mann thought he detected jingo-
ism in his brother's World War position, and he brought up
his heavy guns in attack. Thus began the famous *Brüderkrieg*, in which Thomas battled grimly for the conservative,
bourgeois, antipolitical position, while the ententophile
Heinrich took the part of *die französichen Intellectuellen*.[8]

The conviction that the German man of culture is by nature averse to politics was by no means original with Thomas
Mann. It was almost axiomatic in Germany before 1914.

[6] See Nietzsche's *The Genealogy of Morals,* p. 183.
[7] *The Patrioteer* (New York, 1921), p. 267.
[8] For further discussion of the Mann brothers' disagreement, see Weigand's *Thomas Mann's Novel 'Der Zauberberg,'* p. 172.

There is an interesting passage in the above-mentioned novel of Heinrich Mann, which illustrates this. Weibel, a noisy jingoist, is described accounting for his political interest before a student corps: "He explained to the freshmen that the time had come to take politics seriously. *He knew it was considered vulgar* [writer's italics], but their opponents made it necessary." [9] The nonpolitical attitude of the German bourgeoisie dated from the old days when Germany was a disunited heap of independent states, governed by petty princes. And the greatest *Unpolitische* of all was Thomas Mann's literary hero—Wolfgang Goethe.

During the years 1812-1813, the German states made their first long delayed move to concerted action, and their efforts were crowned by the defeat of Napoleon at Leipsic. In those exciting days, when the fire of newborn patriotism roused all Germany to enthusiastic deeds, Goethe sat still and did nothing, thereby earning for himself the lasting scorn of many of those who had hitherto idolized him. "You have been reproached," remarked Eckermann to the aged writer, "for not taking up arms at that great period, or at least co-operating as a poet." To which Goethe scornfully sniffed "To write military songs and sit in a room! That forsooth was my duty! . . . that was not my life and not my business." [10] Here are some of the venerable writer's dicta to Eckermann on the subject of poets and politics:

The English poet Thomson wrote a very good poem on the Seasons, but a very bad one on Liberty; and that was not from want of poetry in the poet, but from want of poetry in the subject.

If a poet would work politically, he must give himself up to a party; and as soon as he does that he is lost as a poet. I hate all bungling like sin; but, most of all, bungling in state affairs, which produces nothing but mischief to thousands and millions.[11]

[9] *The Patrioteer*, p. 47.   [10] Eck, pp. 359-60.   [11] *Ibid.*, p. 425.

Speaking of the criticism which he had brought upon himself because of his refusal to participate in revolutionary activity, Goethe shouts:

. . . all my labors are as nothing in the eyes of certain people, just because I have disdained to mingle in political parties. To please such people I must have become a member of a Jacobin club, and preached bloodshed and murder. However, not a word more upon this wretched subject, lest I become unwise in railing against folly.[12]

Referring to the political course of Uhland, which had brought that poet so much praise, Goethe is pessimistic:

Mind, the politician will devour the poet. To be a member of the States, and to live amid daily jostlings and excitements, is not for the delicate nature of a poet.[13]

Finally, here is Goethe's stately reply to those who accused him of being deficient in patriotism:

What is meant by love of one's country? What is meant by patriotic deeds? If the poet has employed a life in battling with pernicious prejudices, in setting aside narrow views, in enlightening the minds, purifying the tastes, ennobling the feelings and thoughts of his countrymen, what better could he have done? How could he have acted more patriotically?[14]

Thomas Mann has always been extremely interested in Goethe's antipolitical sentiments, and has never wearied of calling attention to them, pointing out the essentially German character of the poet's attitude. Concerning the hostility Goethe aroused against himself by his indifference to the revolution, Mann remarks in an essay written before his exile:

The hatred he [Goethe] had to endure was essentially political, it had to do with his coldly obstinate and repellent attitude to-

12 *Ibid.*   13 *Ibid.*, p. 426. This is quoted by Mann in *Reflections*, p. 85.
14 Eck, p. 426.

ward the two main tendencies of his century, the nationalistic and the democratic. . . . But will not Goethe's conception of the German people, as unpolitical and intellectual, as centred upon human values, receiving from all and teaching all, will not this always have its profound justification? [15]

In Mann's late novel, *The Beloved Returns*, Mann takes great pains to play up this antipolitical aspect of Goethe, showing among other things how much suffering young August Goethe had to bear on account of his father's hostility to the political sphere. At one point in the book, Goethe is revealed delivering an antipolitical lecture, which carries a conviction similar to that of Mann quoted above:

"The German, instead of confining himself to himself, must take in the whole world in order to have an effect on the world. Our goal must be, not hostile separation from other peoples, but rather friendly association with all the world, cultivation of the social virtues, even at the expense of our inborn feelings or even rights." [16]

And the bourgeois factor! To Thomas Mann, German culture has been essentially a bourgeois culture, and it has always been a mark of the German bourgeois to be nonpolitical. Now did Goethe's political *je m'en fiche* influence the bourgeois tradition? Or did the bourgeois heritage determine Goethe's feelings? Mann answers:

It is hard to say to what extent the German bourgeois idea owes its introspective, cultural, anti-political impress to Goethe, and to what extent Goethe, as an exponent of these qualities, merely reflected the German bourgeois character. Perhaps it is a case of interaction and mutual confirmation.[17]

Why was the German *Bürgertum* essentially unpolitical? The equation sounds a little strained to American ears. In

[15] "Goethe," FGW, p. 89.　　　　　[16]. *The Beloved Returns*, p. 161.
[17] "Goethe," *Yale Review*, XXI, 711.

partial answer, one can point to the peculiar social structure of the old Germany in which matters political were the exclusive concern of the official class. The bourgeoisie left political management to the bureaucracy. Placed between the working classes and officialdom, they looked condescendingly down on the one, and submitted respectfully to the other in the political sphere. An interesting commentary on the German middle-class attitude toward officialdom is Thomas Mann's remark concerning the behavior of the bourgeois hero of *The Magic Mountain*, while he is paying his bill in the office of the sanatorium. Throughout the transaction, Castorp maintained "the solemn, discreet, almost overawed bearing which the young German's respect for authority leads him to assume in the presence of pens, ink, and paper, or anything else which bears to his mind an official stamp." [18]

In Arthur Schopenhauer, Mann finds another nonpolitical representative of German culture, a capitalist bourgeois philosopher. During the revolution of '48, soldiers were quartered in his house, and they shot at the revolutionaries from his window. On one occasion, Schopenhauer handed his own opera glasses over to an officer so that he might see better to direct the fire. It was Schopenhauer who called the common people "souveräne canaille." [19] The phrase recalls old Lebrecht Kröger of *Buddenbrooks*. He stood watching the mob in '48—which now and again timidly threw a stone or two—and growled to Johann Buddenbrook, "Parbleu, Jean, this infamous rabble ought to be taught some respect with a little powder and shot. *Canaille!* Scum!" [20] In the contemptuous epithet which Schopenhauer (and Lebrecht Kröger) bestowed on the revolutionists, Thomas Mann dis-

[18] MM, p. 169.
[19] See *Reflections*, p. 100, and also "Culture and Politics," *Survey Graphic*, LXXV (Feb., 1939), p. 95.   [20] Bud, I, 191.

cerns a "challenge, mockery, denial, not only of Liberalism
and the Revolution, but of politics itself—an unpolitical or
suprapolitical disposition that is German, German-bourgeois,
German-intellectual." [21]

Richard Wagner was a different sort. He was a forty-
eighter and paid for his subversive ardor with exile. Here
then, contrary to rule, is a great German artist who was a
political man—or was he? Thomas Mann never seems to have
made up his mind about Wagner's political bent. In the *Reflections*, he suggests that Wagner's eager youth won him
over to the revolution, that he visioned its goal, not as political, but as cultural:

Wagner found in the German Revolution a little of himself; he
was young and passionate enough, and he had confidence in the
realization of his culture-dream of "The End of Politics" and of
the beginning of humanity. [22]

Nineteen years after the writing of these words, Mann was
more inclined to give the composer credit for genuine political interest. At the time of the 1933 Wagner essay, Mann
had abandoned his old belief that German culture was justified in its remoteness from politics. In this essay, he says of
Wagner:

. . . we find in his writings the opinion—in a certain sense the
very un-German opinion: "Whoever tries to get away from the
political befools himself!" So living and radical a spirit was of
course aware of the unity of the problem for humanity, of the
inseparability of mind and politics; he did not cling to the delu-
sion of the German citizen, that one may be a man of culture,
yet not of politics. [23]

Yet even in this mature essay, Mann equivocates. He hints
that Wagner's revolutionary bias was not really an intimate

[21] *Reflections,* p. 100.   [22] *Ibid.,* p. 92.   [23] "Wagner," FGW, p. 198.

trait of his character at all, that he was political only in a Pickwickian sense, revolutionary in the interest of his art, which was itself a revolt, and in the hope that the new order would favor his purely artistic rather than his political investments. As Ernest Newman says, Wagner "became a revolutionist—not for politics' sake, but for art's sake." [24] In the triumphant refrain from *Die Meistersinger*—"Though Holy Roman Empire sink to dust—There still survives our sacred German art" [25]—Mann finds the catch. The eternity of the German state is not mentioned; it is the survival of German art that matters. Mann's comment is:

It is precisely these lines . . . which attest the intellectuality of Wagner's nationalism and its remoteness from the political sphere; they betray a complete anarchistic indifference to the State so long as the spiritually German, the *Deutsche Kunst*, survives.[26]

Mann's discovery of anticipations of the National Socialist ideal in Wagner's writings, and even in his music, belongs to a later phase of his feelings toward the composer's political character.

The critical examination of his presuppositions, to which Mann forced himself in the *Reflections*, had an interesting effect on him. He realized that this "rearguard action in the grand style" [27] was fought for a lost cause, that the German bourgeois epoch was over and done with. Mann remarked later that a fitting motto for the *Reflections* would have been "No one remains precisely what he is when he knows himself." [28] In any event, Mann never returned to the extreme conservative position outlined in his War book.

A modification is already perceptible in *The Magic Moun-*

[24] *Wagner, as Man and Artist* (New York, 1934), p. 181.
[25] *Die Meistersinger von Nürnberg*, closing scene.
[26] "Wagner," FGW, p. 197.
[27] "Culture and Socialism," PM, p. 203.   [28] Sk, p. 48.

tain, which was published in 1924. Hans Castorp is a non-political man. His isolation from world events is physically and spiritually complete. His "hermetic" existence at Davos has sealed him in completely from the political winds of the Flatland. Hans confesses this on the occasion of his introduction to Naphta, who remarks that he thought he heard Hans and Joachim talking politics, as they were strolling along behind him. Says Hans in protest:

"Oh, no . . . How should we come to be doing that? For my cousin here, it would be unprofessional to discuss politics; and as for me, I would willingly forego the privilege. I don't know anything about it.—I haven't had a newspaper in my hand since I came." [29]

Herr Settembrini does not approve of this cavalier neglect of the newspapers. For he himself is a political man. His faith is pledged to the Holy Alliance of civic democracies. He is the ententophile *par excellence,* the articulate champion of the Enlightenment, the ambassador of Western Europe. One of his conversations with his pupil is very revealing. He is discussing with Hans the political character of Freemasonry, of which brotherhood he is a member, and he takes the occasion to slip in a jibe at the nonpolitical Germans:

"We admit that we are political, admit it openly, unreservedly. We care nothing for the odium that is bound up with the word in the eyes of certain fools—they are at home in your own country, Engineer, and almost nowhere else. The friend of humanity cannot recognize a distinction between what is political and what is not political. Everything is politics." [30]

Everything is politics? Hans Castorp cannot concur in that. He replies that he always thought there was as sharp a dis-

[29] MM, pp. 480-81.   [30] *Ibid.,* p. 649.

tinction between the political and the nonpolitical as there
was between the things that are Caesar's and the things that
are God's.[31] In Settembrini's rejoinder, we hear prophecy:

"*Caro amico!* There will be decisions to make, decisions of un-
speakable importance for the happiness and future of Europe; it
will fall to your country to decide, in her soul the decision will
be consummated. Placed as she is between East and West, she
will have to choose, she will have to decide finally and consciously between the two spheres." [32]

But Germany is the land of mediation, and the German
character, faced with alternatives, refuses to choose one to
the exclusion of the other. To the Italian's eloquent plea,
Hans Castorp is silent; there is a look of stubbornness in his
blue eyes. His Mediterranean friend notes this with chagrin,
and reproaches the young citizen of *das unliterarische Land*
in these words:

"You are silent. . . . You and your native land, you preserve a
silence which seems to cover a reservation—and which gives one
no hint of what goes on in your depths. You do not love the
Word, or you have it not, or you are chary with it to unfriendli-
ness. The articulate world does not know where it is with you.
My friend, that is perilous. Speech is civilization itself." [33]

The Magic Mountain is in many respects the creative
counterpart of the *Reflections*. It embodies the War book's
thesis that Germany is the land of the mean, the inarticulate,
nonpolitical country. The dreaming, music-loving Castorp is
the ambassador extraordinary of the Fatherland. The po-
litico-humanistic moralizing of Settembrini, the representative of Western democracy, is like one never-changing tune
played over and over again on a hand organ. (". . . a gal-
lant gentleman," says Pieperkorn of the Italian, "though

---

[31] *Ibid.*, p. 650 (compare this with *Ibid.*, p. 584).
[32] *Ibid.*, p. 652.   [33] *Ibid.*

obviously unable to change his clothing with any frequency.")[34] But "no one remains precisely what he is when
he knows himself"—and *The Magic Mountain*, brought to
completion six years after the close of the first World War,
does not hold statically to the conservative, rear-guard position of the *Reflections*. Although Hans Castorp refuses to go
over to the democratic humanistic stand of his tutor, the
Italian's influence on the young man is more than superficial.
During his life at Davos, Hans learns how to talk, to make
himself clear. After a year or so, he becomes very articulate,
persuasive even—to such an extent that he can talk rings
around Pieperkorn, and even hold his own with Settembrini
and Naphta. Thomas Mann suggests thereby that Germany
should learn her lesson, and no more stop her ears when
challenged by the literary West, but live up to her destiny,
which is not only to teach all, but to receive from all.

Certainly it is true that through his "hermetic" existence
at the sanatorium, Hans Castorp has developed from honorable mediocrity to a "deep young man";[35] his deck-chair has
given him more food for thought than all the years down on
the Flatland before.[36] But there filters through the pages of
his story the suspicion that his sealing-in has not been without
harmful effects. It is plain that Hans Castorp's isolation from
world affairs has carried with it no small danger. The anti-
Settembrinian neglect of the newspapers is condignly punished. The mine explodes beneath the magic mountain, and
the dazed inhabitants are knocked sprawling down to the
Flatland. Hans Castorp is as bewildered as any. We are left
in little doubt that Life would receive her "delicate child"
again "not by a cheap and easy slipping back to her arms,

[34] *Ibid.*, p. 758.
[35] *Ibid.*, p. 775. This is Clavdia's opinion of Hans expressed late in his
stay at the sanatorium.
[36] *Ibid.*, p. 477.

but sternly, solemnly, penitentially." [37] For Hans Castorp is one of the "German Seven-Sleepers." [38] He finds himself stumbling through a flaming battlefield in Flanders, without knowing why he is there. Tragic ignorance! *The Magic Mountain* was written in full consciousness that "the *Bürger* epoch" had ended, and in the growing, if not yet explicit, conviction that it was the nonpolitical character in the culture of Germany that brought her to her knees before the nations of Western democracy. There are overtones of warning to Germany in *The Magic Mountain*, warning that continued blindness to political exigencies may on some future day bring her to a fate quite as bad as the degradation of the World War.

The essay *Goethe and Tolstoy*, we have noted before, was one of several pieces of critical analysis thrown off during the composition of *The Magic Mountain*. Already in this study, we find more than one advance on the conservative position of the *Reflections*. For the essay contains a candid acknowledgement of the end of the bourgeois era; ". . . for all the world," says Mann, "there is at hand the ending of an epoch: the bourgeois, humanistic, liberal epoch." [39] With two results: first, the classic, Mediterranean, "Settembrinian" concept of civilization is doomed; it has outlived its usefulness, it is worn out. Secondly, Germany can no longer remain static in her culture of music and dreams. Her traditional heritage must be informed with a new leaven. That is— socialism. In striving to unite the best in her conservative, cultural inheritance with the forward moving spirit of the new order, Germany will only be fulfilling her traditional mission as world mediator. "We are a people of the middle," Mann declares in this essay of 1922, "a world bourgeoisie; there is a fittingness in our geographical position and in our

<hr>

[37] *Ibid.*, p. 894.   [38] *Ibid.*, p. 893.   [39] G-T, p. 132.

mores." [40] The people of the "world-middle" must live up to
their ordained function as "the race that moves between
extremes, easily, with a non-committal benevolence." [41]
Germany's destiny, so conceived, is ironic. Her post-war
salvation would lie in a union between Athens and Moscow
—"she will have found herself as soon as Karl Marx shall
have read Friederich Hölderlin." [42]

In the socialist movement of Germany in the twenties,
Mann perceived just the needed stimulation of the German
culture, one of whose hereditary weaknesses was her tendency to underestimate the importance of the social categories. Mann makes this point clear in an essay "Culture and
Socialism," typical of his political writings of the middle
twenties:

The actual inadequacy of traditional intellectualism in Germany,
its powerlessness to aid the mind turned futurewards—however
strong the bond which the latter feels with it—is due to the fact
that traditional intellectualism lacks the social, the socialistic
ingredient.[43]

To the German conservative, Mann goes on to say, his people represented a Folk rather than a Nation—and "Folk"
implies an individualistic antipolitical community concept
hostile to that of the social class.[44] Socialism, to the old-line
German, seemed to threaten the dissolution of the cultural,
antipolitical, community idea, the proud bulwark of German
burgherdom:

All German conservatism, all sincere belief that the traditional
German idea must be left untouched, must, in the political
sphere, repudiate the republican, the democratic form of government as foreign to land and folk, as false and intellectually
repugnant to the realistic sense.[45]

[40] *Ibid.*, p. 137.   [41] *Ibid.*   [42] *Ibid.*, p. 136.
[43] PM, p. 213.   [44] *Ibid.*, p. 210.   [45] *Ibid.*, p. 207.

Now it was Thomas Mann's opinion in the twenties that the time for that antipolitical dream was past, and that a synthesis between the two warring concepts must be effected to stabilize Germany, which was already showing symptoms of internal disruption. "What would be needed," says the *Kulturmensch* trying his political wings, "what would be typically German, would be an alliance, a compact between the conservative culture-idea and revolutionary social thought." [46] The logical conclusion of these pleas in the nineteen-twenties for synthesis between the "music" of the old pre-war nonpolitical culture and the intellectual democratic germ of the new socialism was Thomas Mann's open and outright espousal of the ill-fated cause of the German Social Democrats. In a speech in Berlin on October 17, 1930, he boldly took the stump for that party. "I state my conviction," he declared upon that occasion, "that the political place of the German citizen is today with the social-democratic party." [47] To this was appended a blistering denunciation of National Socialism.

As early as 1922, Thomas Mann had declared against fascism. This is interesting, for there later arose a widely held belief that he preserved complete silence, remaining "above the battle" until some time after the reins of government had been seized by the National Socialists in Germany. But it was the very first stirrings of the new movement that awakened in Mann immediate and instinctive antipathy. His first condemnation was in these words:

I do not propose to dwell upon German fascism, nor upon the circumstances, the quite comprehensible circumstances of its origin. It is enough to say that it is a racial religion, with antipathy not only for international Judaism, but also, quite expressly, for Christianity, as a humane influence; nor do its priests

[46] *Ibid.*, p. 214   [47] "An Appeal to Reason," *Criterion*, X (London), 411.

behave more friendly toward the humanism of our classical
literature. It is a pagan folk-religion, a Wotan cult: it is, to be
invidious—and I mean to be invidious—romantic barbarism.[48]

Mann was revolted by this bellicose nationalism, because he
saw in it reaction, and what was worse, reaction disguised as
revolution. There had been revolutionary elements in the
nineteenth century's stress upon subintellectual categories.
But in German fascism—for all its cult of myth and the
dynamic—Mann could perceive no revolution at all, but only
an attempt to force humanity backwards, a movement all
the more to be distrusted because of the blatant, artificial
complexion of youth it affected:

We have a right to feel impatience, and even aversion, when
hostility to life puts on the garb of youth and the future, and so
distinguished, begins to ply its dismal task . . . there is something new about this ambition of the old to clothe itself in the
garments of the young. For the old was wont to insist upon its
age and rail in no uncertain terms against the new. Today it puts
on the color of youth, and the doubtful light of a very early
dawn helps on the deception.[49]

Nor was Thomas Mann's early hostility to fascism confined
to the home variety. In the first stages of the world movement he saw nothing specifically German, but looked on it
as a world sickness, an international hysteria. In 1922, he
attacked the Mediterranean brand. "Italian fascism," Mann
warned, "is the precise pendant to Russian bolshevism; all
its archaistic gesturings and mummery cannot disguise its
essential hostility to the humane." [50] In 1929, Mann published *Mario and the Magician,* an allegory of Italian fascism.
On the surface, the story is but a simple account of an inci-
dent which occurred during a vacation the narrator spends
in Italy with his wife and children. The key to the allegory

48 G-T, p. 135.   49 "Freud's Position," PM, p. 213.   50 G-T, p. 135.

lies in these remarks of the teller of the tale, apropos a certain hostile arrogance which he senses in the usually gracious Italian atmosphere:

Phrases were dropped about the greatness and dignity of Italy, solemn phrases that spoilt the fun. We saw our two little ones retreat, puzzled and hurt, and were put to it to explain the situation. These people, we told them, were just passing through a certain stage, something rather like an illness, perhaps; not very pleasant, but probably unavoidable.[51]

One evening the narrator and his family attend a performance staged by an itinerant magician, Cipolla by name. The *prestidigatore* does marvels in bending the local yokelry to his hypnotic will. He himself is a hunchback, sickly and repulsive in appearance, and he has to keep up the fires of his semimystic power by continuous, though covert, sips of cognac. One after another of the stout lads of Torre del Venere, chosen at random from the audience, are rendered will-less by the demonic cripple. They are forced to perform stunts, most of them infantile and harmless, but brought about in such a way as to cause qualms of uneasiness in the more intelligent members of the audience. Cipolla passes all bounds when he deludes Mario, a young waiter, into believing that he, the deformed hypnotist, is his sweetheart, and the poor youth is forced to kiss the ugly mouth of his tormentor. But Cipolla's triumph is short-lived. When the spell is broken by the swish of the conjuror's whip, Mario instantly revenges his degradation. He snatches out a pistol and shoots the magician dead on the stage. It is unnecessary to interpret the parable at length. Cipolla, of course, is the symbol of the fascist leader, and the effect of his conjuror's power is the hypnotic domination of fascism over the masses. His death is an artistic wish fulfillment. Riddance, even if vio-

[51] *Mario and the Magician*, STD, p. 535.

lent, is riddance. "An end of horror," reflects the narrator, concluding his tale, "a fatal end. And yet a liberation—for I could not, and cannot but find it so." [52]

It was in 1930, we noted, that Thomas Mann openly attacked National Socialism in his political appeal at Berlin for the cause of the Social Democrats. He called German fascism "a wave of anomalous barbarism, of primitive popular vulgarity." [53] He refused to believe that his beloved Germany could be sucked in by this fanaticism, so foreign to her traditions. "Is there any deep substratum of the German soul," he asked, "where all that orgiastic denial of reason and human dignity is really at home?" [54] He saw in the growing power of the new movement another manifestation of the characteristic deficiency in sound governmental instinct, the same tendency toward isolation from politics which contributed to Germany's downfall in 1914-1918. Here are some of the words from Mann's Berlin polemic against the National Socialist Party:

It [the National Socialist Party] addresses the Germany of 1930 in a high-flown wishy-washy jargon full of mystical good feeling, with hyphenated prefixes like race- and folk- and fellowship- and lends to the movement a concomitant of fanatical cult-barbarism, more dangerous and estranging than the isolation and the political romanticism which led us into the war. [55]

This was pretty strong language. One can see why Mann did not trust himself to the kindly mercies of the victorious party. In 1933, he was lecturing in Switzerland when Hitler seized power. His children telephoned him that "the weather was unpleasant" at home. [56] Mann did not return to Germany, but took up residence in Switzerland. For some time

[52] *Ibid.*, p. 567.
[53] "An Appeal to Reason," *Criterion*, X (London), 401.
[54] *Ibid.*, p. 402.   [55] *Ibid.*, p. 401.
[56] See Klaus and Erica Mann, *Escape to Life* (New York, 1939), p. 87.

he preserved silence, withholding any further criticism of the new order in his homeland, although his fellow exiles urged him to denounce it before the world. In 1934, he visited the United States for the first time. In 1935, he crossed the ocean again, this time to receive an honorary degree from Harvard. He had nothing to say in public about Germany. In 1936, his German citizenship was taken from him with the result that his exile was no longer purely voluntary. His honorary doctorate from the University of Bonn was canceled, and this action brought forth the celebrated letter to the dean of that institution.[57] The year 1937 saw him assume editorial guidance of a Swiss magazine, printed in the German language, entitled *Mass und Wert* ("Standards and Values"). In the pages of this publication he began his long series of attacks upon fascism before a world public. The year 1938 brought him again to the United States, this time with the intention of taking up permanent residence in the country he regarded as the repository of all that was best in democracy.

It is clear that Thomas Mann's views on the relation of the artist to politics have passed through three stages. First, there is a period summed up in the *Reflections,* which sets forth the thesis that the artist, particularly the German artist, has no concern with the political sphere; since politics belongs to the realm of the moral and the critical, while the task of the artist is creative and thus unconcerned directly with this sphere. German culture, moreover, has been traditionally unpolitical, and the German artist reflects this character. Second, there is the stage of transition, beginning with the writing of *The Magic Mountain* and *Goethe and Tolstoy.* In this stage, the nonpolitical attitude of German men of culture is subjected to gradually rising suspicion, and Mann's

[57] Mann, *An Exchange of Letters* (New York, 1937).

slowly growing consciousness of the need of synthesis between art and the political is suddenly quickened by the manifest weakness of the Weimar republic and the ascendancy of National Socialism. Third, there is the period which follows the interval of silence Mann preserved immediately after his voluntary exile. This is marked by complete and final repudiation of the nonpolitical attitude, violent polemics against German fascism, and an enthusiastic defense of the principles of democracy. Let us touch briefly on some aspects of this third and final stage of Mann's political orientation.

Once, we recall, it was Mann's cherished belief that Germany was destined to play the part of mediator between Europe and Asia. Placed geographically between the rational literary West and the sensuous inarticulate East (represented by Russia), Germany, through her "musical" culture, world receiving and world teaching as it was, would one day effect a synthesis in which the two antithetic worlds would be united. When the Nazis seized power in Germany, Mann abandoned this hope as a lost dream. In 1937 he declared to an interviewer, "Today I should no longer insist on the idea of Germany as the land of the middle. The notion of the mean is one of those which satisfy for a while and then wear out." [58] But that Mann in his late maturity had not completely forgotten this concept of Germany is evident from the words of his Goethe in *The Beloved Returns*, which was completed after the beginning of the second war:

"So should the Germans be, I am their image and pattern. World-receiving, world-giving, hearts wide open to admire and be fructified. Great in understanding and in love, mediating spirits—

[58] Interview by Harry Slochower in *The New Masses* (April 27, 1937), p. 15.

for mediation is of the spirit too—so should the Germans be, and such their destiny." [59]

The responsibility for the "new" Germany, Mann declares, does not rest with Hitler; the blame for the victory of the Nazis in Germany cannot be put off on the shoulders of a single scapegoat. Mann brings home this responsibility to the representatives of German culture, himself included, who thought they could safely remain aloof from politics. He says in 1938:

I must regretfully own that in my younger years I shared that dangerous German habit of thought which regards life and intellect, art and politics as totally separate worlds. In those days we were all of us inclined to view political and social matters as non-essentials that might as well be entrusted to politicians. And we were foolish enough to rely upon the ability of these specialists to protect our highest interests. [60]

The severity of German political astigmatism is well demonstrated, thinks Mann, when one considers the character of the leader to whom Germany's destiny was handed over in 1933.

The haughty contempt which this race feels towards politics is most clearly revealed in the type of person to whom it entrusts the revelation and execution of this unnatural "Weltanschauung," in short the leadership of its political affairs, and upon whom devolves the decision in all questions of "nationalism" and "Machtpolitik" as to just what is German and what is not . . . his selection is proof of the boundless pessimism of the nation's attitude toward politics. [61]

The old Germany's indifference to politics has borne bitter fruit. "This political passivity and remoteness from democ-

---

[59] *The Beloved Returns*, p. 338.
[60] *The Coming Victory of Democracy*, trans. Agnes Meyer (New York, 1938), pp. 64-65.   [61] "Standards and Values."

racy," says Mann, "has frightfully avenged itself." [62] All her music, all her metaphysics could not save Germany when the test came. She yielded. Her once proud and jealously individualistic bourgeoisie had to pay homage to the goose-step and the *Horst Wessel Lied;* they had to accept the outrages against the Jews, the concentration camps, the legal assaults and murder perpetrated by "a pack which there is no fit language to describe." [63] And even in bowing to these degradations, the nonpolitical bourgeoisie permitted themselves to be duped into believing that all this was for the glory of Germany. Yet before all the world, the country of Bach and Lessing and Goethe, of Dürer and Beethoven and Heine, became known as the enemy of humankind:

Enemy of Humankind! To this has the German spirit come with its anti-democratic cultural pride. This awful name, a name accursed, has become its name. The intellectual German bour-geois could never have dreamed it, and thinks he is dreaming now that it has become the truth. But true it is. His refusal to realize that politics are part of the human problem has issued in political frightfulness, enslavement to power, the totalitarian state. The fruit of his aesthetic bourgeois culture is barbarism: a savagery of convictions, purposes and methods like to nothing in the world before. His elegant disdain of democratic revolution has made him the tool of another revolution: an anarchic one, running amok to threaten the foundations and props of all our Western morality and civilization; a world revolution to which no invasion of the Huns in olden times can even be compared.[64]

Once the Nazis were in the saddle, Mann insists, war was inevitable. War was implicit in the doctrine of National Socialism. War was simply the logical conclusion to the premises to which Germany committed herself in 1933. This

[62] "Culture and Politics," *Survey Graphic,* LXXV (Feb., 1939), p. 96.
[63] Mann, *This War,* trans. Eric Sutton (New York, 1940), p. 7.
[64] "Culture and Politics," p. 97.

the Western democracies could not see. They had prepared themselves for an era of peace. They were convinced that if they were nice to the Nazis, these worthies would behave like good fellows. They did not realize that the Munich agreement was futile, that appeasement was hopeless, since if the drive toward war were eliminated from the structure of National Socialism, the whole thing would fall to pieces. Three years before the war began, Thomas Mann made this point plain in his famous letter to the dean of Bonn University:

The meaning and purpose of the National Socialist State is this alone and can be only this: to shape the German people for the "coming war" by a process of merciless spiritual isolation and repression and by extirpating every stirring of opposition; to make of them an absolutely malleable instrument, impervious to any impulse of criticism and driven by a blind and fanatical ignorance. Such a system can have no other meaning and purpose, nor any other *excuse*. All the sacrifices of freedom, justice, human happiness, including all the abominations secretly and openly committed, the guilt of which has been so lightly undertaken, can only be justified by the idea of an absolute fitness for war. If the concept of war as an aim in itself disappeared, the whole system would be merely a crime against humanity—and, as such, utterly meaningless and superfluous.[65]

To these almost frantic denunciations of totalitarian Germany is coupled an impassioned plea for democracy. Thomas Mann admits that his allegiance to democracy is an acquired loyalty. Once, he had defined democracy as the political functioning of the intellect and had opposed it in the name of culture. But some time after the first World War, he confesses:

I came to see that there is no clear dividing line between the intellectual and the political; that the German bourgeoisie had

[65] Mann quotes this passage from his letter in *This War*, p. 24.

erred in thinking that a man of culture could remain unpolitical; that our culture itself stood in the greatest danger wherever and whenever it lacked interest and aptitude for the political. In short, an acknowledgement of democratic feeling rose to my lips.[66]

In 1938, Thomas Mann defines democracy once again as the political functioning of the intellect, but this time upholds and defends it in the name of culture and freedom. To Mann, democracy implies four principles which humanity cannot abandon if it hopes to save itself: truth, freedom, justice, and the dignity of man.[67] Mann goes so far indeed as to assert that when one denies the political, one denies necessary elements of Christianity and morality. The German bourgeois "did not know that democracy is nothing but the political stamp of occidental Christianity; that politics itself is nothing but intellectual morality, without which the spirit perishes." [68]

Has Thomas Mann a final and specific word concerning the artist and his relation to politics? "I do not hold," he said in his Berlin speech of 1930, "with that remorselessly social point of view which looks upon art—the beautiful and the useless—as a private pastime of the individual, which in times like these may almost be relegated to the category of the criminal." [69] On the other hand, he declared later, the man of art who "shrinks the human problem when presented politically" has lost his soul.[70] If it would preserve its freedom and dignity, humanity cannot remain indifferent to the social and the political. And the artist is the most human of men. It is his duty to speak out as the representative of humanity, to denounce, to fight with every weapon at his

[66] "Culture and Politics," p. 95.
[67] *The Coming Victory of Democracy*, pp. 16-17.   [68] *Ibid.*, p. 97.
[69] "An Appeal to Reason," *Criterion*, X (London), 394.
[70] "Epilogue to 'Spain,'" *Life and Letters of Today*, XVI (London, Summer, 1937), No. 8, p. 16.

command, when anticultural, antihumane forces threaten to prevail:

Whose affair is it, if not the creative artist's—the man whose emotions are free—to assert the human conscience against the bareness of interest, at once so presumptuous and so petty; to protest against the stultifying, all-embracing confusion made in our time between politics and villainy? [71]

The confidence a man earns as an artist, Mann claims, is not merely aesthetic. It is a human confidence, and he should use it for the good in life as well as for the good in art. For the artist to say "I take no interest in politics" is an egoistic piece of self-deception. For

the politico-social field is an undeniable and inalienable part of the all-embracing human; it is one section of the human problem, the human task, which the non-political man thinks to set off, as the decisive and the actual, against the political sphere. The decisive and the actual: it is indeed that; for in the guise of the political, the problem of the human being, man himself, is put to us with a final life-and-death seriousness unknown before. Then shall the artist—he who, by nature and destiny, ever occupies humanity's furthest outposts—shall he alone be allowed to shirk a decision? [72]

One can discern in Thomas Mann's early aloofness from politics the natural concomitant of his youthful Byronic isolation from the human world, an isolation which he regarded as the inevitable penalty of the artist's vocation. We saw in an earlier chapter that Mann regarded this consciousness of isolation as inseparable from his inherited bourgeois character. And we remember that in the *Reflections* he defended the nonpolitical position as a legitimate and necessary aspect of the German bourgeois tradition. He insisted that he was nonpolitical because he was a bourgeois. At the same time, in this very bourgeois element in Mann's

[71] *Ibid.*, p. 15.   [72] *Ibid.*

personality one also finds the seeds of his later political consciousness. The early polarity between the artistic and the bourgeois in Mann must be considered against the background of a personal development. We observed that even in his nonpolitical days, Mann had a strong, if suspicious, interest in the political sphere, and that, after the *Reflections,* he began to acquire a gradual recognition of that sphere's importance. The crisis in Germany, which put the challenge of governmental leadership squarely up to the bourgeoisie, brought him to the Social Democratic party. His conservative roots, his bourgeois love of order and uprightness compelled him to open political allegiance. That bourgeois factor, to which he once attributed his nonpolitical character, turned out to be the very thing which made him acknowledge the political realm, and accept political responsibility. The appearance of National Socialism in Germany dissipated a nonpolitical residue the years may have left. Thus Mann's transition from nonpolitical to political man should be viewed as not so much a *volte-face* as a personal integration. The political task was not just a burden thrust upon him, it was a task for which he was inwardly prepared by long reflection and self-criticism.

Art cannot be cut off from human responsibility, of which the political trust is today so large a part. For, says Mann, "art is intensely human, intensely humane, since it is the mediator between spirit and life, and nothing would be more erroneous than to regard its irony—the irony of all mediation—as a nihilistic escape from struggle and from human obligation." [73] Before concluding our study, we must try to sketch Mann's conception of the relation between those two realms of which art is the mediator and from which humanity draws its being.

[73] "Standards and Values."

6

ART AS MEDIATOR BETWEEN
NATURE AND SPIRIT

THAT MAN IS a member of two worlds, one of spirit, the other of nature, that art has a cosmic role to play, that the artist has a hermetic task of mediation between the two spheres—these are themes that concern our final reflections and recapitulation. To clarify Thomas Mann's doctrine of nature and spirit, we must fix our attention upon some metaphysical implications in his work. There is a danger here; for it is a common practice among critics to furnish an eminent artist with a complete and highly abstract *Weltanschauung* which has every virtue except that the artist in question is totally innocent of it. To read into Mann's work a systematic metaphysics which is not there at all is quite possible. On the other hand, it is difficult to overlook tendencies in Mann which reach out toward the metaphysical realm. Even a first reading of Mann's books reveals a philosophical bent. Although he has written no single essay which explicitly outlines his world view, it is impossible to read even his novels without being struck by his habit—exasperating to some—of stopping periodically to indulge in speculative discourse on art, time, nature, man, morality, life, and a host of other classical topics of philosophy. In the maturity brought him by sixty years, Mann openly declared his faith in metaphysics. We remember that declaration: "I believe that in actual fact philosophy ranks before and above the natural sciences, and that all method and exactness serve its intuitions and its intellectual and historical will." [1]

When one is concerned with an artist's philosophical tendencies, there are two possible approaches to the problem. One may regard his metaphysical concepts as pointing to an inclusive system which provides the basis of interpretation of any specific element in his work. Or, one may view them as further extensions of ideas, as developments which carry over into an abstract plane themes which had first been set in particular contexts. In Thomas Mann's case, the second is the more appropriate interpretation. Mann does not place a metaphysical staging around his creative products, nor should his critics claim that this story or that novel cannot be "understood" without applying as a key some philosophic concept or other in order to make the meaning clear. Mann does extend feelings and insights, which we find in his creative work in specific contexts; he makes these feelings and insights point to certain broader categories, certain wider relations that go far beyond the concrete situation yet do not constitute a formal summary of all his themes, through which alone they can be comprehended. Mann himself puts it this way: "I should say that a work of literature may and often does contain a metaphysical idea; yet it is not necessary that the reader, nor even the artist at the moment of creation, be aware of this." [2]

Thomas Mann's antithesis of nature and spirit represents an extension into the metaphysical sphere of certain elements present in his art in concrete form, and at the same time constitutes a vision of the place of art in the hierarchy of reality. Art, to Mann, has a cosmic significance, for it mediates between nature and spirit. So too the artist plays

[1] "Freud," FGW, p. 22.
[2] Author's interview with Thomas Mann, Princeton, Jan. 27, 1941.

a role not only of aesthetic but of metaphysical importance, bridging as he does the gap between the two worlds, the natural and the spiritual.

Some interesting cosmological reflections can be found in *The Magic Mountain*. We recall that during his biological studies Hans Castorp reflected long upon the nature of life and the contrasting character of matter. Which is prior in the order of being, he wondered, the organic or the inorganic, matter or spirit? These speculations imply his answer:

Was that which one might call the original procreation of matter only a disease, a growth produced by morbid stimulation of the immaterial? The first step toward evil, toward desire and death, was taken precisely then, when there took place that first increase in the density of the spiritual, that pathologically luxuriant morbid growth, produced by the irritant of some unknown infiltration: this, in part pleasurable, in part a motion of self-defense, was the primeval stage of matter, the transition from the insubstantial to the substance. This was the Fall. The second creation, the birth of the organic out of the inorganic, was only another fatal stage in the progress of the corporeal toward consciousness.[3]

In other words, there are three cosmic epochs. The first, when spirit is alone and supreme; the second, when spirit breaks down into physical nature; the third, when spirit is born anew from nature. This reminds us of Goethe's description of the hermetic cosmology which his readings of the old alchemists helped to inspire in him; how the primal spirit Elohim ruled at first unrivaled in the heavens, how Lucifer revolted and was deposed, becoming by this Fall the prince of matter, and how the gulf between the lord of spirit and the demon of nature was finally bridged by man,

[3] MM, p. 362.

through whom the original connection with the Godhead was restored to nature.[4]

Thus we are brought to the world of myth. In the prelude to the first volume of the *Joseph* series, Thomas Mann reflects on the primordial antithesis of spirit and nature. This extraordinary overture is a sounding of the Well of Time. It is a recapitulation, a casting up of certain sacred old stories of primeval events, which Joseph knew by heart—the tradition of the Flood, of Abraham, of the Tower of Babel, of the Lost Continent, and others of these "Time-coulisses," these focal points of consciousness wherein is caught up some measure of things holy and inscrutable. These ancient legends are myths, that is, distillations, compressions into story form of certain primal happenings, whose source and beginnings are lost in the darkness of the prehistoric and buried deep down in the womb of the unconscious. The prehistoric and the unconscious both, we say, because the myth has two faces, it tells a double story. It weaves parallels between the outer world and the inner man, between past-veiled happenings of prehistory, and the source experiences of the preconscious.

The oldest story of all, the last time-coulisse to which Thomas Mann comes in his searching of the Well of Time, is the sacred tradition of the Fall, the descent of the soul from heaven to earth, the account of God's love for the soul and His sending of an emissary to restore it to its former high station.[5] Here is the cosmogony which Mann finds symbolized by this holy tradition. In the beginning, there were three primal entities—God, soul, and matter. Moved by an inner yearning that could not be gainsaid, the soul—that is to say, the primeval human—went adventuring; it plunged

[4] *The Autobiography of Goethe* (London, 1874), VIII, 300-302 ("Poetry and Truth").   [5] *Joseph and His Brothers*, p. 38.

into matter, activated by a sensuous almost sinful desire to mingle itself with the formless and to bring forth forms.[6] But matter, in its sluggishness and inertia, resisted the passionate activity of the soul, and would have defeated it had not God lent His aid to the soul in its struggles, and helped it to bring forth form from matter. Thus was the world created, nature came into being, the consequence of the mingling of soul and matter. But then God sent forth spirit, out of the substance of His very Being, to dissolve this sinful union, to call the soul back to her high place, to bring about the end of the world—for once soul should withdraw from matter, nature would disappear, and matter would return to its original formless state.[7] But the soul would not be won away, and to this day there exists that primal tension between nature (that is, soul-informed matter) and spirit. The soul resists spirit, yet soul and spirit are one, or rather will be one when that final interpenetration of spirit and nature has been reached, which will "bring about a present humanity with blessing from heaven above and from the depths beneath." [8]

Thomas Mann's preoccupation with the nature-spirit antithesis suggests an interesting parallel with the efforts of the post-Kantian philosophers, and indeed this is not the only side of Mann which is kin to the spirit of German Idealism. We remember those philosophers who strove, amid the manifold metaphysical tasks they set themselves, to close the gap which Kant had left between the moral law within and the starry heavens above, between the "I" and the "not-I," between spirit and nature. "The transition from the insubstantial to the substance—" Thomas Mann declares, "this was the Fall." Fichte commenced the exposition of his system by asserting that the first principle of reality was the

[6] *Ibid.*, p. 40.   [7] *Ibid.*, p. 41.   [8] *Ibid.*, p. 481.

"I" or spirit, and then posited, as a lever which would start off the necessary deductive movement, the "not-I" or nature. Was not this second metaphysical principle of Fichte, this process from the absolute to the relative, the fall of the angels from heaven? It was Fichte who said that man is a member of two orders, the one purely spiritual, the other sensuous.[9] Indeed it may be suggested that the whole gigantic task of post-Kantian philosophy was the systematic attempt to close this breach between nature and spirit, with Fichte attacking from one side in his deduction of a metaphysic of spirit, Schelling from the opposite flank with his philosophy of nature, and Hegel, striving to succeed where they fell short, with his essay at final synthesis of spirit and nature in the self-conscious Absolute.

Even more distinctly within the tradition of German idealism is Thomas Mann's interest in the theory of knowledge. In one of his disputes with Settembrini, Naphta insists that the idea of a material world existing by and for itself is as much a laughable contradiction as is the dogma of science that time, space, and causality are actual conditions existing independently of the mind.[10] One must remember that Hans Castorp admits that Naphta, disagreeable as he is, "is nearly always right." [11] That this declaration of allegiance to Kantian criticism in *The Magic Mountain* is no mere whimsy of its author is proved by Mann's reiteration of his Idealist epistemology in his Schopenhauer essay written fifteen years after the publication of the Davos novel. Mann reflects in this piece that:

Our conceptions, created out of the phenomenal world, out of a highly conditioned point of view, are, as a critical and discriminating philosophy admits, applicable in an immanent not in a

---

[9] *The Vocation of Man* in "Modern Classical Philosophers," ed. Rand (Boston, 1936), p. 516.   [10] MM, p. 869.   [11] *Ibid.*, p. 603.

transcendent sense—that is, they deal with knowledge vouchsafed to us in time, space and causality, and are conditioned by these, instead of being obtained by applying reason upon itself. The subject-matter of our thinking, and indeed the judgements we build up upon it, are inadequate as a means of grasping the essence of things in themselves, the true essence of the world and of life. Even the most convinced and convincing, the most deeply experienced definition of that which underlies the manifestation, does not avail to get at the root of things and draw it to the light.[12]

Mann, like Hegel, views reality as antithetic, as a cosmic play of opposites. But to the novelist, the antitheses must not be argued into the status of secondary levels of being in favor of an all-embracing oneness. To Mann, monism of any sort is suspect. When Settembrini insists that nature herself is spirit, Naphta queries "Doesn't your monism rather bore you?"[13] To the unorthodox Jesuit, the attempt to reduce irreconcilable differences to one comfortable principle is just another mark of flabby bourgeois insufficiency. To him, any "monistic position was an insult to the spirit."[14] That Naphta's opinion on this point is Mann's own is clear from the author's indictment of the nineteenth century in his Wagner essay: "Its monistic solution of the riddle of the universe" was "full of shallow complacency."[15] Thomas Mann views reality as dualistic and antithetic; there is a conflict of opposites in everything, every phenomenon has two facets. Disease, looked at in one way, is degrading and renders the sufferer doubly physical; in another aspect, it is ennobling, and heightens man's humanity. The finished product of art may be chaste and beautiful; yet how often does it have its origin in darkness and the forbidden. Morality, regarded in one light, is asceticism and self-control; in

---

[12] *Schopenhauer Presented by Thomas Mann*, pp. 1-2.
[13] MM, p. 474.　　[14] *Ibid.*, p. 869.　　[15] "Wagner," FGW, p. 102.

another, it is yielding to adventure and the harmful. Time, in its external character, is rigid, regular, and absolute; but internally, it is relative—fluid and compressible. Hegel would have delighted in Pieperkorn's talk on toxicology:

> . . . the truth was, in the world of matter, that all substances were the vehicle of both life and death, all of them were medicinal and all poisonous, in fact therapeutics and toxicology were one and the same, man could be cured by poison, and substances known to be the bearers of life could kill at a thrust in a single second of time.[16]

Perhaps a source of Thomas Mann's intuition as to the nature of reality can be found in, Goethe's metaphysical speculations. In the poet's world view, one of the primal archetypes (*Urphenomena*) was the principle of polarity (*Polarität*). Goethe conceived of a dynamic world process, bound and governed by a series of equal and opposing forces—something like the equilibrium brought about by the Heraclitean strife of Opposites. To Goethe, the paired opposites in the phenomenal world—attraction-repulsion, pleasure-pain, heat-cold, systole-diastole—were proofs of the existence of this basic law of polarity. His perception of this law followed upon his readings in Kant's natural philosophy, and in his own words: "From this I perceived the primal polarity of all things, which permeates and animates the infinite variety of phenomena." [17] Another of Goethe's primary archetypes was the principle of ascent (*Steigerung*). By this he meant a tendency in everything to rise from lower to higher levels, an upward striving, a "stepping-up" universally present in nature. This law of ascent was responsible

---

[16] MM, p. 729.

[17] *Campaign in France* in "The Miscellaneous Travels of Goethe," ed. Schmitz (London, 1882). The translation used above is that of Calvin Thomas who discusses Goethe's principles of Ascent and Polarity in his *Goethe* (New York, 1929), pp. 183-88.

for a variety of phenomena, from the refinement of plant juices to the spiritual instincts in man.[18]

It is not too wide of the mark to discern the expansion of the Goethean principles of polarity and ascent in Thomas Mann's suggestion that the growth of the human spirit is conditioned from without by the effect of antithetic "pedagogic" forces, and from within by a certain upward nisus. The Davos novel's allegory of the development of the *homo humanus* is, of course, the story of Hans Castorp's transformation from a "mediocre" youth to a "deep young man."[19] During his stay at the sanatorium, Hans runs a gauntlet of opposing forces. To say that Joachim and Clavdia are poles apart is to be right in two senses. The tenderly drawn character of Ziemssen stands for honor, loyalty, and uprightness, while Madame Chauchat represents the sweet, perilous forbidden. Castorp has ties to both. He is also pulled between the influence of the bumbling Behrens, who in his blunt physical approach to his cases symbolizes the view of disease as organic, and of the dubious Krokowski, who by his role of psychoanalyst of the establishment stands for the concept of illness as nonorganic, with its roots in the psyche. The polar pedagogic forces of Settembrini and Naphta are almost too obvious to mention. The Italian would convert the plastic youth to the enlightened philosophy of Western humanism, and the Jesuit scholastic would win him over to his strange faith, a *guzzabuglio* in which antibourgeois proletarianism is mingled with spiritual terrorism. "You and he," Hans mentally addresses the bellicose pair, "come to grips over my paltry soul like God and the Devil in the medieval legends."[20] But when Pieperkorn appears on the scene, the two masters of dialectic swing away from him together to form the pole of intellect ("cerebrum, cerebral,

[18] Eck, p. 545.   [19] MM, pp. 41, 775.   [20] *Ibid.*, p. 603.

you understand!"),[21] while in the person of the Dutch East Indian Dionysus we perceive the pole of feeling. Hans Castorp loses Joachim and Pieperkorn in death, Clavdia in renunciation; he refuses final assent to the tenets of either Settembrini or Naphta. But in his "egoistic craving for experience"[22] he learns much from each, takes from each warring force its measure of stimulus to the never quite achieved goal of his spiritual Odyssey.

Taking the concept of polarity from Mann's situations by abstraction, one finds that he uses the term "ascent" (*Steigerung*) explicitly. The reader of *The Magic Mountain* is left in no doubt that despite the necessity of yielding himself to the enriching irradiation of antithetic forces playing in upon the soul, man must also have something of himself which is capable of rising under the influences of these forces. Naphta talks of this *Steigerung* when, in a discussion of medieval Freemasonry, he tells his young auditor of the old masters' concept of the sacred purpose of alchemy:

. . . it was purification, refinement, metamorphosis, transubstantiation, into a higher state, of course; the *lapis philosophorum*, the male-female product of sulphur and mercury, the *res bina*, the double-sexed *prima materia* was no more, and no less, than the principle of levitation, of the upward impulse due to the working of influences from without.[23]

That Naphta's discourse on the hermetics of olden times has been thoroughly assimilated by Castorp is clearly evident by the youth's subsequent confession to Clavdia that he knows he has this upward impulse within him; that in his case it is nothing other than his inborn love of death, not, of course,

---

[21] *Ibid.*, p. 734. Pieperkorn's words.
[22] *Ibid.*, p. 754. Clavdia's words.
[23] *Ibid.*, p. 644. Compare Naphta's discussion of the mystical alchemy of Freemasonry with Pierre's reflections on the same subject in Tolstoy's *War and Peace* (pp. 407 and 410 of the "Modern Library" edition).

as negation and annihilation, but as the dangerous path to life and love of life:

". . . you, of course, do not know that there is such a thing as alchemistic-pedagogy, transubstantiation, from lower to higher, ascending degrees [*Steigerung*], if you know what I mean. But matter that is capable of taking those ascending stages by dint of outward pressure must have a little something in itself to start with. And what I had in me, as I quite clearly know, was that from long ago, even as a lad, I was familiar with illness and death." [24]

The dual principle of ascent and polarity—the latter itself essentially antithetic—guides that dialectical process which is human development. Yet we must note one more use of antithesis in *The Magic Mountain*, this time not in content but in form, not in the subject matter but in the craftsmanship itself. This, of course, is irony, a literary method with an honorable background in the German romantic tradition.[25] Like so many other concepts which absorb Thomas Mann, irony to him has two aspects. It is at once literary and metaphysical. As a literary device, irony is the principle of objectivity. It is that delicate self-scepticism by which a literary creator prevents himself from taking his own convictions overseriously, thereby alienating the reader by too passionate a subjectivism. It is that which enables a writer to smile down on his own masterpiece, and even to poke kindly fun at his own characters. *The Magic Mountain* is a playground for this stylistic aspect of irony; all the talk, for instance, of Hans Castorp being a "simple-minded though pleasing young man," [26] is illustrative of it.

[24] MM, p. 752.
[25] For more detailed discussion of Mann's use of irony, as well as its relation to the German romantic tradition, see Weigand's *Thomas Mann's Novel 'Der Zauberberg,'* Chapter V. See also Käte Hamburger's *Thomas Mann und die Romantik*, I, 3.   [26] MM, p. 1.

But the Davos novel is also the locus of another kind of irony. The ironic has a significance over and above that of purely literary contrivance; it has the function of exposing the two sides of every fundamental question, and thus it mirrors the antithetical character of reality. The handling of personages like Settembrini and Naphta is replete with irony of this sort. During their prodigious speeches, the reader feels that Hans Castorp (and his creator) are thinking "Yes, yes—true enough, but there's a lot to be said for the other side." In Mann's view, irony must be more than the Settembrinian "direct and classic device of oratory," to fulfill its cosmic function; it must be two-sided, equivocal. "Irony that is 'not for a moment equivocal,'" Hans muses on Settembrini's strictures, "what kind of irony would that be? . . . It would be a piece of dried up pedantry." [27] In an essay written during the composition of *The Magic Mountain*, Mann speaks of

irony which glances at both sides, which plays slyly and irresponsibly—yet not without benevolence—among opposites, and is in no great haste to take sides and come to decisions; guided as it is by the surmise that in great matters, in matters of humanity, every decision may prove premature; that the real goal to reach is not decision, but harmony, accord.[28]

Thus when Hans is badgered by Settembrini, who wishes him to make up his mind on a fundamental question, the youth is silent and a stubborn look comes into his blue eyes.[29] He is a German, a man of that country whose very geographical position is "ironic"—between the East and the West—whose cultural character opposes sharp-cut decisions.

The full resources of Thomas Mann's irony are turned on Hans Castorp's illness. Since it may be approached either

[27] For Settembrini's remarks on irony, see MM, pp. 281-82.
[28] G-T, pp. 136-37.   [29] MM, p. 652.

as a purely physical aberration or as a psychic phenomenon, disease itself is a highly equivocal affair, and is consequently well suited to ironic treatment. That Hans Castorp plans a three weeks' vacation at Davos under the impression that he is the victim of a slight and purely physical *malaise,* and then comes gradually to realize that his illness is psychic in origin and character, that it is, in fact, the organic manifestation of his unconscious will to escape from the purposeless bourgeois mold down on the Flatland and the physical counterpart of his love for Clavdia—that situation, it goes without saying, is in the highest degree ironic.

"Irony is the pathos of the middle," declares Thomas Mann.[30] Man's position in the universe is thereby ironic in the metaphysical sense of the term. For man, the delicate child of life, is caught between two realms by his double bond to spirit and sense. "Thus one might call man the romantic being," Mann observes, "in that he, a spiritual entity stands outside of and beyond nature and . . . in this double essence of nature and spirit finds both his own importance and his own misery." [31] Nature and spirit—here is the fundamental antithesis, the irreducible dualism of the cosmos. Spirit stands over and apart from nature, in opposition to her, even hostile to her. "Nature is not spirit," Mann asserts, "in fact, this antithesis is, I should say, the greatest of all antitheses." [32] Spirit is the cause of this primary antithesis, for spirit is in essence dualistic. It is spirit which sets itself off from nature, rather than nature from spirit; it is spirit which is responsible for the manifold of less universal polarities which shade on down through the world. "Dualism, antithesis," says Naphta, "is the moving, the passionate, the dialectical principle of all spirit." [33]

[30] G-T, p. 137.   [31] *Ibid.,* p. 31.
[32] *Ibid.,* p. 25.   [33] MM, p. 474.

Spirit, Mann affirms, distinguishes man from all other forms of organic life. Man's peculiar predicament, at once tragic and heroic, lies in that he is at once part of nature, and yet distinct from her. Dr. Riemer of *The Beloved Returns* asserts:

"Man belongs fundamentally, with a large part of his being, to the world of nature; but with the other, one might say decisive part, to the world of spirit. We may say, employing a rather comic metaphor, which yet brings out quite well the apprehension I mean, that we stand with one leg in one world and the other in the other." [34]

Hans Castorp, of *The Magic Mountain,* finds himself between the polar forces of *Leben* (Clavdia, Pieperkorn) and *Geist* (Settembrini, Naphta) and thus he is a symbol of man, whose unique cosmic importance lies in his stand between nature and spirit. The question of choice between the two poles is the "aristocratic problem" and Castorp's attitude toward it is ironic; he is convinced that the problem cannot be solved by choice, for the choosing, since it must fix on one aspect of reality to the exclusion of the other, would be self-stultifying. Antithesis is of value only if through it synthesis may be achieved. The universe is the scene of the mighty antithetic play of nature and spirit; yet *The Magic Mountain* hints that they approach synthesis in man. The insight vouchsafed to Hans Castorp during the mountain snowstorm emboldens him to cry:

"Their aristocratic questions! Disease, health! Spirit, nature! Are those contradictions? I ask, are they problems? No, they are no problems, neither is the problem of their aristocracy. The recklessness of death is in life, it would not be life without it—and in the centre is the position of the *Homo Dei*, between recklessness and reason, as his state is between mystic community and

[34] *The Beloved Returns,* pp. 83-84.

windy individualism. . . . Man is the lord of the counter-positions, they can be only through him, and thus he is more aristocratic than they." [35]

As for art: all artists, says Mann in his *Goethe and Tolstoy,* stand under one or other of two banners—that of nature, or that of spirit. Although they cannot belong completely to either realm, since they are human and therefore inescapably compounded of the two principles, the scale never balances; it is always weighted in one direction or the other, either toward nature or toward spirit, by each man's personality and his art—which of course are indistinguishable, since an artist *is* what he *does.*[36]

According to Mann, two kinds of nobility, natural and spiritual, are found in the world of art. The artist allied to nature is, when the highest of his type, "godlike." The artist whose allegiance is to spirit is "saintly." [37] Goethe and Tolstoy are examples of the one, Schiller and Dostoyevsky of the other. To the sons of nature, in virtue of their bond to her, are accorded health and long life. To the sons of spirit, since they are cut off from nature, disease and early death are meted out. Goethe and Tolstoy lived to a venerable age, while the lives of Schiller and Dostoyevsky—one ridden by consumption, the other by epilepsy—were brought to a sudden and early close. In the contrasting character of the work of these men may be found clear evidence as to whether they turned toward or away from nature. The "mighty sense-appeal of Tolstoy's art," says Mann, stands over against "Dostoyevsky's sickly, distorted dream-and-soul world." [38] Goethe's art is rooted in sense, marked by tranquillity and repose, while Schiller's vision is all fever and intensity. "And to all eternity," Mann is confident, "the truth, power, calm,

[35] MM, p. 625.   [36] "Wagner," FGW, p. 191.
[37] G-T, p. 28.   [38] *Ibid.,* p. 45.

and humility of nature will be in conflict with the dispro-
portionate, fevered, and dogmatic presumption of spirit." [39]

Thomas Mann writes in a brief essay on Tolstoy that "the
world of the soul is the world of disease, but the world of
health is the world of the body." [40] In other words, to the
kingdom of spirit pertains disease, to that of nature, health.
Goethe's way of saying the same thing was to insist that
classic art was "healthy" and romantic art "diseased." To
Thomas Mann disease has an importance which is metaphysical, as well as artistic. For disease is one facet of spirit.
Spirit is that aspect of reality which is separate from and
opposed to nature. Illness too is separation from nature, and
man is human in that he stands apart from nature. Thus in a
sense disease may be more human than health. In the
phenomenon of illness, Mann thinks we can perceive a manifestation of spirit. "It may be going too far to say that disease
is spirit," we recall Mann saying, "still the two conceptions
do have very much in common." [41]

Further, the children of spirit are marked by moral sense,
by Christianity, even saintliness; while moral issues are not
at home in the realm of nature—her favored sons being less
Christian saints than pagan gods. "Spirit is good," Mann has
it, "nature is by no means good. One might say she is evil, if
moral categories were admissible with reference to her." [42]
We recall that Settembrini of *The Magic Mountain* did think
that moral categories were admissible of nature; he pronounced nature to be both evil and stupid,[43] and praised
Voltaire because he had protested against the Lisbon earthquake in the name of reason.[44] At any rate, in Mann's view,

[39] *Ibid.*   [40] "Tolstoy," PM, p. 160.
[41] G-T, p. 29.   [42] *Ibid.*, p. 69.   [43] MM, p. 129.
[44] See *The Magic Mountain*, p. 318. Settembrini's attitude (and Voltaire's) may be compared with the feeling of Goethe's friend Tischbein,
who also resented nature as anti-human. In his *Letters from Italy* (ed.

nature is the principle of innocence and health, spirit that
of morality and disease.

Creation, love of form—this is the prerogative of nature
artists, while men of spirit tend toward criticism and analysis. "Critique is spirit," says Thomas Mann, "whereas creation is the preoccupation of the children of God and nature." [45] Pantheistic necessity rules in the sphere of nature,
final causes do not trouble her; while freedom and purpose
are vital to spirit.[46] Not without significance was Goethe's
admiration of Spinoza's nonteleological universe in which
attributes and modes necessarily proceed from the divine
Substance, just as the conclusion of a syllogism is determined
by its premises. No accident was Schiller's bias for Kantian
philosophy in which the phenomenal world ruled by necessary laws is transcended by moral man. And speaking of
Schiller, Mann would say his concept of the "naïve" or
"simple" falls under the heading of nature, while his "sentimental" is nothing other than the category of spirit. Further: the art of nature is instinctive, rooted deep in the earth,
in the senses, in *eros;* while the art of spirit is conscious, and
strains upward toward mind and thought. Men of nature are,
more often than not, aristocrats with little interest in the
masses, but men of spirit are of democratic character and
socially conscious.[47] In addition, "all national character belongs to the natural sphere and all tendency toward the
cosmopolitan to the spiritual." [48] Finally, to the kingdom of

Bell, p. 240), Goethe says, "Most reluctantly, yet for the sake of good
fellowship, Tischbein accompanied me to Vesuvius. To him—the artist of
form, who concerns himself with none but the most beautiful of human
and animal shapes, and one also whose taste and judgment lead to human-
ize even the formless rock and landscape—such a frightful and shapeless
conglomeration of matter, which, moreover, is continually preying on itself,
and proclaiming war against every idea of the beautiful, must have appeared abominable."

[45] G-T, p. 37.   [46] *Ibid.*, pp. 37-38.
[47] Ibid., pp. 58-59.   [48] *Ibid.*, p. 76.

spirit belongs time, and hence interest in progress and the political, while the laws of the kingdom of nature are timeless and eternal. "The antithesis between life and religion," Hans Castorp was moved to say, "went back to that between time and eternity. Only in time was there progress; in eternity there was none, nor any politics either." [49]

In art, which is more valuable, which ranks higher—natural or spiritual nobility? Is Tolstoy greater than Dostoyevsky? Is Goethe greater than Schiller? Is feverish intensity better than measure and repose? Is saintly nobility higher than the godlike? This again is the "aristocratic problem." And the question it poses, Mann assures us, cannot be answered with finality. Faced with a choice between the art of nature and the art of spirit, we must act on Plato's suggestion, and reply as children do, "Give us both!" In Mann's own words:

Which is greater? Which is more aristocratic? I shall not answer either of these. I will let the reader come to his individual conclusion in this matter of value, according to his own taste. Or, less glibly put, according to the conception he has of humanity, which—I must add *sotto voce*—will have to be one-sided and incomplete to admit of his coming to any conclusion at all.[50]

Here is a schema by which we may attempt a summing-up of Thomas Mann's all-inclusive antithesis of nature and spirit. Under these headings, we may subsume various concepts which stand as predicates of species of the two genera.[51]

---

[49] MM, p. 584.   [50] G-T, p. 11.
[51] Compare Goethe's schema in his essay "Shakespeare ad Infinitum," *Goethe's Literary Essays*, ed. Spingarn, p. 179.

Ancient	Modern	Idealistic	Realistic
Natural	Sentimental	Freedom	Necessity
Pagan	Christian	Will (*wollen*)	Duty (*sollen*)
Classic	Romantic		

Nature	*Spirit*
Health	Disease
Body	Soul
Classic	Romantic
Objective	Subjective
Simple	Sentimental
Nonmoral	Moral
Pagan	Christian
Form	Analysis
Creation	Critique
Sense	Mind
Eros	*Logos*
Necessity	Freedom
Instinct	Consciousness
Eternity	Time
Aristocratic	Democratic
Nonpolitical	Political

If we wish to consider the opposition metaphysically, we may place "man" between the two spheres, for both meet in him, he is "the lord of the counter-positions." If we wish to look at the antithesis from the viewpoint of aesthetics, we can insert "art" or "artist"—for art, as we shall see, has a mediating function between nature and spirit. Should there be any question as to why "man" and "artist" are interchangeable, we must remember that to Mann art is the finest expression of all that is human, and the artist is the human being *par excellence*. Schopenhauer and Thomas Mann agree about the artist; to one, he is the universal man, to the other the apogee of humanity.

It must be emphasized that no artist has all the characteristics of nature and none of spirit, nor has any artist all the characteristics of spirit and none of nature. Thomas Mann does not think for one moment that there is any man, any artist who belongs wholly to one sphere. Man is neither completely of nature or spirit, but he is placed between them, bound with indestructible ties to both, participating in both. Every artist, since he is a human being, has a double alliance with nature and spirit. Through art comes a union of the two kingdoms. To understand this, it is first necessary to set the two realms off against each other. Antithesis must be stressed before we look for synthesis.

Nature and spirit: "The field of art," Thomas Mann maintains, "has at all times been full of blends of the two." [52] Tolstoy was one of nature's own. Yet why did Tolstoy, at one notable period of his life, became a Christian ascetic, don a peasant blouse, and proceed to repudiate his earlier work. Because, Mann answers, there was in Tolstoy—more violently than in most nature artists to be sure—the involuntary urge toward spirit which lies under the skin even of those dearly beloved of nature: "Nature too is sentimental, she yearns to be spirit." [53] Richard Wagner's art is sensual, erotic, strong in physical appeal. Yet there is a strain in it—implicit in *The Flying Dutchman,* more definite in *Tannhäuser,* and finally open and explicit in *Parsifal*—which embodies a nostalgia for faith and redemption, for ascetic Christianity. Something of the same sort may be observed in Claude Debussy's music, from *L'Après-midi d'un Faune* to his last work of significance, *Le Martyre de Saint-Sébastien.* As far as Wagner is concerned, Thomas Mann claims that at different stages of his life art appeared to him in two widely differing aspects. In one light, art seemed to the composer a principle of release, a sedative, a Schopenhaurian condition of contemplation and surrender of the will. Yet in another mood, Wagner thought of art as a hindrance to spiritual safety, as the broad path which Buddha declared led away from salvation. Commenting on this latter convic-

[52] "Goethe, Novelist," PM, p. 103.   [53] *Ibid.*

tion of the composer, Mann remarks, "What we have here is a variation of the Tolstoyan repudiation of art, the cruel denial of one's own natural endowment for the sake of the 'spirit.'" [54]

In certain consummate artists, the powers of nature and spirit nearly, if not quite, balance. Such a man's creative faculty does not preclude a highly developed critical sense; his bond with nature does not entail moral insensitivity nor does his preoccupation with form keep him from paying homage to intellect. It is unfortunate, Mann thinks, that there has been in Germany the traditional belief in a sharp distinction between the creative writer and the critic; the line between *Dichter* and *Schriftsteller* has been all too much overdrawn. Mann is definite about this in a tribute to Lessing, an artist whom he considers at once a creator and a critic:

Most personally and vividly he represents the ideal productive type, the kind of intellectual whose performance is viewed in some quarters with a jaundiced eye, as mere profane writing, sharply and contemptuously distinguished from the sacred sphere of the afflatus. We all know how popular this distinction is, particularly in Germany, . . . nor is its position tenable, since the line between creative authorship and mere "writing" runs, of course, not outwardly, between the products, but inwardly, within the personality itself; and because it is possible to imagine, combined in one person, the trained writer endowed with initiative and the conscious, clear-eyed creative artist.[55]

Goethe too, godlike son of nature though he was, approximated this ideal. With the poet in mind, Dr. Reimer of Mann's *The Beloved Returns* declares:

"In the great man the spirit reaches its height without derogation of the natural; for in him spirit confides in nature as in the element of creation itself, because it is in some way bound up

[54] "Wagner," FGW, p. 151.   [55] "Lessing," PM, p. 122.

with it, and its familiar in creation—it is brother, so to speak, to
nature, and to it she reveals her secrets. For the creative is the
common brother-sister element, it binds together nature and
spirit, and in it they are one." [56]

The sage of Weimar was both poet and critic, and because
he was both, he nearly always dwelt in peace with both
spirit and nature. Mann does not mention a letter from
Schiller to Goethe in which Schiller tells his friend, "Your
characteristic way of alternating between reflection and production is truly enviable and admirable. Both species of
activity are wholly present in you, and this is precisely the
reason why both are so well developed." [57]

In Thomas Mann's own case, criticism has always accompanied creation. The epic novel which absorbed twelve years
of labor made way time and again for the composition of
critical studies. Besides the *Goethe and Tolstoy,* there were
written in this period *Frederick the Great, An Experience in
the Occult,* the massive "Reflections" and numerous shorter
pieces. For the creative power does not stand alone in
Thomas Mann. Accompanying it and inseparable from it is
the power of criticism and analysis, the intellectual transmu-
tation of inherited bourgeois discipline.

Thus we come to a resolution of our antithesis. If the artist
in his moments of highest success unites the natural and the
spiritual, this need not surprise us. For art is the great rain-
bow bridge between nature's earth and the other world of
spirit. Art is the mediator between mind and sense, the synthesis of the greatest of all antitheses. To Thomas Mann,
man himself is the result of a "high encounter of nature and
mind in their yearning way toward each other." [58] And in

[56] *The Beloved Returns,* p. 84.
[57] Letter 404, *Correspondence between Schiller and Goethe,* ed. Schmitz.
[58] "Goethe, Novelist," PM, p. 103.

man's most characteristic activity—art—we should expect a
force which has the power to bind the two realms. In Mann's
words, "Great art was always the herald of the third kingdom." [59] This third kingdom is the ideal sphere wherein
nature and spirit are fused. "Art must be both body and
mind," Mann reminds us, "she is like Proserpina in belonging to the powers of the underworld and the powers of
light." [60] A completely unintelligent artist is as nonexistent
as one totally cut off from nature. In the idea of Form, the
touch-stone of art, the hero of *The Magic Mountain* per-
ceives a common denominator between knowledge and creation, a mystic span between the two kingdoms of nature and
spirit. Here is Castorp's reflection:

"I find it a simply priceless arrangement of things, that the
formal, the idea of form, of beautiful form, lies at the bottom of
every sort of humanistic calling . . . you can see how the things
of the mind and the love of beauty come together, and that they
always really have been one and the same—in other words,
science and art; and that the calling of being an artist surely
belongs with the others, as a sort of fifth faculty, because it too
is a humanistic calling, a variety of humanistic interest, in so far
as its most important theme or concern is with man." [61]

In Goethe's *Elective Affinities*, Ottilie makes this note in
her diary, "One cannot withdraw from the world more se-
curely than through art, one cannot knit oneself more se-
curely to the world than through art." [62] This is a testament
to the synthetic mission of art, its function as mediator between sense and spirit. The artist moves between polar forces
of mind and flesh; his powerful erotic nature cannot avail
without loyalty to thought. Beauty which does not have

[59] *Ibid.*, p. 114.
[60] *Ibid.* The exact words are repeated in *"Freud's Position in the History
of Modern Thought,"* PM, p. 181.   [61] MM, p. 330.
[62] "Elective Affinities," in *Novels and Tales of Goethe* (London, 1868),
pp. 153-54.

truth on its side is a chimera. Therefore the artist, Thomas Mann points out in his 1938 Schopenhauer essay, is a Hermes who travels between the heaven of the mind and the world of nature:

He it is who may owe his bond to the world of images and appearances—be sensually, voluptuously, sinfully bound to them, yet be aware at the same time that he belongs no less to the world of the idea and the spirit, as the magician who makes the appearance transparent that the idea and the spirit may shine through. Here is exhibited the artist's mediating task, his hermetic and magical role as broken between the upper and lower world, between idea and phenomenon, spirit and sense. Here, in fact, we have what I call the cosmic position of art.[63]

The artist's domain is beauty, and just as Plato's *Eros* is the mediator between the divine and the mortal, so beauty, which is of the third kingdom, stands between heaven and earth. This was the thought of Mann's Gustave von Aschenbach, when he paraphrased the words of Socrates spoken under a plane tree on the banks of the Ilissus, and declared that beauty is the Idea shining through the world of sense. "For beauty, my Phaedrus," Aschenbach mentally addressed his beloved, "beauty alone is lovely and visible at once. For, mark you, it is the sole aspect of the spiritual which we can perceive through the senses." [64]

An emphasis on the place of beauty in the cosmos, a little different from Aschenbach's, can be found in a lively nature-spirit parable which Mann wrote between the third and final books of the *Joseph* story. This is the little fantasy, *The Transposed Heads*, composed on the theme of an old Indian myth.

The tale concerns two youths, Shridaman and Nanda, and a beautiful girl, Sita. Shridaman, thoughtful and sensitive,

[63] Schopenhauer Presented by Thomas Mann, p. 4.
[64] DV: STD, p. 413.

has a fine, delicate head, and an indifferent body, inclined to softness. Nanda, a healthy normal fellow, possesses a splendidly developed body, but his head is mediocre, even goatlike. Shridaman falls in love with and marries the beautiful Sita. She admires his finely formed head, but covets his friend's magnificent body. The three go on a journey at a time when Sita is with child by her husband. Shridaman pays a visit to the shrine of the death goddess Kali. In a sudden religious ecstasy, he cuts off his own head with the sacrificial sword. Nanda discovers the corpse of his friend, and in his anguish he too beheads himself. Sita finds both bodies. Horror-struck, she prays to Kali for help. Kali appears and tells the girl to set the heads back on the bodies so that her divine power may restore the young men to life. Sita does so, but she makes a "mistake." She sets the wrong heads on the bodies.

The two youths now spring to life, one with the Shridaman head and the Nanda body, the other with the Nanda head and the Shridaman body. The question is, which is Sita's husband? The three seek out an old hermit and submit their case to his judgment. He decides that the head determines the identity, and that Sita's rightful husband is the man with the *spirituel* head of Shridaman and the nature-blessed body of Nanda. So Sita and her husband go off to their housekeeping, while the disappointed one flees to the forest to become a hermit.

But the transformation is not a stable one. The heads and bodies of the newly assembled man-units begin to cast a reciprocal influence on each other. Slowly, the refined head of Sita's husband tends to coarsen while his strong hard body loses something of its firm structure and becomes softer. And the young hermit's head little by little loses its goatlike quality, and his soft body grows firmer.

The dénouement comes when Sita, now mother of a little boy, deserts her husband to seek her other spouse in the forest—after all, it was his body which begot the son. But Sita's husband, he of the coarsening Shridaman head and the softening Nanda body, follows her and finds her in the arms of the young hermit. The two men fight and slay each other, not in wrath but in resignation to the inevitable. Sita burns herself on their funeral pyre.

The little son, Samadhi-Andhaka, grows up to be a scholar in the court of the King of Benares. It does not detract from his fortune that he is fair-skinned and near-sighted. (Samadhi-Andhaka was conceived before the heads were transposed. His father was the original Shridaman. Sita, at the moment of begetting, remembered Nanda's stalwart body, grew pale with misery and shut her eyes to blot out the sight of Shridaman.)

The tale poses a question, and Mann answers it in interpreting the allegory.[65] Does beauty belong to the realm of sense or of mind? Some say that beauty pertains to the natural sphere, and that spirit, since it stands over against the world of nature, has nothing to do with beauty. But this is not so. For spirit yearns toward beauty set in the world of sense, and out of this love there arises a spiritual, an intellectual beauty. Beauty in the natural realm welcomes the love of spirit, and in turn reaches out to the spiritual world. Divided, they cannot exist. The world's goal is a union between the two. "This tale of ours," says Thomas Mann, "is but an illustration of the failures and false starts attending the effort to reach the goal." [66]

Beauty, therefore, cannot be fulfilled through either na-

[65] *The Transposed Heads*, pp. 167-68.
[66] *Ibid.*, p. 168.

ture or spirit alone. There must be a joining of the two kingdoms. In man, *homo humanus* and *homo Dei,* nature and
spirit find their point of contact. In the artist and in his work
they achieve their highest interpenetration.

BIBLIOGRAPHY

THE FOLLOWING lists have been prepared with American readers in mind. These lists are not exhaustive. Most of Mann's writings have been translated into English and have been published in this country by Alfred A. Knopf. In Germany, Mann's works were published up to 1935 by S. Fischer, Berlin. For the longer works of fiction, the original date of publication is given, followed by the English title, with the original title and place of publication in parentheses.

LONGER WORKS OF FICTION

1901 Buddenbrooks (Buddenbrooks. Berlin). Trans. H. T. Lowe-Porter. New York, 1924.

1909 Royal Highness (Königliche Hoheit. Berlin). Trans. A. Cecil Curtis. New York, 1926; new ed., 1939.

1924 The Magic Mountain (Der Zauberberg. Berlin). Trans. H. T. Lowe-Porter. New York 1927.

1933 Joseph and His Brothers (Joseph und Seine Brüder). Trans. H. T. Lowe-Porter.
Vol. I. Joseph and His Brothers (Die Geschichten Jaakobs. Berlin). New York, 1934.

1934 Vol. II. Young Joseph (Der junge Joseph. Berlin). New York, 1935.

1936 Vol. III. Joseph in Egypt (Joseph in Ägypten. Vienna). New York, 1938.

1939 The Beloved Returns (Lotte in Weimar. Stockholm). Trans. H. T. Lowe-Porter. New York, 1940.

1939 The Transposed Heads (Die vertauschten Köpfe. Stockholm). Trans. H. T. Lowe-Porter. New York, 1941.

SHORTER WORKS OF FICTION

THE ENGLISH TRANSLATIONS of practically all Mann's shorter works of fiction, including his single drama *Fiorenza,* are published by Knopf under the title *Stories of Three Decades* (New York, 1936). The translations are by H. T. Lowe-Porter. The date of original publication is followed by the English title, with the original title in parentheses.

1896 Disillusionment (Enttäuschung).

1897 Little Herr Friedemann (Der kleine Herr Friedemann).

1897 The Dilettante (Der Bajazzo).

1897 Tobias Mindernickel (Tobias Mindernickel).

1897 Little Lizzie (Luischen).

1899 The Wardrobe (Der Kleiderschrank).

1901 The Way to the Churchyard (Der Weg zum Friedhof).

1902 Gladius Dei (Gladius Dei).

1902 Tristan (Tristan).

1902 The Hungry (Die Hungernden).

1903 Tonio Kröger (Tonio Kröger).

1903 The Infant Prodigy (Das Wunderkind).

1904 Fiorenza (Fiorenza).

1904 A Gleam (Ein Glück).

1904 At the Prophet's (Beim Propheten).

1905 A Weary Hour (Schwere Stunde).

1905 The Blood of the Walsungs (Wälsungenblut)

1907 Railway Accident (Das Eisenbahnunglück).

1911 The Fight between Jappe and Do Escobar (Wie Jappe und Do Escobar sich prügelten).

1911 Felix Krull (Bekenntnisse des Hochstaplers Felix Krull).

1911 Death in Venice (Der Tod in Venedig).

1918 A Man and His Dog (Herr und Hund).

1925 Disorder and Early Sorrow (Unordnung und frühes Leid).

1929 Mario and the Magician (Mario und der Zauberer).

ESSAYS

"Appeal to Reason, An," *Criterion,* X (London, 1931). A speech, "Deutsche Ansprache, ein Appell an die Vernunft," delivered in Berlin, Oct. 17, 1930, and reprinted in Achtung Europa! (Stockholm, 1938).

Bemühungen. Berlin 1925. See under Past Masters; Three Essays.

"Culture and Politics" *Survey Graphic,* LXXV (Feb., 1939).

"Epilogue to 'Spain,' " *Life and Letters of Today,* XVI (London, Summer, 1937), No. 8.

Exchange of Letters, An. Trans. H. T. Lowe-Porter. New York, 1937. Published separately as Ein Briefwechsel (Zurich, 1937), and reprinted in Achtung Europa! (Stockholm, 1938).

Forderung des Tages, Die. Berlin, 1930. See under Past Masters.

Freud, Goethe, Wagner. New York, 1937.

"Freud and the Future, trans. H. T. Lowe-Porter. Published separately as Freud und die Zukunft (Vienna, Fischer, 1936).

"Goethe's Career as a Man of Letters, trans. Rita Matthias-Reil. Delivered as a commemorative address at Weimar, 1932, and later included as "Goethes Laufbahn als Schriftsteller" in Leiden und Grösse der Meister (Berlin, 1935).

"The Sufferings and Greatness of Richard Wagner," trans. H. T. Lowe-Porter. From *Neue Rundschau,* April, 1933; also included in English in Past Masters and, as "Leiden und Grösse Richard Wagners," in Leiden und Grösse der Meister.

"Germany's Guilt and Mission," *Decision,* July, 1941.

"Goethe," trans. H. T. Lowe-Porter, *Yale Review,* XXI (Summer, 1932). Originally published separately as Goethe als Repräsentant des bürgerlichen Zeitalters (Berlin, 1932).

"How to Win the Peace," *Atlantic Monthly,* Feb., 1942.

"I Believe," trans. H. T. Lowe-Porter. In the anthology I Believe, comp. Clifton Fadiman. New York, 1939.

Past Masters. Trans. H. T. Lowe-Porter. New York, 1933.

"The Sufferings and Greatness of Richard Wagner." See under Freud, Goethe, Wagner.

"Goethe, Novelist." Epilogue to the Epicon edition of Goethe's Die Wahlverwandtschaften (Berlin, 1932).

"Lessing." From Die Forderung des Tages (Berlin, 1930).

"Nietzsche and Music." From Bemühungen (Berlin, 1925).

"Durer." From Die Forderung des Tages.

"Tolstoi." From Die Forderung des Tages.

"Freud's Position in the History of Modern Thought." From Die Forderung des Tages.

"Culture and Socialism." From Die Forderung des Tages.

"On the Theory of Spengler." From Bemühungen.

"Joseph Conrad's 'The Secret Agent.'" From Die Forderung des Tages.

"Cosmopolitanism." From Bemühungen.

"On the Film." From Die Forderung des Tages.

"Sleep, Sweet Sleep." From Rede und Antwort (Berlin, 1922).

"Problem of Freedom, The," Association of American Colleges Bulletin, XXV (Fall, 1939). Address at Rutgers University, April 28, 1939; Phi Beta Kappa address at the commencement of Hobart College and William Smith College, May 29, 1939. Published as Das Problem der Freiheit (Stockholm, 1939).

Rede und Antwort. Berlin, 1922. See under Past Masters; Three Essays.

Reflections of a Non-Political Man. Published as Betrachtungen eines Unpolitischen (Berlin, 1918); not translated into English.

Schopenhauer Presented by Thomas Mann. New York, 1939. The essay which forms the Preface was published separately as Schopenhauer (Stockholm, 1938).

This Peace. Trans. H. T. Lowe-Porter. New York, 1938.

This War. Trans. Eric Sutton. New York, 1940.

Three Essays. Trans. H. T. Lowe-Porter. New York, 1929.
"Goethe and Tolstoy." From Bemühungen (Berlin, 1925).

"Frederick the Great and the Grand Coalition." From Rede und Antwort (Berlin, 1922).

"An Experience in the Occult." From Bemühungen.

Sketch of My Life, A. Paris, 1935. Published as "Lebensabriss," in *Neue Rundschau* (1930), pp. 732-69.

"Standards and Values," trans. Agnes Meyer, New York *Times*, Aug. 15, 1937. Published as "Mass und Wert," in *Mass und Wert* (Zurich, Summer, 1937) and reprinted in Achtung Europa! (Stockholm, 1938).

BOOKS ABOUT THOMAS MANN AND HIS WORK

Cleugh, James. Thomas Mann, a Study. London, 1933.

Baer, Lydia. The Concept and Function of Death in the Works of Thomas Mann. Dissertation, University of Pennsylvania. Philadelphia, 1932.

Slochower, Harry. Three Ways of Modern Man. New York, 1937. Contains "Bourgeois Liberalism: Thomas Mann's 'The Magic Mountain.'"

—— Thomas Mann's Joseph Story. New York, 1938. Includes reviews of Mann's books by various writers.

Weigand, Hermann J. Thomas Mann's Novel 'Der Zauberberg.' New York, 1933. While this volume does not pretend to be an exhaustive treatise of Mann's great novel, it is a valuable and brilliant study.

Alberts, Wilhelm. Thomas Mann and Sein Beruf. Leipzig, 1913.

Back, Hanne. Thomas Mann: Verfall und Uberwindung. Vienna, 1925.

Brüll, Oscar. Thomas Mann. Vienna, 1923.

Eloesser, Arthur. Thomas Mann: sein Leben und sein Werk. Berlin, 1925.

Erlacher, Louis. "Untersuchungen zur Romantechnik Thomas Manns." Inaugural dissertation, University of Basel, 1931.

Hamburger, Käte. Thomas Mann und die Romantik. Berlin, 1932.

Havenstein, Martin. Thomas Mann: der Dichter und Schriftsteller. Berlin, 1927.

Hebling, Carl. Die Gestalt des Kunstlers in neueren Dichtung; eine Studie über Thomas Mann. Berlin, 1932.

Jacob, Gerhard. "Thomas Mann und Nietzsche zum Problem der Decadence." Inaugural dissertation, University of Leipzig, 1926.

—— Das Werk Thomas Manns. A Bibliography. Berlin, 1926.

Kasdorff, Hans. Der Todesgedanke im Werke Thomas Manns. Leipzig, 1932.

Leppmann, Franz. Thomas Mann. Berlin, 1915.

Lion, Ferdinand. Thomas Mann in seiner Zeit. Zürich, 1935.

Peacock, Ronald. Der Leitmotiv bei Thomas Mann. Berne, 1934.

Peter, Hans Arnim. Thomas Mann and seine epische Charakterisierungkunst. Berne, 1934.

Rohmer, Charlotte. "Buddenbrooks und The Forsyte Saga." Inaugural dissertation, Julius-Maximilians Universität, Munich, 1931.

Rosenkranz, Hans. Thomas Mann und das zwangzigste Jahrhundert. Berlin, 1925.

INDEX

Abandonment, role in artist morality, xii, 118 ff.; nature of, 126; not pusillanimity, 130

Aesthetics, morality and the artist, 109-33; antithesis of nature and spirit, 179; place of beauty in cosmic, 184-87; see also Art and the Artist

Aïda (Verdi), 97, 99

Anaxagoras, philosophy, 84

Après-Midi d'un Faune, L' (Debussy), 98, 99, 180

Aristocracy, principle represented by Catholicism, 31; aristocratic problem in field of art, 178

Ascent, principle of, 168 ff.

Associations, Mann's fondness for, 104

"At the Prophet's" (Mann), 116

Art and the Artist, x-xv; artist human being par excellence, x, 50, 179; bond with disease and death, xi, xii, xiii, 37-75, 87, 89, 102, 122, 167, 175, 176; criminal akin to artist, xii, 115-18, 126; music and the romantic, xii, 76-108; morality and the artist, xii, 109-33, 167, 176; art and politics, xiii, 104, 134-60; mediation between nature and spirit, xiii, 161-87; effect of German bourgeois culture, 6, 24-26, 33; German middle-class suspicion, 10, 13, 25, 118; isolation from rest of world, 13-36; hard work provides refuge, 15; effect of knowledge upon, 21; relation to normal humanity, 21; artist and philosopher compared, 22; Mann's use of metaphor "marked man," 23n; tuberculosis

disease most commonly associated with genius, 58 f.; relation to the erotic, 63, 125; tendency toward the neurotic, 65, 125; charge of degeneracy, 73 f.; Germany's characteristic arts, 107; bridge between nature and morality, 110; relation to sin, 111, 113, 119 f., 123; equivocal sources, 114 ff., 167; "art for art's sake," 114; role of abandonment, 118 ff.; importance of form, 128, 183; potentially tragic elements in artist nature, 129; morality of genius is for the few, 129; hostile to morality? 130 f.; artist resembles soldier, 130; value in common with morals, 132; work not private pastime of individual, 158; "godlike" and "saintly" types, 175 ff.; natural or spiritual nobility of more value? 178; double alliance with nature and spirit, 180; synthesis of greatest of all antitheses, 182 ff.

Balzac, Honoré de, Cousin Betty, 38

Bashkirtseff, Marie, effect of tuberculosis upon, 58

Baudelaire, Charles, captivated by Wagner's music, 77

Beauty, Kant's attitude toward, 109; place in cosmos, 184-87; belongs to realm of nature or of spirit? 186; see also Aesthetics

Beloved Returns, The (Mann), xi, 33, 48n; originally Lotte in Weimar, xv; decries frowning sublimity in art, 50; disease motif,

Beloved Returns, The (*Continued*) 66, 71; Goethe's antipolitical aspect, 140; Germany as mediator between Europe and Asia, 154; nature-spirit conflict, 174; nature and spirit balance in great man, 181

Betrachtungen eines Unpolitischen (Mann), *see Reflections of a Non-Political Man*

Bie, Oskar, responsible for publication of "Little Herr Friedemann," 95n

Bizet, Georges, *Carmen*, 97,99

Blood and race myth, doctrines of, 86

"Blood of the Walsungs, The" (Mann), 64; emphasis on music, 96

Bohemianism, Mann holds aloof from, 129

Bonn, University of, cancels Mann's honorary doctorate, 153; Mann's letter to dean, 157

Bourgeois class, 3-36, 136, 137; significance in Mann's work, xi, xiii, 3 ff.; derivation of word "bourgeois," 4n; communism and fascism repudiate value of, 5, 35; treatment of, in *Buddenbrooks*, 6-8; suspicion of art and artists, 10, 13, 25, 118; principle represented by Protestantism, 31; nonpolitical attitudes of German, 138, 140, 147, 156, 158, 159

Brandes, Georg, Nietzsche's letter to, 94

Brill, A. A., American translator of Freud, 63

Brinkman, Carl, on German bourgeois class, 5

Britain, *see* England

Brothers Karamazov, The (Dostoyevsky), 38

Bruhns, *see* Silva-Bruhns, Julia da

Buddenbrooks (Mann), 3, 6-8, 18, 136, 141; bourgeois epic full of autobiographical overtones, 6, 8, 10, 16, 67; isolation motif, 16; treatment of disease and death, 41-43, 44, 68; role of music, 95, 99, 100

Byron, George Gordon, sixth Baron, 34; fondness for portraying solitary genius, 13-15, 23; *Don Juan*, 14; *Manfred*, 14

Capitalism, rise of bourgeois class, 4

Carmen (Bizet), 97, 99

Catholicism, represents aristocratic principle, 31; importance of death, 102

Chamberlain, Houston Stewart, Wagner's son-in-law, 79, 88

Classic, relation between romantic and the, 74

Common Sense, articles on affinity between Wagner and Hitler party, 78 f.

Communism, repudiation of bourgeois values, 5

Cosmogony, Mann's depiction, 164 f.

Cousin Betty (Balzac), 38

Creative writer, *see* Writer

Criminal, morality akin to artist's, xii, 115-18, 126

Critic, distinction between creative writer and, 181

Critique of Judgment (Kant), aesthetic theory, 109, 110

Culture, German, ix, x; romantic tradition, xii, xiv, 13 ff., 39, 40n, 74, 76-108, 171; too much emphasis on feeling and music, xii; interest in prehistory, xiv; tragic aloofness from politics, 134, 136 ff., 152, 155-60; essentially bourgeois, 136, 137, 138, 140; socialism provides stimulation, 148; "Culture and Socialism" (Mann), 148

Dawn of Day (Nietzsche), 47

Death in Venice (Mann), x; autobiographical overtones, 9; isolation motif, 26; tension between bourgeois and genius, 27; disease motif, 46-48, 68, 122; prototype for protagonist, 47*n;* parallel with Freud's teachings, 63, 64; emphasis on infra-rational, 89; emphasis on music, 96; equivocal origins of the beautiful, 115; capitulation to disease and sin, 122; morality of abandonment, 127-29; role of beauty, 184

Debussy, Claude, *L'Après-Midi d'un Faune,* 98, 99, 180; *Le Martyre de Saint-Sébastien,* 180; nostalgia for faith and redemption, 180

Degas, Edgar Hilaire Germain, on equivocal origins of the beautiful, 115

Degeneration (Nordau), 73 f.

Democracy, Mann's attitude toward, xiii, 35, 157 f.

Dichter, distinction between *Schriftsteller* and, 181

Dickens, Charles, role of illness in works, 38

"Dilettante, The" (Mann), autobiographical overtones, 8, 15; isolation motif, 15

Disease and death, Mann's preoccupation with, xi, xii, xiii, 37-75, 87, 89; lively subject for literary treatment, 38-40; ennobling quality of, 38, 48; German romantic attitude, 39, 40*n,* 74, 87; humanistic attitude toward death, 44, 57; dual aspects of illness, 48, 52, 53-58, 69 f., 167; effect of tuberculosis upon genius, 58 f.; curiosity about death leads to preoccupation with symptoms of disease, 67; should not be exalted over life, 68; Catholic view of death, 102; relation of sin to, 122;

relation to kingdom of spirit, 175, 176

Disorder and Early Sorrow (Mann), isolation theme, 26; disease and death motif, 66

Don Juan (Byron), 14

Dostoyevsky, Feodor Mikhailovich, *The Brothers Karamazov,* 38; *The Idiot,* 38, 39; compared with Mann, 39; relation to illness and health, 69-71; man of spirit, 114, 175

Dualism, Mann's view, xiii, 70

Dumas, Alexandre, literary treatment of disease, 38

Eckermann, Johann Peter, on Goethe, 138

Elective Affinities (Goethe), 123; synthetic mission of art, 183

England, bourgeois class, 5; role of illness in literature, 38; Undset compares English genius with German variety, 74*n*

Enlightenment, attitude toward instinct, 86; noble conception of *Humanität,* 111

Epistemology, *see* Knowledge

Erotic, relation of art to the, 63, 125

Europe, bourgeois society, 4-6; *see also* England; Germany, etc.

Experience in the Occult, An (Mann), 182

Fall, sacred tradition of the, 164 f., 166

Falsehood, artist cannot tolerate, 131

Fascism, repudiation of bourgeois values, 5, 35; Mann's attitude, 35, 85, 149-60; romanticism linked to, 86-88; *see also* National Socialism

Faust (Goethe), 34, 62, 121, 127

Faust (Gounod), 97, 99

Feeling, romantic emphasis upon, 82, 83 ff.

"Felix Krull" (Mann), 64; inter-relation of criminal and artistic elements, 117

Fichte, Johann Gottlieb, denounced as precursor of Hitler's Germany, 88; metaphysic of spirit, 165 f.

Fiorenza (Mann), disease motif, 44 f.; treatment of sin and morality, 124

Fischer, S., Mann's German publisher, 6

Flying Dutchman, The (Wagner), 180

Forbidden, the, see Abandonment

Form, artist's creative discipline, 128, 183

Forsyte Saga (Galsworthy), resemblance between Buddenbrooks and, 6

France, bourgeoisie, 4, 5

Francis of Assisi, Saint, effect of tuberculosis upon, 59

Franz von Sternbald (Goethe), 92

Frederick the Great and the Grand Coalition (Mann), 135, 182

Freemasonry in The Magic Mountain, 144, 170

Freud, Sigmund, ix, x; Mann's sympathy with doctrine, 62-65, 68; connection between artistic impulse and erotic drive, 63; exploration of infra-rational, 84, 85, 86; Mann's rebuke, 90; theory of art, 125

"Freud's Position in the History of Modern Thought" (Mann), 85, 87

Galsworthy, John, Buddenbrooks resembles Forsyte Saga, 6

Genius, relation between disease and, xi, 37-75; finds morality in abandonment, xii; study of, in The Beloved Returns, xv; tuberculosis disease most commonly associated with, 58 f.; morality of, 129; see also Art and the artist

Germany, culture, ix, x, xii, xiv, 134, 136 ff., 148, 152, 155-60; bourgeois class, xi, 5, 10, 32-36, 136, 137, 138, 140, 147, 156, 158, 159; romantic tradition, xii, xiv, 13 ff., 39, 40n, 74, 76-108, 171; music, xii, 76 ff., 91-108, 136; characteristic arts, 107; aesthetic theory, 109 ff.; reason for Nazi control, 134; Mann's attitude toward role in First World War, 135; defeat of Napoleon at Leipsic, 138; mediator between Europe and Asia, 148, 154; socialist movement, 148; spirit of idealism, 165 ff.; "ironic" geographical position, 172; distinction between creative writer and critic, 181

Ghosts (Ibsen), 38

Giorgione, Pater's essay on, 92

Gladius Dei (Mann), treatment of sin and morality, 124

God, role in primal struggle between soul and matter, 164 f.

"Godlike" type of artist, 175

Goethe, Johann Wolfgang von, ix, x; central figure in The Beloved Returns, xv, 33, 48n, 50, 66, 71, 140, 154, 181; on isolation of the poet, 22; Wilhelm Meister's Apprenticeship, 28n, 111; strength from bourgeois inheritance, 33 f.; Faust, 34, 62, 121, 127; Hermann and Dorothea, 34; love for Ulrike Levetzow, 47n; on the classic and romantic, 74, 176; Franz von Sternbald, 92; concept of artist morality, 109, 110, 111, 127; Mann's essay on, 115; Elective Affinities, 123, 183; art theory, 131; attitude toward politics, 138-40; cosmology, 163; metaphysical speculations, 168; "godlike" type, 175; admiration of Spinoza's non-

Goethe, Johann Wolfgang von (*Continued*)
teleological universe, 177; creator and critic, 181
"Goethe" (Mann), 115, 140
Goethe and Tolstoy (Mann), 69-71, 182; on Germany's destiny, 147, 153; nature-spirit conflict, 175
"Goethe as Representative of the Bourgeois Age" (Mann), 33 f.
Götterdämmerung (Wagner), 78
"Good," Mann's definition of term, 131, 132
Gounod, Charles François, *Faust*, 97, 99
Gray, Cecil, music as the romantic art, 92
Great Britain, *see* England
Greek philosophers, morals in political sphere, 133

Hamlet (Shakespeare), 49; hero compared with bourgeois artist, 24
Hauptmann, Gerhart, *Poor Henry*, 38
Hegel, Georg Wilhelm Friedrich, 168; attempt to close breach between nature and spirit, 166, 167
Hermann and Dorothea (Goethe), 34
History, romantic interest in prehistory, xiv
Hitler, Adolf, idolizes Wagner, 78 f.; seizure of power exiles Mann, 152; Mann's opinion of, 155; responsibility for "new" Germany, 155
Hoffmann, E. T. A., attitude toward illness, 40; attraction to music, 92, 93
Humanism, attitude toward death, 44, 57
Humanity, relation of artist to, 21; art and morals cannot be separated from, 131
"Hungry, The" (Mann), isolation

motif, 16-18, 21; use of metaphor "marked man," 23n
Huxley, Aldous, attitude toward suffering in *Those Barren Leaves*, 54
Hymns to Night (Novalis), 80

Ibsen, Henrik, *Ghosts*, 38; charge of degeneracy, 73
Idealism, spirit of German, 165 ff.
Idiot, The (Dostoyevsky), 38, 39
Ignatius Loyola, St., 102
Illness, *see* Disease and death
Immorality, sin not to be confused with, 119 f., 123; *see also* Morality
Impressionist painters, charged with degeneracy, 73
"Infant Prodigy, The" (Mann), emphasis on music, 96
Infra-rational, romantic emphasis upon, 84 ff.
Insight, role of, in art, 21
Instinct, *see* Feeling
Intellect, romantic attitude toward, 82, 88; Mann's attitude toward, 90
Irony in *The Magic Mountain*, 171-75
Isolation theme in Mann's early work, xi, xiii, 13-26, 67, 159; not predominant in later work, 26
Italian fascism, Mann's attack on, 150-52

Jacobson, Arthur, connections between tuberculosis infection and genius, 59
Joseph story (Mann), 35; romantic nature, xiv f.; influence of Freud, 64; disease and death motif, 66; development of myth-psychology, 67, 69; infra-rational emphasis, 89; sin is spiritual, 122; antithesis of spirit and nature, 164
Joyce, James, *Ulysses*, 57
Judgment, Critique of (Kant), 109, 110

Kant, Immanuel, *Critique of Judgment*, 109, 110; influences Mann, 166; natural philosophy, 168; Schiller's bias for philosophy of, 177

Kaunitz, Prince von, engineers coalition against Prussia, 135

Keats, John, effect of tuberculosis upon, 59

Knowledge, effect upon the artist, 21, 24; primordial sin committed in pursuit of, 127 f.; Mann's interest in theory of, 166

Kreutzer Sonata, The (Tolstoy), indictment of modern art, 113

Kultur, opposed to *Zivilisation*, 136 f.

Last Puritan, The (Santayana), on funeral services, 57

Legend, *see* Myth

Leipsic, Napoleon's defeat at, 138

Lessing, Gotthold Ephraim, creator and critic, 181

Levetzow, Ulrike, Goethe's love for, 47n

Libertinism, morality of artist not to be confused with, 129

Linden Tree, The (Schubert), 87, 98, 99

Lisbon earthquake, Voltaire's protest against, 176

Literature, disease a lively subject, 38-40, 73 f.; *see also* Art and the artist

"Little Herr Friedemann" (Mann), xi, 40, 67; role of music, 95; accepted for publication, 95n

"Little Lizzy" (Mann), 40

Lohengrin (Wagner), 77, 78, 95

Lotte in Weimar (Mann), xv

Louis Philippe, king of France, bourgeois attitude, 4, 5n

Loyola, St. Ignatius, 102

Lucinde (Schlegel), 40; worship of night, 81

Ludwig, king of Bavaria, captivated by Wagner's music, 77

Magic Mountain, The (Mann), xiv, 48-63; tension between bourgeois and genius, 28-32, 35; disease motif, 43, 44, 48 ff., 66, 67-69, 72, 87, 89, 98, 122; allegory of artist nature? 49, 51; different levels of signification, 49 f., 52; Hans Castorp a genius? 51; dual aspect of disease and death, 53-58; choice of tubercular ailment, 58; nature of Hans Castorp's illness, 59 ff., 172; influence of Freud, 62, 64 f., 68; emphasis on infra-rational, 89; emphasis on music, 97-99, 100-8; use of leitmotiv, 99, 100, 101; morality of abandonment, 120-23, 130; German middle-class attitude toward officialdom, 141; political stand, 144-47, 153; creative counterpart of *Reflections*, 145; cosmological reflections, 163; interest in theory of knowledge, 166, 167; principles of polarity and ascent, 169-71; use of irony, 171-75; nature-spirit antithesis, 173 f., 176, 178, 183

Mahler, Gustave, source for protagonist of *Death in Venice*, 47n

Mallarmé, Stephané, 98

Manfred (Byron), 14

Mann, Carla, sister to Thomas, suicide, 69n

Mann, Heinrich, brother of Thomas, 3; *Brüderkrieg*, with Thomas, 137; *The Patrioteer*, 137, 138

Mann, Johann Heinrich, father of Thomas, 3, 4, 8 ff.

Mann, Thomas, quality of synthesis, ix; eye toward future, ix; concern with art and the artist, x ff.; bourgeois environment, xi, xiii, 3-36, 67, 159, 182; motif of isolation in early stories, xi, xiii, 13 ff., 67,

159; preoccupation with disease and death, xi, xii, xiii, 37-75, 176; attitude toward music, xii, 76-108; romantic tendencies, xii, xiv, 76 ff.; morality and the artist, xii, 109, 114-33; art as mediator between nature and spirit, xiii, 161-87; stand on world politics, xiii, xiv, 35, 85, 134, 149-60; use of irony, xiii, 171-75; birth, 3; parents, 3 f., 6, 8 ff.; nonbourgeois element, 6; autobiographical overtones in writings, 6, 8 ff.; forbears, 8; spiritual conflict, 8, 24; "bad conscience" theme, 11; preference in attire, 12; compared with Byron, 15; marriage, 18; sympathy for humanity, 26; later work does not feature isolation theme, 26, 35; motif of polarity between bourgeois character and creative instinct, 27-32, 35; emphasizes psychic connotations of disease, 38 f.; earliest work, 40 f., 67; early antipathy and distrust toward life, 41, 67; combination of disease and genius in heroes, 43; artist most human of men, 50; emphasis on disease and death diminished, 67 ff.; development of myth-psychology, 67, 69; personal contact with illness and death, 69; on decadent tendencies in German romanticism, 74; worship of the night, 81; emphasis on infra-rational, 88 ff.; attitude toward intellect, 90; use of leitmotiv, 99 ff.; fondness for associations, 104; self-criticism, 107; attitude toward Tolstoy, 114, 176; self-portrait, 116; truth and the general public, 129; art and politics, 134-60; claim to non-political character, 134 ff.; Brüderkrieg with Heinrich, 137; attitude toward socialism, 147, 148; on Germany as

mediator between Europe and Asia, 148, 154; espousal of cause of Social Democrats, 149, 152, 160; exile, 152 f.; editor of Mass und Wert, 153; honorary doctorate from Bonn canceled, 153; takes up permanent residence in U. S., 153; attitude toward Hitler, 155; letter to dean of Bonn University, 157; metaphysical implications, 161 ff.; closeness to German Idealism, 165 ff.; interest in theory of knowledge, 166; principles of polarity and ascent, 169; on value of natural and spiritual nobility in art, 178; schema summing up his antithesis of nature and spirit, 178 f.; tribute to Lessing, 181; criticism always accompanies creation, 182; attitude toward beauty, 184 ff.

Dominant influences: Freud, 62-65, 68, 84, 85, 86, 90, 125; Goethe, x, xv, 28n, 33 f., 47n, 48n, 50, 66, 71, 111, 115, 123, 131, 140, 154, 168, 175, 181; Nietzsche, x, xii, 17, 37, 47, 61, 72 f., 76, 78, 84, 87, 88, 94, 106, 107, 112, 127; Schopenhauer, x, 11, 37, 50, 67, 84, 88, 111, 125, 141, 166, 179, 184; Wagner, x, xii, 34, 71 f., 76-80, 81, 82, 84, 87, 88, 95-97, 99, 142 f., 167, 180

Works: "At the Prophet's," 116; Beloved Returns, xi, xv, 33, 48n, 50, 66, 71, 140, 154, 174, 181; Betrachtungen eines Unpolitischen, see Reflections of a Non-Political Man; "Blood of the Walsungs," 64, 96; Buddenbrooks, 3, 6-8, 10, 16, 18, 41-43, 44, 67, 68, 95, 99, 100, 136, 141; "Culture and Socialism," 148; Death in Venice, x, 9, 26, 27, 46-48, 63, 64, 68, 89, 96,

Works (*Continued*)
115, 122, 127-29, 184; "Dilettante," 8, 15; *Disorder and
Early Sorrow*, 26, 66; *Experience in the Occult*, 182; "Felix
Krull," 64, 117; *Fiorenza*, 44 f.,
124; *Frederick the Great* . . . ,
135, 182; "Freud's Position in
. . . Modern Thought," 85, 87;
"*Gladius Dei*," 124; "Goethe,"
115, 140; *Goethe and Tolstoy*,
69-71, 147, 153, 175, 182;
"Goethe as Representative of
the Bourgeois Age," 33 f.;
"Hungry," 16-18, 21, 23n; "Infant Prodigy," 96; *Joseph* story,
xiv f., 35, 64, 66, 67, 69, 89,
122, 164; "Little Herr Friedemann," xi, 40, 67, 95; "Little
Lizzy," 40; *Lotte in Weimar*,
xv; *Magic Mountain*, xiv, 28-
32, 35, 43, 44, 48-69 *passim*,
72, 87, 89, 97-108, 120-23, 130,
141, 144-47, 153, 163, 166, 167,
169-75, 176, 178, 183; *Mario
and the Magician*, 150-52;
"Nietzsche and Music," 76, 87;
preface to Goethe's *Elective
Affinities*, 123; *Reflections of a
Non-Political Man*, xiii, 32, 88,
107, 119, 134, 135, 142, 143,
145, 146, 147, 153, 159, 160,
182; *Royal Highness*, 9, 18 f.,
46, 69n; *Schopenhauer Presented by Thomas Mann*, 166,
184; "Sleep, Sweet Sleep," 81 f.,
119; *Sufferings and Greatness
of Richard Wagner*, 71 f.;
"Tobias Mindernickel," 40;
Tonio Kröger, 9, 11-13, 17, 19-
21, 23 f., 25 f., 32, 44, 100 f.,
114, 116; *Transposed Heads*,
xv, 124n, 184-87; *Tristan*, 16,
43 f., 95 f.; *Vertauschten Köpfe,
see Heads Transposed*; "Wagner," 167; "Way to the

Churchyard," 40; "Weary
Hour," 45
Manolescu, Rumanian adventurer,
117
Mansfield, Katherine, effect of tuber-
culosis upon, 59
Mario and the Magician (Mann),
allegory of Italian Fascism, 150-
52
"Marked man," metaphor applied to
artist, 23n
Martyre de Saint-Sébastien, Le
(Debussy), 180
Mass und Wert, Swiss magazine un-
der editorship of Mann, 153
Matter, soul's primal struggle with,
164 f.
Maugham, Somerset, role of illness
in works, 38; on suffering, 53;
artist's standard of conduct, 126
Medici, Lorenzo de', protagonist of
Mann's *Fiorenza*, 44, 124
Meistersinger, Die (Wagner), 34,
77, 78, 96, 143
Metaphysics, Mann's faith in, 161-
87; antithesis of nature and spirit,
179
Middle class, *see* Bourgeois class
Mind, realm of, *see* Intellect; Spirit
Molière, effect of tuberculosis upon,
59
Monism, Mann's attitude toward,
167
Moorman, Lewis J., *Tuberculosis
and Genius*, 58 f., 115n
Morality, connection between art
and, xii, 109-33; role of abandonment, xii, 118 ff.; art a bridge between nature and, 110; sin not to
be confused with immorality,
119 f., 123; of the genius, 129;
art hostile to? 130 f.; value in
common with art, 132; both personal and civic, 133; dual aspects,
167; not at home in realm of nature, **176**

Munich agreement, futility of, 157

Music, role in German life, xii, 136; Mann's attitude, xii, 76 ff., 91-108; in romantic tradition, xii, 91 ff.; political significance of, 104; linked with psychology, 104; Tolstoy's view, 113

Myers, J. A., connection between tubercular infection and genius, 59

Myth, infra-rational sphere, 90; Mann's work in field of, 164 f.; see also Joseph story

Napoleon, defeat at Leipsic, 138

National Socialism, 131, 149-60; fascism's repudiation of bourgeois values, 5, 35; Mann's attitude, 36, 85, 149 ff.; apotheosis of Wagner, 78 f., 143; romanticism linked to fascism, 86-88; reason for rise of, 134

Natural sciences, see Sciences

Nature, art as mediator between spirit and, xiii, 161-87; art a bridge between morality and, 110; hostility to spirit, 162 ff., 173 ff.; creation of, 165; sons accorded health and long life, 175; morality not at home in realm of, 176; value in field of art, 178; schema summing up antithesis of spirit and, 178 f.; beauty belongs to realm of? 186

Nazis, see National Socialism

Neue Deutsche Rundschau, 95n

Neurotic, artistic tendency toward, 65, 125

Newman, Ernest, on Wagner's political stand, 143

Nietzsche, Friedrich, ix, x, xii, 17, 21, 87; on man's ability to suffer, 37; Dawn of Day, 47; on cause of illness, 61; classic example of union of disease and genius, 72 f.; charged with degeneracy, 73; atti-tude toward Wagner, 76, 77, 78, 85, 94, 97, 106, 112; Night and Music, 82; exploration in realm of infra-rational, 84, 85, 86; de-nounced as precursor of Hitler's Germany, 88; passion for music, 93-95, 106, 107; on art and moral-ity, 112, 131; insists on morality of abandonment, 127

"Nietzsche and Music" (Mann), 76, 87

Night, worship of the, 80, 81, 82

Night and Music (Nietzsche), 82

Nordau, Max, Degeneration, 73 f.

Novalis, on sickness, 40; Hymns to Night, 80; attracted to music, 92, 93; on sin, 124

Officialdom, German middle-class attitude, 141

Painting, Impressionists charged with degeneracy, 73; Tolstoy's view, 113

Parsifal (Wagner), 77, 180

Pater, Walter, all art tends toward music, 92

Patrioteer, The (H. Mann), 137, 138

Patriotism, Goethe's stand on, 139

Pericles, imprisonment of Phidias, 118

Philip II, king of Spain, 31, 102

Philosophy, artist and philosopher compared, 22; ranked above natu-ral sciences, 91

Plato, on poet's creative activity, x; attitude toward music in Repub-lic, 104 f.; on truth and the gen-eral public, 129; on natural and spiritual nobility in field of art, 178; Eros mediator between di-vine and mortal, 184

Poets, creative activity akin to mad-ness, x; isolation from rest of the world, 22; Symbolists charged with degeneracy, 73; morality and

Poets (*Continued*)
the, 110 ff.; Mann's attitude toward, 116; and politics, 138
Polarity, principle of, 168 ff.
Politics, Mann's stand on world,
xiii, xiv, 35, 134-60; political significance of music, 104; art and,
134 ff.; tragic aloofness of German
culture from, 134, 136 ff., 152,
155-60; and poets, 138
Poor Henry (Hauptmann), 38
Prehistory, romantic interest in, xiv
Pre-Raphaelites, charged with degeneracy, 73
Pringsheim, Alfred, Mann's father-
in-law, 18
Protestantism, represents bourgeois
principle, 31
Prussia, comparison with 20th-century Germany, 135
Psychoanalysis, concern with infra-
rational, 85
Psychology, music linked with, 104

Race myth, doctrines of, 86
Reality, a cosmic play of opposites,
167; antithetical character, 172
Reflections of a Non-Political Man
(Mann), xiii, 32, 107, 134, 160,
182; emphasis on infra-rational,
88; concept of artist morality, 119;
thesis, 135, 145, 153, 159; on
Wagner's political interests, 142;
extreme conservative stand, 143,
146, 147; *The Magic Mountain*
is creative counterpart of, 145
Renaissance, rise of bourgeois class,
4
Republic (Plato), attitude toward
music, 104 f.
Rheingold (Wagner), 85
Ring des Nibelungen (Wagner), 96
Roman Catholicism, *see* Catholicism
Romanticism, German, inclination to
decadence, xii; interest in prehistory, xiv; isolation of the artist,

13 ff.; disease regarded sympathetically, 39, 40n, 74; Mann's
attitude toward, 76-108; worship
of the night, 80; emphasis on feeling, 82, 83 ff.; stress on infra-
rational, 85; link with fascism, 86-
88; equivocal and harmful elements, 87, 88; role of music in,
91 ff.; use of irony, 171
Royal Highness (Mann), autobiographical overtones, 9, 69n; isolation theme, 18 f.; disease motif,
46

Schiller, Friedrich, Mann's portrait
of, in "A Weary Hour," 45; effect
of tuberculosis upon, 58, 69-71;
on romanticism, 87; concept of
artist morality, 109-11, 114, 119,
127; *Simple and Sentimental
Poetry*, 110; *The Stage as a Moral
Institution*, 110; "The Veiled
Image of Sais," 127; definition of
art, 132; "saintly" type, 175; bias
for Kantian philosophy, 177;
recognizes Goethe as both poet
and critic, 182
"Saintly" type of artist, 175
Santayana, George, *The Last Puritan*,
57; on moral and aesthetic values,
132
Savonarola, Girolamo, protagonist
of Mann's *Fiorenza*, 44, 124
Schelling, Friedrich Wilhelm Joseph
von, philosophy of nature, 166
Schlegel, Friedrich, *Lucinde*, 40, 81;
on morality of a book, 131
Schopenhauer, Arthur, ix, x, 11, 67,
166, 184; on artist knowledge, 22;
The World as Will and Idea, 37,
93, 111; theory of suffering, 37,
42; artist most human of men, 50;
exploration in realm of infra-rational, 84, 86; denounced as precursor of Hitler's Germany, 88;
love of music, 93; on art and

morality, 111; on art and the erotic drive, 125; attitude toward politics, 141; attitude toward the artist, 179

Schopenhauer Presented by Thomas Mann (Mann), 166, 184

Schriftsteller, distinction between *Dichter* and, 181

Schubert, Franz Peter, *The Linden Tree*, 87, 98, 99

Sciences, natural, philosophy ranked above, 91

Sense, realm of, *see* Nature

Sensibility, *see* Feeling

Shakespeare, William, *Hamlet*, 24, 49

Shaw, Bernard, answers Nordau's *Degeneration*, 74; captivated by Wagner's music, 77

Shelley, Percy Bysshe, effect of tuberculosis upon, 59

Siegfried Idyll (Wagner), 77

Silva-Bruhns, Julia da, mother of Thomas Mann, 3, 6, 8 ff.

Simple and Sentimental Poetry (Schiller), autonomy of art, 110

Sin, relation of art to, 111, 113, 119 f., 123; spiritual aspect, 122; relation to disease, 122

"Sleep, Sweet Sleep" (Mann), 81 f.; revaluation of sin, 119

Social Democrats, Mann's espousal of cause, 149, 152, 160

Socialism, in Germany, 148

Society, attitude toward criminal and the artist, 10, 13, 25, 118, 126; attitude toward the poet, 117

Socrates, 104 f.

Soldier, resembles artist, 130

Soul, primal struggle with matter, 164 f.

Spinoza, Baruch, nonteleological universe, 177

Spirit, art as mediator between nature and, 161-87; nature's hostility to, 162 ff., 173 ff.; sent to dissolve union between soul and matter, 165; distinguishes man from all other forms of organic life, 174; disease and early death meted to sons of, 175; value in field of art, 178; schema summing up antithesis of nature and, 178 f.; beauty belongs to realm of? 186

Stage as a Moral Institution, The (Schiller), 110

Stevenson, Robert Louis, effect of tuberculosis upon, 58

Suffering, Schopenhauer's theory of, 37, 42; Maugham's view, 53; Huxley's view, 54

Sufferings and Greatness of Richard Wagner, The (Mann), 71 f.

Symbolist poets, charged with degeneracy, 73

Tannhäuser (Wagner), 180

Thompson, Francis, effect of tuberculosis upon, 59

Thomson, James, Goethe's criticism of, 138

Those Barren Leaves (Huxley), 54

Tieck, Ludwig, worship of night, 80; attraction to music, 91, 92, 93

Time, dual aspects, 168

Tischbein, Johann Heinrich Wilhelm, nature as anti-human, 176n, 177n

"Tobias Mindernickel" (Mann), 40

Tolstoy, Lev Nikolayevich, Mann's essay on, 69-71; charged with degeneracy, 73; discussion of art and immorality in *What Is Art?* 113 f.; *The Kreutzer Sonata*, 113; "godlike" type, 175; involuntary urge toward spirit, 180, 181

Tonio Kröger (Mann), 44; autobiographical overtones, 9, 11-13, 25 f.; isolation motif, 17, 19-21, 23 f., 32, 100, 116; influence of Freud, 64; use of leitmotiv, 100 f.;

Tonio Kröger (*Continued*)
equivocal origins of the beautiful, 114, 116
Transposed Heads, The (Mann), xv; ascetic's equivocal nature, 124n; place of beauty in cosmos, 184-87
Travemünde, scene of Mann's summer holidays, 3, 8
Tristan (Mann), isolation motif, 16; theme of disease, 43 f.; role of music, 95 f.
Tristan und Isolde (Wagner), 77, 96, 112; affinity for darkness, 80
Truth, art and morality meet in, 131; *see also* Knowledge
Tuberculosis and Genius (Moorman), 58 f.; equivocal origins of the beautiful, 115n

Uhland, Johann Ludwig, Goethe's criticism of, 139
Ulysses (Joyce), discussion of death, 57
Undset, Sigrid, on relation of disease to German literature, 74n
United States, Mann takes up permanent residence, 153

"Veiled Image of Sais, The" (Schiller), 127
Verdi, Giuseppe, *Aïda*, 97, 99
Vertauschten Köpfe, Die (Mann), xv
Viereck, Peter, on affinity between Wagner and Hitler party, 78 f.
Virtue, Mann's definition, 119
Voltaire, François Marie Arouet de, effect of tuberculosis upon, 59; protest against Lisbon earthquake, 176

Wackenroder, Wilhelm Heinrich, attraction to music, 92
Wagner, Richard, ix; Mann's attitude toward, x, xii, 34, 71 f., 76-80, 81, 82, 84, 87, 88, 95-97, 99,

142 f., 167, 180; bourgeois heritage, 34; effect of illness upon, 71 f.; charge of degeneracy, 73; Nietzsche's attitude toward, 76, 77, 78, 85, 94, 97, 106, 112; romantic element, 76, 77, 78, 79; two aspects, 77; idol of Hitler, 78 f.; equivocal character of music, 79; cult of night, 80, 81, 82; exploration in realm of infra-rational, 84; stand on politics, 142 f.; attitude toward art, 180; nostalgia for faith and redemption, 180
Works: *Flying Dutchman,* 180; *Götterdämmerung,* 78; *Lohengrin,* 77, 78, 95; *Meistersinger,* 34, 77, 78, 96, 143; *Parsifal,* 77, 180; *Rheingold,* 85; *Ring des Nibelungen,* 96; *Siegfried Idyll,* 77; *Tannhäuser,* 180; *Tristan und Isolde,* 77, 80, 96, 112; *Walküre,* 77, 96
Walküre, Die (Wagner), 77, 96
Wanamaker, John, suppression of Tolstoy's *The Kreutzer Sonata,* 113n
"Way to the Churchyard, The" (Mann), 40
"Weary Hour, A" (Mann), portrait of Schiller, 45
What Is Art? (Tolstoy), on art and immorality, 113 f.
Wilhelm Meister's Apprenticeship (Goethe), 28n, 111
World as Will and Idea, The (Schopenhauer), 37, 93; on art and morality, 111
World War I, effect, 5; Germany forced into? 135
Writer, distinction between critic and creative, 181

Zivilisation, opposed to *Kultur,* 136 f.
Zola, Émile, charged with degeneracy, 73